Nature and Wildlife Photography

A Practical Guide to How to Shoot and Sell

Susan McCartney

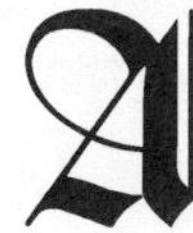

ALLWORTH PRESS, NEW YORK

© 1994 by Susan McCartney

Published by **Allworth Press**, an imprint of Allworth Communications, Inc. 10 East 23rd Street, New York, NY 10010.

Distributor to the trade in the United States and Canada:
Consortium Book Sales & Distribution, Inc.
1045 Westgate Drive
Saint Paul, MN 55114-0165.

Distributor to photographic supply outlets:
Amphoto Books
1515 Broadway
New York, NY 10036

Book design by Douglas Design Associates, New York

ISBN: 1-880559-12-9

Library of Congress Catalog Card Number: 93-71919

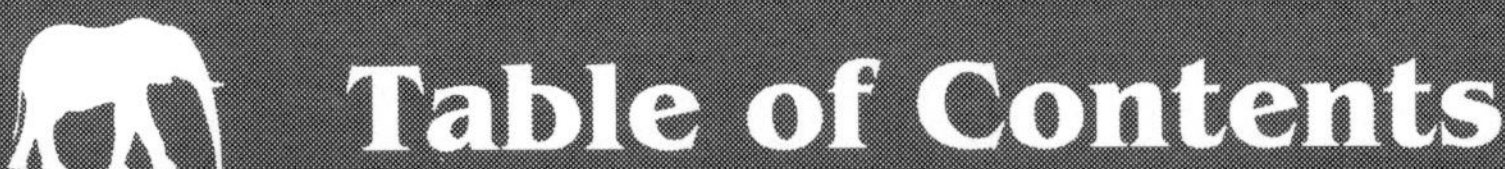

Table of Contents

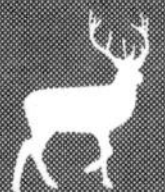 Introduction

I had fun writing this book and would like to thank most sincerely the top nature photographers and other specialists who took time from their busy schedules to talk about their work, and the very different ways that they approach nature.

I am very much indebted to Heather Angel, Jim Brandenburg, Patricia Caulfield, Nathan Farb, Dwight Kuhn, Frans Lanting, Robert Rattner, Dr. Roger Tory Peterson, Dr. Leonard Lee Rue III, Len Rue, Jr., Curtice Taylor, Dr. Merlin D. Tuttle, and Art Wolfe.

Thanks also for informative interviews to nature- and stock-picture specialists Ann Guilfoyle, John Kapriellian, and Norman Owen Tomalin. I was also fortunate to talk about stock to experts: Peter Arnold, Arie Kopelman, Len Lessin, and Jim Pickerell, who all helped a lot.

Phillip Leonian as always freely gave me of his deep knowledge of photographic theory and practice, especially small electronic flash; he also helped me to make some gadgets. Ivan Eberle, Bernard Furnival, and Gregory Papin supplied information on light-beam triggers, and Dr. John Cooke, A. Kenneth Olsen, and Norman Stuessy talked to me about their custom-made flash units.

Dr. Robert Cappel of Eastman Kodak reviewed the section on chemicals and safe disposal, and corrected me on a couple of points. Robert Bosmann of Agfa, Warren Mauzy of Ilford, and John De Luca, Inder Mohadarin, and Susan Shaw also supplied information on this important topic.

Rick Lewis of the U.S. National Parks Service; Craig Reben, Georgia Parham, and Nancy Marks of the U.S. Fish and Wildlife Service, and Christine Indoe of the National Audubon Society, gave me literature and information on top wildlife and nature locations.

I should also like to thank Deborah Allen, José Aygun, Gerard Bailey, Stephanie Bruzemas, Andrew Childs, Pat Collyns, Tad Crawford, Jon Falk, Pat and Wayne Fisher, Sam Garcia, Ewan Gillies, Elizabeth Hutz, Edith Leonian, Zvi Livnat, Dr. Thomas E. Lovejoy, Jan Meyers, David and Luba Milme, Daniel Paris, Dian Rattner, and Herb Zimmerman for answering questions, making suggestions, or providing hospitality.

Robert Rattner not only gave me a great interview on underwater photography, but read the manuscript and made many valuable suggestions.

Any errors that have crept into the book despite my best efforts, are no-one's resposibility except mine.

I wish you success on your own terms, joy in your photography, and a beautiful clean earth teeming with animal life to hand down to your childrens' childrens' children. Save the planet!

Susan McCartney

How To Use This Book

Each chapter of the book is self-contained, and can be read independently, skipped, or referred back to, as needed. The book is meant to be a useful tool, and a guide for finding in-depth information, and the index is as complete as I can make it. I have not been given any financial inducements for recommending anything.

This book is dedicated to Caroline.

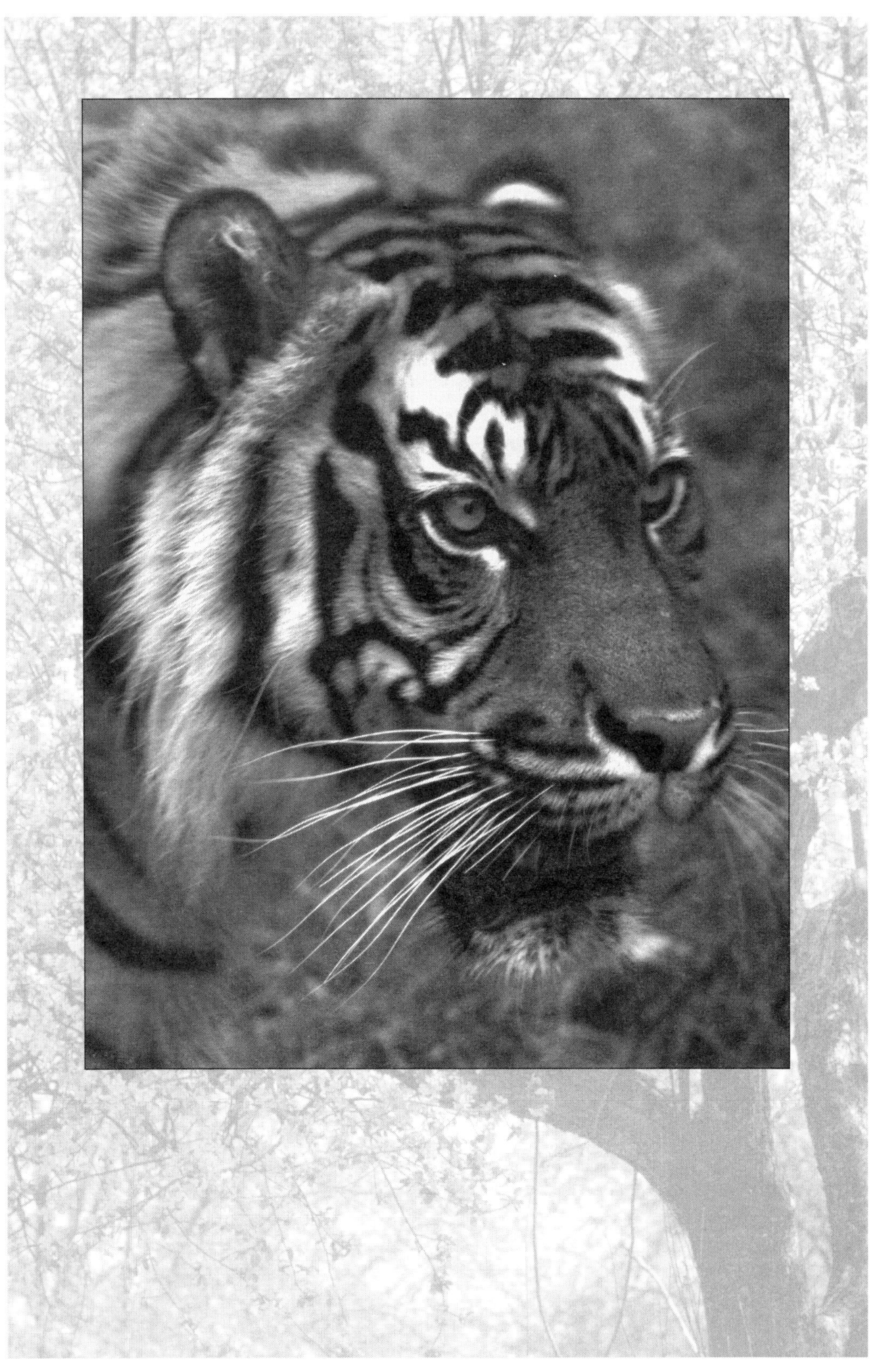

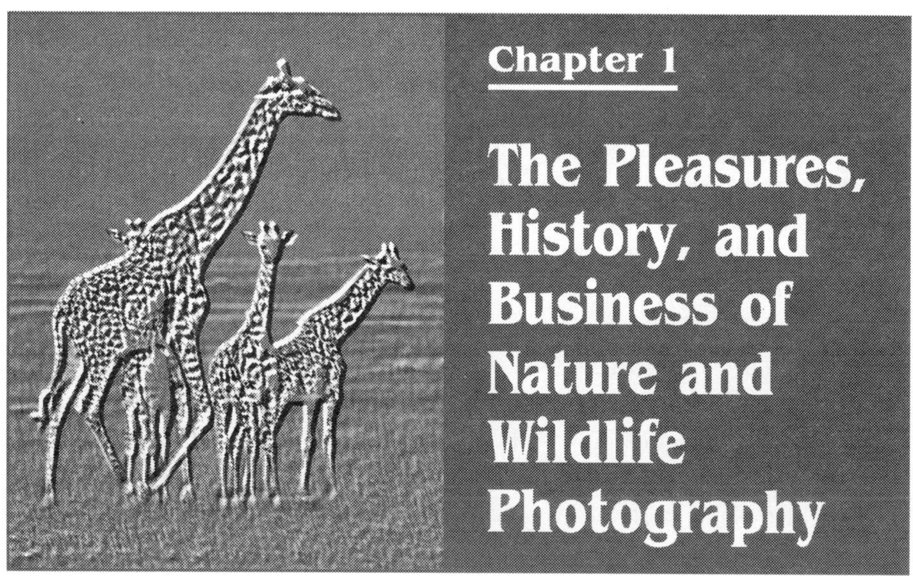

The Pleasures, History, and Business of Nature and Wildlife Photography

One of the best days of my life was spent on the Serengeti Plain in Tanzania, photographing for an African safari program. The art director who sent me had a very specific idea of what he wanted on the cover of the brochure—the head and neck of a giraffe silhouetted against a setting sun, with plenty of space left for type. My travelling companion and I had a rented Land Rover with a shooting platform and a sunroof. One day, we hired a Tanzanian guide called Ben (his real name was unpronounceable to us) who promised he could find giraffes. He did, a herd of about thirty of them. We followed the giraffes' slow progress across the plain for hours. Sometimes the beasts browsed on bushes, sometimes they galloped in circles with a strange rocking-horse gait; long legs and huge hooves seeming to stretch out in front and behind at the same time. As the sun sank lower, the giraffes moved towards distant trees. Ben told us that giraffes sleep in groves and would be hidden by the time the sun set.

I drew Ben a sketch of a giraffe's head with a big setting sun behind it, and let him look through my 500mm lens at the low sun. He became very enthusiastic and said that if we kept the Land Rover between the giraffes and the trees, we could delay their retirement for a few minutes. We drove very, very slowly, closer and closer. The giraffes were not alarmed. With hand signals, I directed the driver. Finally a giraffe was between me and the sun. Through the 500mm lens his head and neck filled the vertical frame. The creature stood peacefully for a few minutes with the sun directly behind his head, almost exactly as the art director had envisioned. I had time to expose two rolls of film, and there was enough time to let guide Ben admire the scene through the long lens and take a picture. When the sun went below the horizon we moved and the giraffes went to the trees. Of course guide Ben was rewarded well, and the client was ecstatic when he saw the pictures.

Another day I will never forget was on my first visit to the Pacific Northwest. I spent it on Ruby Beach, Washington, watching big waves booming against fantastically shaped rocks and offshore islets with pine trees growing on them. At noon the sky was blue and the sunlight harsh. A few people sat on stones near me. A family with kids threw sticks to a dog and played in the surf. Slowly, a mist came down, and around 5:00 p.m. the tide had fallen enough to walk along the deserted beach. The whole scene became monochrome. Ghostly pine and spruce trees crowded to the very edge of the vertical cliffs that rose high above the beach; the elephantine-looking remains of hundreds of dead trees lay on the stones at the high-tide line; the islets, sand, sky, and ocean were luminous shades of gray. Only shiny conical black rocks and white surf gave contrast. I photographed the totally monochrome scene using color film. In a few of the (I think) beautiful pictures I made that afternoon, I sat down and included my own pinky brown feet, just for their color.

Another good memory is from the village in upstate New York where I have a house. One early December, I got up at dawn and walked by the Wallkill River. Soft snow had fallen the previous night, then there had been a hard freeze. Little spikes of sparkling frost covered every surface—thick tree trunks, branches, shrubs, ground plants, and dead leaves. The river was partly frozen with a bluish snow cover, the unfrozen river just below a dam was swirling and steaming. The sky, water, and mist were deep pink from a red sunrise. I took rolls and rolls of close-ups and wide-angle shots of the best effects; at nine o'clock the frost coating the trees and the beautiful light were both gone.

My deepest involvement in nature photography comes when I travel, or in upstate New York, but I also take pictures in Manhattan's great Central Park. This park is a "hot spot" for birds, (more than 200 species have been spotted there), has nice plantings including spectacular cherry trees, and the Central Park Zoo has a good collection of animals in pleasant surroundings.

The pleasure of nature photography is available to just about anyone, no matter whether they live in suburb, town, city, or rural area. Perhaps you live near a wildlife refuge, or the shore, a great lake or river, or close to rolling meadows with flowers and butterflies at the right season. The plains and deserts are full of wildlife if you know where to look.

Mountains and deep woods, swamps and marshes are the best places of all to find wild creatures. There are some wonderful parks and hidden gardens in the suburbs. Get a book from the library and learn about the ecology of your region. Also check out commercial nature reserves, botanic gardens, zoos, city, state, and national parks, wildlife refuges, even animal/bird rehabilitation centers. All offer serious nature-photo opportunities.

You can start taking nature and wildlife pictures with almost any camera, though if you are serious and can afford it, I recommend getting an electronic TTL/dedicated camera that measures daylight and flash exposure Through The Lens. (The advantages will be detailed in the next chapter.)

At first anyway, no highly technical knowledge is required to get good pictures of flowers and plants, bugs and butterflies, zoo animals and nearby landscapes. These are all good subjects to start with. Try and shoot fairly spontaneously, don't agonize over each picture. Let one subject lead you to the next. Shoot several frames on any good subject, varying your composition by moving around. Early and late on sunny days are the times for pretty light, sunrise and sunset often the best times of all outdoors.

On Any Nature Photography Outing, Don't Forget To Carry:

Your camera out of its case, with lens protected by a filter

Film—more than you think you will need

Spare batteries of all sizes used

Camera instruction book — I carry mine, electronic models are complex!

Local map

Notebook

A few feet of gaffer tape wound round a sharp pencil

Swiss Army knife or Leatherman tool

Thin waxed twine

Odorless sunblock, SP 15 (beware of greasy ones)

Odorless, greaseless insect repellent (Deet is effective)

Rain poncho, green or camouflage — can be used as a blind in an emergency

Long-peaked cap

Jacket for the season/climate

White and black plastic trash bags

When you have been working at your photography for a while, you will probably be quite good, have produced some decent shots, and perhaps been told that you should sell your pictures. Most photographers would like to sell, and it's quite possible if you have a quantity of sharp, clear, well-exposed, interesting pictures, but this doesn't happen by accident. You will need to know something about the photography business in general, and have a plan.

The Business of Nature and Wildlife Photography

Professional photography is a big business, and today a very competitive one. If you have any intention of marketing your work as stock, as fine art, or perhaps of approaching publishers with picture stories, you should know at least the basics of this business. To learn more, read chapter 11 of this book, and read some business books. Ask photographers you know about the business side of their operation. Attend meetings of one the professional photographers' associations; the American Society of Media Photographers (ASMP) has chapters nationwide, and most meetings are open to nonmembers. If you qualify, join a photographers' association to learn, make friends in your business, and help support professional photography in general. Learn about copyright laws, pricing strategies, and prevailing rates for assignment and stock photography.

Take a general small-business course at a local community college to learn about business income-tax laws, sales taxes, insurance, amortization, depreciation and more. Some camera clubs may occasionally have meetings about marketing pictures.

Potential markets for nature/wildlife pictures include national and regional magazines and newspapers, small specialist magazines, and books of all kinds. Stock (existing) pictures are sold by individual photographers, but mostly are marketed by specialized stock-picture agencies (sometimes called stock libraries). Stock may be used for advertising, promotion, magazines, books, and especially textbooks. Today it is a very big business, and the most likely market for good nature or wildlife pictures. A smaller market is in so-called "paper goods" — greeting cards, posters, postcards (that can be reached by stock) — and there is some market for fine-art nature images sold inexpensively as posters, or as expensive original prints in galleries. A few photographers sell original prints through decorators, sometimes referred to as making "wall art."

If you build your files of needed, wanted, and popular subjects, and promote your work, users of nature and wildlife photographs will become aware of you as a source, and you will then have an excellent chance of marketing stock pictures through an agency or direct or both, and selling picture stories to newspapers, and local and specialist publications. You can build from those beginnings if your ultimate aim is to be top-class professional.

A fairly small number (I have heard 500 given as an estimate) of people make a living entirely from landscape/nature and/or wildlife photography. There are many different styles and approaches. Some concentrate on shooting in a loose, "editorial" style for magazines, others prefer to shoot for scientific illustrations aimed at textbooks, encyclopedias, and childrens' books. Some top photographers like the freedom and high income that shooting high-quality stock of in-demand subjects gives them, working closely with one or more stock agencies to keep up with trends and needs.

Some nature photographers write stories and articles as well as shoot; some own or are partners in stock-picture agencies. Some famous photographers lecture, give workshops, endorse film and gear, and design and market specialist equipment.

The best of the best produce wonderful picture books, which are great for study to improve your "eye" as well as just looking at for pleasure.

A handful of nature and wildlife photographers, superb at what they do, dedicated, and sometimes courageous, have advanced scientific knowledge as well as made wonderful images, and have become international celebrities.

As well as looking at books and videos by old and contemporary masters of photography, go to exhibits, and, especially, illustrated lectures. Look at original photographs whenever you possibly can. No book or video can ever completely capture the quality of a beautiful print or projected transparency.

Study Art and the Masters of Photography to Improve Your Own Work

In my opinion, to learn how to "see" well, and to refine your eye for a picture, you should have some knowledge of great photographs and great paintings. Perhaps some outdoor types think that going to museums is for wimps. But great painters and photographers know how to create effects of movement and depth on a still, two-dimensional surface. They attract the viewer's eye to the center of interest by varied arrangements of subjects in a given space, and they see and make the most of natural light in all weathers and seasons. These are all invaluable lessons.

Check out how classical painters manage to have a lot going on in their compositions without them seeming too cluttered. Chinese scroll painters "saw" in black-and-white, long before photographers did. Study color—color in nature is not there just to look pretty, but to attract, repel, intimidate, camouflage, and ensure survival. Painters can teach photographers an enormous amount about the use of hue and shade, color juxtaposition and contrast.

I have met students who told me that they were afraid of looking at others' art, because they believed it would stifle their own creativity. Do not be afraid. Creativity is as strong as the humble grasses that sometimes grow through concrete sidewalks. Don't worry that in the early stages of looking your photographs resemble the style of someone you admire. Sophisticated artists and photographers are always influenced to some degree by others (in fact the usual definition of "naive" art is that it has not been exposed to outside influences). If you take enough pictures, and persist, you will sooner or later synthesize other influences into your own style, with a contemporary aesthetic, and your work will have a "look" all its own.

Nature and Animals in Art

Artists have always recorded the natural world. The earliest known paintings, in caves at Altamira, Spain, and Lascaux, France, were of hunting scenes, and portraits of bison, reindeer, long-horned bulls, and spotted horses. (The caves are closed to all but scholars, but you can enjoy the images in books.) Assyrian, Egyptian, Greek, and Roman sites were decorated with sculptures, mosaics, and frescoes of lions, eagles, elephants, dolphins, camels, and hawks. In the Italian Renaissance, religious frescoes and later secular portraits showed enchanting landscapes—behind the main subject. Classical painters showed horses in battle (look especially at Paolo Ucello's superb work). The sixteenth-century German artist Albrecht Durer made many delightful engravings of animals (including my favorite of an almost perceptively quivering hare). Dutch artists painted landscapes for their own sake starting in the seventeenth century; later Dutch masters created superb seascapes and botanically accurate flower studies, some including butterflies.

In the late eighteenth and early nineteenth century, British artists (and poets) romanticized the misty mountains of the English Lake District and soaring, jagged Swiss Alps. John Constable painted the changing light over the Suffolk countryside, and his contemporary J.M.W. Turner painted classical, then romantic and industrial landscapes, eventually dissolving them in golden mists. Turner is now considered the forerunner of French Impressionism.

In the United States, a great movement in landscape painting arose in New York State in the 1820s and 1830s. Thomas Cole and other members of the Hudson Valley School painted the great river and its seasons in light that was both sensuous and realistic. Two of the greatest American landscapists were Frank Church and German-born Albert Bierstadt. They both went out West, and gained great fame (and fortune) with enormous, highly realistic paintings of the wilderness, mountains, and even weather of Wyoming, Montana, Colorado and California. Church

14

later traveled overseas, and painted volcanoes in the Andes and Aegean scenes. Another great western artist, George Catlin, loved the Great Plains, portraying the last wild buffalo herds and making great pictures of Native American life and ritual. And also in nineteenth-century America, John James Audubon made his marvellous bird lithographs.

Early European paintings of exotic animals were often amusing, the artists worked from tales recounted by explorers, not from life. One who marvelously caught the feeling of wild animals amid dense jungles (even though they were far from accurately drawn) was the French customs officer Henri (Douanier) Rousseau. A nineteenth-century American naive artist, George Hicks, made paintings in which the spirit of animals was deeply felt. You perhaps have seen prints of his most famous work, *The Peaceable Kingdom.* One of America's greatest artists, Winslow Homer, made some of his finest paintings with natural themes. His *The Fox Hunt* is a chilling study of the survival of the fittest, his Caribbean paintings are full of the intense light of the region and his late seascapes are masterpieces.

A Brief History of Nature and Wildlife Photography

Today's cameras evolved from the "camera obscura" (which means darkened room) used since the sixteenth century to help artists draw landscapes accurately. Early camera obscuras were huge. They worked something like a cross between an old 20-by-24-inch view camera and today's single lens reflex, with a forward-facing lens that focussed and angled an internal mirror that reflected the chosen scene onto a ground-glass screen on top. The artist traced the reflected image.

French philosopher Michel Montaigne once said: "Nothing has the power of an idea whose time has come." Many people in the early nineteenth century wanted to fix a light image focussed on ground glass. (The word photography comes from the Greek "photos"—light.) In France, Louis Jacques Mandé Daguerre, a former artist and exhibitor of spectacular "dioramas" of Greek and Roman classical scenes, spent years on the quest. He worked with metal plates used by lithographers. By experimenting with various coatings on the metal plates, and highly toxic developers and fixers, he eventually succeeded and in 1839 published details of his Daguerrotype process. He was rewarded by great fame, and a lot of cash from a grateful French government.

In England, Daguerre's contemporary William Henry Fox Talbot was both wealthy and a gifted scientist. He made a "grand tour" of Europe with his wife in 1833, and took along a camera lucida to help him paint watercolors of the scenery. This was a compact drawing aid employing a prism so an artist could look at the view and the paper simultaneously. Fox Talbot was not very successful with this device, and soon went back to using the big camera obscura, but together they gave him the germ of an idea that he worked on obsessively: to fix an image onto sensitized paper. He succeeded after years of work, but published details of his Calotype or Talbotype process only after Daguerre declared he had invented photography. Fox Talbot never gained the Frenchman's fame.

Daguerreotypes fixed an image onto a copper plate coated with silver, but could not be duplicated. They were beautifully detailed, and initially were much more popular than paper Calotypes, which made rather fuzzy images. But, the Calotype process made multiple copies of pictures possible, and was the basis for photography as we know it today. (British astronomer Sir John Herschel, who first used sodium thiosulfate as fixer, is now considered a co-inventor of positive-negative photography, along with Fox Talbot.)

City-dweller Daguerre photographed people, Paris, and still-life subjects, but Fox Talbot was a countryman. His earliest "photogenic drawings" were of ferns and leaves exposed directly by sunlight onto sensitized paper. Then he used a camera to make tiny pictures of light coming through leaded windows of his home, Lacock Abbey, and fixed the images. They were the first negatives. Fox Talbot kept improving his process and in 1844 he published *The Pencil of Nature*, a periodical devoted to photography, illustrated with tipped-in prints of his work. This was bound as the first photographic book.

Fox Talbot photographed country things: haystacks, ladders against barn walls, a misty river with a bridge, picturesque folk in traditional dress, and trees and flowers. Fox Talbot was a great scientist, but probably not a great photographer. Other nature photographers soon followed him.

In France, in the 1840s Gustave Le Gray made deeply felt landscapes. In 1862 the Bisson brothers were the first photographers to accompany an alpine expedition, climbing Mont Blanc and documenting the ascent. They used the glass-plate collodion process and the cumbersome cameras of the day.

In America, pioneer photographers followed the Hudson River School painters west, in the 1880s and 1890s. The purpose of the photographs they made was to record and survey, not to make art. But some of these American landscapists were masters; the greatest include Carleton Watkins and William Henry Jackson, Timothy O'Sullivan and Edweard Muybridge. Their works were reproduced in steriopticon viewers, (the television of the mid-nineteenth century), and made people in the Midwest and East aware of the glorious scenery of the West. William Henry Jackson's pictures especially were a crucial factor in gaining the political support needed to establish Yellowstone as the world's first national park, and ultimately to the creation of the U.S. national parks system.

In England, Peter Henry Emerson, an Anglo-American writer, physician, and photographer, was a superb observer of the country scene at the beginning of the twentieth century. His studies of the landscape and way of life on the still rather isolated Norfolk Broads are now considered masterpieces.

In the 1920s, Alfred Steiglitz made pioneering photos of clouds—his *Equivalents* series—and studies of the scenery around Lake George, New York, in addition to the big-city scenes, nudes, and portraits for which he is best known. In California in the 1930s Edward Weston started to photograph the dunes, tree forms, and ocean around Point Lobos.

The most admired landscape photographs ever made, perhaps the best-known photographs ever made, were done by the great Ansel Adams, who worked from the 1920s to the 1970s. (You can still use his book on the U.S. national parks, first published in the 1940s, his zenith, as a guide to photographing the parks today.) A few years ago I saw an exhibit of his original black-and-white prints at the National Gallery of Art in Washington, D.C. Some were six or eight feet tall, rich and lush in tone, powerful in feeling; it was a great experience.

In 1962, another physician-turned-photographer, Eliot Porter, published his first book at the age of sixty, after photographing for thirty years. This book of large-format color landscapes and close-ups, *In Wildness Is the Preservation of the World,* using Thoreau's words, revolutionized nature photography and probably did as much as anything to inspire its current popularity.

In the late 1970s Ernst Haas published his classic *The Creation*, interpreting Genesis with impressionistic and realistic photographs of fire, earth, water, air, and creatures and plants taken in East Africa, Hawaii, the Galapagos, and the American West. That book, still in print, inspired Jim Brandenburg and Frans Lanting among other contemporary nature masters.

Historic Animal and Bird Photography

Wildlife photography began much later than landscape for the obvious reason that early films and lenses were far too slow to record moving subjects. The earliest wildlife photos were of dead beasts with some hunter's foot on the trophy or of stuffed specimens. Pioneering live-bird pictures, studies of storks that almost any bird photographer could still be proud of, were made in a German zoo by Ottomar Anshütz, in the mid-1880s.

L.A. Huffman made some rather static, but definitely live, images of some of the last great wild buffalo herds, grazing in the Dakotas in about 1890.

In 1891 Edweard Muybridge, a great scientist as well as a great photographer (after years of experimentation and failure) was able to scientifically document the motion of a galloping horse on film. He used a measured run against a white background, fast lenses imported from England, and twelve cameras evenly spaced, with the horse breaking strings and tripping the specially built 1/1000th-of-a-second shutters in succession. Muybridge, of course, went on to make thousands of other motion studies, and was also the inventor of the Zoöpraxiscope (a forerunner of the motion-picture camera).

The First Animal Photographs in the Wild

After Anshütz and Muybridge had broken the motion barrier, others soon started photographing animals in the wild.

A book I love (and wish I owned) is *Early Wildlife Photography,* by C.A.W. Guggisberg (published in 1979). The text is entertaining and illustrated with great shots such as A.W. Dugmore's charging rhino, Marius Maxwell's galloping giraffes, and F.W. Champion's leopard with a kill taken with flash. Plus, there are amusing pictures of people struggling with huge field cameras while strapped to trees, as well as still lifes of the first, wooden, rickety-looking telephoto lenses. (The book is out of print; you can refer to it at good libraries.)

Most early wildlife photographers were well-to-do people. Among them was the team of Mr. and Mrs. A.G. Wallinan who photographed in Colorado in the 1890s and spent years experimenting with flash. Their images include an elk in the snow, a treed cougar, mule deer, and pronghorn antelopes. A book of their work, *Camera Shots At Big Game*, published in 1901, had a foreword by future President Theodore Roosevelt.

Carl G. Schillings, a German who studied photography in Berlin, made three East African expeditions. After much trial, error, and failure (mishaps sometimes included his flashpowder setting his camera blind on fire!) he finally succeeded in obtaining fine night pictures of lions, elephants, and other big game, and published *With Flashlight and Rifle* in 1906.

George Shiras III was a lawyer, one-term congressman from Pennsylvania, and lifetime outdoorsman, and was for sixty years a dedicated outdoor photographer. His excellent flash photographs, with descriptive essays, were regularly published in the *National Geographic* magazine, starting in January 1906. Amusingly, two members of the NGS board resigned at that time to protest that "nature photographs are not a suitable subject for a geographical magazine"! I own Shiras's classic two-volume book *With Flashlight and Camera* (published in the 1930s). See it, if you can find it.

Carl Akeley worked for the American Museum of Natural History in New York, as a sculptor, taxidermist, and photographer. He used some of his fine African photographs as reference for creating the great nature dioramas at this museum. He was killed in Africa by a charging elephant in 1927.

The best known of all early wildlife photographers were the husband-and-wife team, Martin and Osa Johnson. They were not wealthy, but earned their living showing films and lantern slides, and lecturing, and became media stars of their day. Martin was raised in Kansas and Missouri, and accompanied novelist Jack London on a round-the-world odyssey by yacht, in about 1910. When he married Osa, also a Kansan, they travelled the world photographing and filming together, from the 1920s to 1940, when Martin was killed in a plane crash. A recent book about them, *They Married Adventure,* by Pascal and Eleanor Imperato has many fine illustrations. A flash picture by Martin of a lioness with a newly killed zebra, included in the book, is superb.

Eric Hosking in Britain was the world's best bird photographer, from about the 1940s to the 1960s. (His son David carries on the family tradition today.)

Serious underwater photography began when French oceanographer Jacques Yves Cousteau invented the scuba (self-contained underwater breathing apparatus) in the 1950s, and made pioneering images.

Today's landscape, nature, and wildlife masters include James Balog, Jim Brandenburg, Nathan Farb, Douglas Faulkner, Frans Lanting, David Muench, Leonard Lee Rue, and Art Wolfe, all from the United States; Heather Angel and Stephen Dalton from Britain; and, from Ecuador, Japan and Lichtenstein respectively, Tui de Roi, Mitsuako Iwago, and André Bäartschi, (the winner of the 1992 BBC International Wildlife Photographer of the Year award). Study any of their work for pleasure and to improve your own photography.

And, look at magazines like *Airone, Animals, Audubon, BBC Wildlife, Geo, International Wildlife, Life, National Geographic, Natural History, Outdoor Photography, Sierra, Smithsonian, Terre Sauvage,* and *Wildlife Conservation* that regularly use the best established and up-and-coming landscape, nature, and wildlife photographers, and scientist photographers.

There is just one drawback to looking at great work. The very best nature-picture stories in magazines or books, or the fine nature shows on TV usually take months or years of patient work to complete. Don't compare your work to these at first anyway, or you may get discouraged. If your attempts at photographing wintering geese on a local pond, butterflies in a summer meadow, a woodchuck by the side of the road, a lion in a zoo, or a cheeky chipmunk in a western national park are not yet terrific, keep practising. You will improve. Don't expect your early efforts to look like scenes from *Nature or Wild America* or a *BBC* special, or pages from the *National Geographic.*

Instead, study the *feeling* in the work of photographers you most admire, travel as much as you can to broaden your subject matter, and most of all, keep shooting what you love the most.

Nature and Wildlife Photography Skills

I assume that the reader of this book has basic photography skills. These of course include camera operation, understanding of fundamental principals like the correlation between f/stops and shutter speeds, and the ability to normally get sharp, clear, well-exposed pictures.

Basic Nature/Wildlife/Landscape Skills

The principal requirements for making good nature photographs are a love of the outdoors and wild things, a keen eye, good reflexes, great patience, and the willingness to practice and reshoot until use of the equipment owned, whatever it is, becomes instinctive, or almost so. (The wild things you have waited patiently to capture on film can be gone in seconds. If you fumble with a camera or lens, the moment is gone.)

Good nature photographers "compose" well. Composition is a word that frightens many people; it just means to make interesting arrangements of a three-dimensional subject within a two-dimensional picture area. There are no rules that can truly teach composition, but looking at great pictures of all kinds and studying your own work to see how it could be improved is important.

Good wildlife photographers know something about their subjects, at least enough to be able to anticipate behavior. You can learn some of these these things from nature and zoology books, and much more from your own observations.

Local farmers, park rangers, hunters, fishermen, zoo employees, bird watchers, and gardeners, are all possible information sources too.

Learn to look at light as well as plants, birds, butterflies, or whatever else you are most interested in. All good outdoor photographers, especially landscape photographers, make the best possible use of existing light.

A way to learn a lot is to give yourself assignments, rather than to just wander around taking pictures of whatever comes along. When you assign yourself any subject, plan to work on it for a while. You probably won't get what you want on one or two rolls of film. Realistically study and appraise results; go back and reshoot, as often as necessary, to correct technical errors and to get varied coverage of your subject. Watch exposure especially, focus on the eyes of wildlife almost always, and avoid the blur of camera shake by using a solid tripod.

As you gain experience, choose a couple of favorite films and learn their characteristics (for more see chapter 2.) When you have licked basic problems of exposure and sharpness, you will be free to concentrate on capturing peak moments. Practice anticipation, pressing the shutter just before you think something is about to happen; this gets easier the more you do it. Learn how to best use the beautiful variations of daylight and practice making picture stories or series, rather than single images.

If your aim is to to sell nature stories to magazines, books, or newspapers, or to market a serious amount of stock, you should shoot at all times of the year, in as many different places as you can. The more varied your subject matter the better.

Photographers for fine art or pleasure should of course choose any subjects they enjoy, and work to acquire good skills with equipment, and to acquire the sharpest possible eye to capture your subjects well on film.

Intermediate Technical Skills

The skills most needed by nature photographers include the ability to make extremely sharp close-ups, with macro lenses, extension tubes or bellows attachments—or all three combined for the tiniest subjects.

The bird photographer or wild-animal photographer must acquire skill in handling long heavy telephoto lenses, which have very limited depth of field. The landscape photographer most needs a feeling for composition and light.

The ability to know how light records on film is crucial. Very long exposures, or the use of polarizing filters, or graduated neutral-density filters to record both bright sky and dark ground in a backlit scene, are sometimes needed. The most innovative photographers today often use flash as "fill" (supplementary light) for nearby subjects in harsh sunshine or low light. Sometimes flash can be used as the sole source of illumination to stop action of fast moving subjects, like small birds for instance.

Many creatures are active at night and flash must always be used then—very carefully to avoid harsh effects. Many underwater pictures are taken with with flash. To perfect these techniques takes one thing above all others: practice, practice, and more practice. To acquire the best possible physical technique photograph every day if you possibly can. Shoot at least every weekend if you can't use the camera every day.

Advanced Skills

The advanced nature and wildlife photographer will know their equipment, film, and how to use light extremely well, almost by reflex. He or she will then be free to concentrate on the really important things: beauty, mood, action, behavior, and information.

You may or may not need technical skills with flash, depending on what you prefer to shoot. A good knowledge of lighting, though, never hurt any photographer. Ultra-high-speed flash is used to stop motion, sometimes cameras or flashes are triggered by infrared or radio signal, or hard-wire (sync cord) remote control, or an animal or insect can break an invisible infrared light beam and take it's own picture.

Long exposures and blur, alone or combined with action-stopping flash, are techniques used to express motion. "Panning"— following action — is one of the hardest things to do with long heavy lenses and requires a heavy tripod, a big solid ball-head that can be adjusted to different tensions, and practice, practice, and more practice. To catch distant birds taking off may be the most difficult nature photography skill of all.

All top specialist skills (for panoramic and large-format photography, photomicroscopy, bird pictures with the longest lenses, extreme close-ups of insects, advanced underwater photography) are acquired slowly as a rule, by people who practice continually, who work very hard to gain knowledge of the subject matter, and mastery of the equipment used.

With top skills, especially when you are in peak practice, you will be ready to make the most of picture opportunities anywhere, close to home, or in remote areas of the world.

Business Skills

There is a big difference between a being skilled amateur or semiprofessional photographer however talented, whose primary income is from another source, than in being a full-time professional. A good photographer who wants to make serious money from their nature and wildlife photography must have at least an idea of what types of pictures are in demand, and normally sell well, and shoot some of them. (But, superb, creative, original pictures of just about *anything* will eventually sell well!)

Shooting some of what sells doesn't mean selling out, but being practical. Study books and magazines and stock catalogs to see the types of picture most used. If you look at bird magazines for instance, you will soon learn that many more pictures of bright-colored birds are published than of brown ones!

To be professional you have to study the market (the money-making opportunities available); spend at least part of your time providing photo users with what they want (or with what they would want if they knew it existed) and, you must be alert to future trends. Of course, this does not mean giving up what you love to do most. Pictures made with love or even passion are the finest of all and may bring you great success eventually.

Costing and Budgeting

Beginning and part-time professionals should know how much it cost to produce a given picture, in order to charge a fair price—anyone should charge at least enough to cover direct costs, even if you do not charge for the use of your equipment, time, or the years you spent becoming a good enough photographer! Established professionals will have to charge enough to make a decent profit.

Full-time professionals have to consider the cost of equipment, processing, travel, assistance if any; self-promotion, daily living, taxes, insurance, savings for emergencies, retirement, and more. Few full-time professional photographers today would want to be without a telephone answering machine, fax, and photocopier; a large number of professionals now own basic computers with business programs. A small but fast-increasing number of photographers are going into high-end computers, scanning, retouching, and manipulating their own images.

If all this sounds daunting, I suppose it is when looked at as whole, but don't be discouraged. Most people work their way into professional photography, including landscape, nature, and wildlife photography, slowly. Graduates of good photography schools often start as assistants to established talent, a great way to learn. Scientists take photographs for research purposes, to record data, and illustrate their specialty, at first anyway. And, artist-type people have always worked at a wide range of part-time jobs to support themselves as they were getting established.

Photographers' associations, community colleges, and art and photography schools teach business courses. There are good computer programs to help small businesses, including some designed especially for photographers.

Photography, even commercial photography, is considered one of the arts as well as business. All arts professionals who have succeeded know that the greatest quality anyone who wants to make it can have is persistence. Practice. Experiment. Dare. Do not be afraid to fail, or to pick yourself up if you make a mistake and start over.

I truly believe that if you care enough and love photography enough, are willing to work hard and long enough, you can make your life in photography. If you succeed I don't promise riches. I do guarantee you'll have spiritual rewards and considerable prestige, and you'll probably meet a lot of interesting people, go to a lot of interesting places, and have a lot of fun!

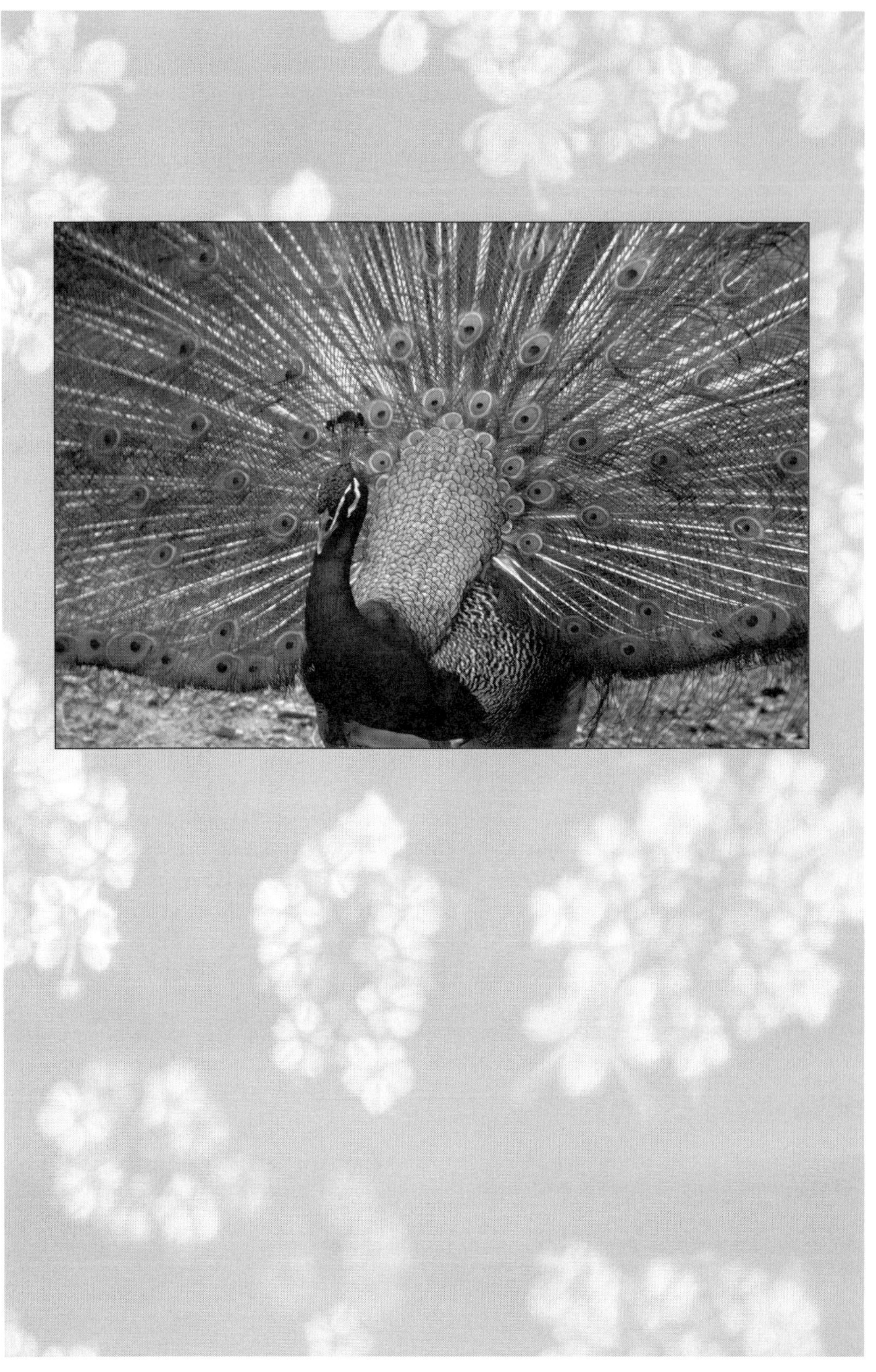

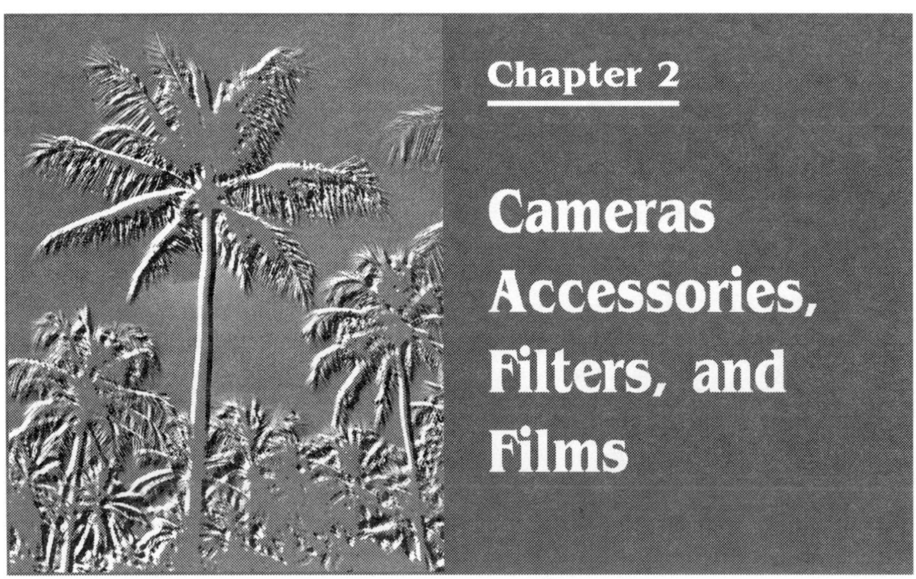

You can take some good nature or wildlife photographs with virtually any camera that focuses. It's a cliché, but true, that the photographer, not the camera or the lens, sees and makes the picture! But certain things are only possible with specialized equipment. This chapter is to help you decide what is basic to your needs now, and what if anything to add to solve particular problems later as you become more proficient and demanding. It will also cover accessories, most useful filters, and the most popular films used in professional nature/wildlife photography.

Get very familiar with the equipment you have at first and spend available cash on shooting, film, and processing, especially if funds are tight. Practice until you can operate your camera instinctively. That's a must for all serious photography, but is even more critical for wildlife, which moves swiftly and unpredictably. Also practice learning to "see" photographically, which means being able to make a good two-dimensional rendition in a limited space of a three-dimensional subject in a large space. The best way to achieve this is to look at your subjects through the lens all the time, this is not as elementary as it sounds. Practice above all to find out what nature subjects interest you most and concentrate on those. See what approach works best for you. The finest photographs of all kinds express deep feelings and create a mood, they are not merely competent renditions of any subject.

If your equipment limits what you can do, then you will probably need to acquire a better camera, or a longer telephoto, or maybe a wide-angle or close-up lens, or other specialized items. But, in my opinion, you should always think of cameras, lenses, and gadgets as fine tools, no more or less. They help you get the images you want onto film, but they are not miracle makers.

Choosing First Lenses

The beginning nature photographer can start with any lens; the 55mm lens has been the "normal" lens on 35mm cameras for years, though you don't have to choose it when you buy a new camera.

Some camera outfits now come with 35-70mm or 28-80mm zoom lenses as standard; these are okay for beginners who only want to carry one lens. (I recommend a owning a good wide angle lens, plus a good telephoto zoom lens, closeup extension tubes and a 1.4x tele-extender, at first.) **Caution:** Inexpensive zooms tend to have a small aperture at the long end of the range. Do not buy any lens slower than f/5.6.

The best of today's zoom lenses are extremely sharp, those in the 80-200mm or 70-210mm range are good for photographing many animals, for the largest birds, and for precise framing of distant landscapes. Get one not slower than f/4, (f/2.8 is best) so that you can use it with a tele-extender (which reduces the light reaching the lens; see later in this chapter).

A good telephoto lens, of a minimum of 300mm or 400mm focal length is needed for photographing small birds, and distant animals. Again, get a lens no slower than f/5.6 so you can use it later with a "doubler" (tele-extender) for larger image size. (If you are serious, and can afford a very fast telephoto lens, get one now, and avoid trading up later!)

Get a wide-angle lens if you plan to photograph landscapes. I frequently use a 28mm lens for gardens, intimate landscapes, and animals in landscapes. A 20mm lens is a good choice for sweeping landscapes.

Wide-angle zoom lenses in the 20-35mm range are available also.

Popular Close-Up Accessories

Macro lenses focus very close without attachments. Magnification of moderate-size subjects like flowers or frogs is easy. The degree of magnification depends on the lens. Macros sold today usually permit showing objects about the size of an average spider at half life-size in the 35mm picture area. Macro lenses can be used with extension tubes, singly or in combination, for life-size or greater magnifications and with a bellows permit enlargements to about 10X life-size or larger (with considerable loss of light reaching the lens).

A Basic Nature Photography Outfit

A single-lens reflex camera - 35mm, or 6x4.5cm, 6x6cm, or 6x7cm, as preferred. (By far the greatest number of published nature/wildlife pictures are taken on the 35mm format.) If you can afford it, get a motorized, TTL (through-the-lens metering) /dedicated camera. Any camera you use should have interchangeable lens capability, and a cable-release outlet. Ideally it should also have:

- A hot shoe for a flash.
- A sync outlet for using a flash off-camera.
- A stop-down preview button (this is essential for close-ups, helpful for previewing depth of field, and spotting problems caused by flare).

A TTL/dedicated, or electronic/program camera should permit choice of mode of operation:

(P)—program mode—is where the aperture and shutter speeds are chosen by the camera computer, not by you. A camera used only on P is essentially a point-and-shoot camera. Program exposures are usually good with average subjects, but do not work so well with subjects that are not average. For instance, chosen shutter speed may be too slow to stop action in low light, resulting in a well-exposed but blurred subject.

(A)—aperture-priority mode—controls lens the opening and depth of field (zone of sharp focus), critical for long lens and close up work.

(S)—shutter-priority mode—is used to alter shutter speeds, to stop action, blur motion, or make very long time exposures for instance.

(M)—manual mode—is used to put all decisions under the photographer's control for creative purposes. You may need or prefer to deliberately over- or underexpose part of a contrasty scene for example, to get correct exposure on your main subject.

(These modes are all helpful, at different times.)

Basic Accessories

By far the most important accessory for any nature or wildlife photographer is a sturdy tripod. Ideally, get a tripod that extends to your eye level without the center column extended, and made so that the legs can be spread for low-angle shooting.

An 18 percent gray card (sold in professional camera stores) will help you get better exposures. (For more see chapter 3.)

A cable release, dedicated if needed for a TTL camera, is a must.

A lightweight, round, collapsible white reflector and/or diffuser, is helpful in a great many outdoor situations, the 36-inch size is good.

A water resistant camera bag or a camera backpack is useful.

Additions to the Basic Nature Photography Outfit

Besides the essentials you may wish to add:

A small flash unit can be extremely useful. Automatic, or TTL/dedicated units are easiest to use. Any tiny flash will do to start.

A sync/PC cord, or dedicated cord, is needed for off-camera flash use. (If your camera does not have a built-in sync/PC outlet, to use flash off-camera you must also get a sync/PC cord adaptor for the hot shoe.)

A lightweight flash bracket will help you aim your flash accurately. (For much more on flash, and brackets, see chapter 4).

A few basic color filters are useful:

Skylight IA (pinkish) or UV filter (clear) filters (screw-in type) can be kept on each lens, instead of lens covers. They protect the lens, but leave you ready to shoot at all times.

A gray polarizing filter can cut glare, and darken blue skies. Polarizers reduce the light reaching the lens by about two stops. For TTL cameras, a circular polarizer is required.

An FLD filter cuts the green effect of most types of fluorescent light on film. This is a useful filter to own if you photograph by available light in zoos or aquariums.

A "straw" filter (81A, 81B, or 81C) cuts blue light of overcast days

A square or oblong graduated to clear neutral-density filter is useful for back-lit landscapes. You will need a filter holder for this.

If you shoot occasional close-ups of flowers and plants, life along the shore, and the like, a 55mm macro lens is extremely useful. The 105mm macro is excellent for insects that can't normally be approached too close without disturbing them, and for some zoo portraits, but it is fairly expensive.

Extension tubes are hollow tubes that are put between camera and lens, singly or combined, to permit close focussing. They are often sold in sets of three; manual ones are inexpensive, automatic ones though are easier to use.

Bellows are used to make magnifications of up to about 10X life-size in combination with macro or special lenses. A bellows is a concertina-like flexible tube on two rails, used between camera and lens. The bellows attachment is sometimes used with a short-mount lens, sometimes with a 55mm macro or "normal" lens reversed with an adaptor ring. Manufacturers' literature on all the above give specific details for close-up equipment. (For more, see chapter 8.)

Long Telephoto Lenses and Tele-Extenders

If animals and especially birds are your passion, you will soon find you need a long telephoto lens if you don't already own one. A 300mm lens is fine for many animals; 400mm is considered a good minimum length for smaller birds; or, do as I sometimes do, and use an f/2.8 80-200mm zoom lens with a 1.4X or 2X tele-extender.

Because you must often use high shutter speeds to stop action and/ or camera shake with long lenses (even when used on a tripod), and because most nature clients prefer pictures made on slow, fine-grain film, always get the fastest telephoto lenses you can afford.

Tele-extenders (sometimes called doublers) are convenient, lightweight, and increasingly popular. 1.4X and 2X extenders are used between the camera body and lenses longer than about 100mm, to increase the focal length (with a one or two f/stop decrease in the light reaching the film). Unlike extension tubes, they permit focussing on infinity.

A 1.4X tele-extender will make a 200mm f/4 lens into a 280mm f/5.6.

A 2X extender will make a 200mm f/4 into a 400mm f/8 lens. Either will help you get closer shots of large birds and distant mammals. I love tele-extenders because they are so light and convenient to carry. I have used both sizes for years and have had no problems using them with tele-zooms. But, be sure to get the extenders made for your good lenses. They cost about the same as some lenses.

Caution: Cheap tele-extenders can badly degrade images.

The Most Essential Accessory, the Tripod

Apart from the camera and a lens, the first accessory you should own is a good tripod. You can live without filters, cable releases, or even a camera bag (pad any strong backpack with foam) if you must. In my opinion, you won't be a serious nature photographer without a tripod.

However much you may hate carrying it, a sturdy tripod is absolutely essential for use in low light with long exposures (often the most beautiful pictures are taken around dawn and dusk); the tripod is needed for close-ups made with the small f/stops and slow shutter speeds needed for maximum depth of field. Tripods are a big help when shooting with telephoto and zoom lenses to minimize blur caused by lens shake. Tripods are essential with any medium-format, large-format, and panoramic cameras, again to prevent blur caused by camera shake.

No serious nature, wildlife, outdoor, travel, location or stock photographer would consider going anywhere without a sturdy tripod. Don't use false economy and get a cheap tripod, you will soon regret it! The ones listed below are excellent.

Gitzo: These superb, expensive tripods are made in France, and they come in all sizes from table toppers to heavyweights extending to about eleven feet. They are used by photographers round the world who work with the fastest, heaviest, longest telephoto lenses. I own two Gitzos. When I must carry one any distance, I use a lightweight, compact Tota-Luxe Performance model. It comes to my eye level (64") when fully-extended; mostly, I use the Studex Safari Performance model, which reaches eighty inches extended. The legs of Performance Gitzos can be spread low.

Bogen: These very good tripods are quite moderately priced, the legs can be spread low. I own a midsized Bogen model # 3001, which is sturdy and reasonably lightweight. Italian-made Bogen tripods are marketed as Manfrotto in Europe and come in several sizes.

Benbo: These tripods are very popular in Britain where they are made, adjust to amazing angles, but you must get used to operating them. The light Trekker model might be a good choice for a close up photographer.

Slik: These Japanese tripods come in budget and professional models, but the legs do not spread. They have a fairly stable superlight model.

Linhof: Top German tripods used by many large-format specialists.

Ball heads are just about essential for following movement, and are used by most nature and wildlife photographers. The best tripods have removable heads, so you can choose the head you prefer. Whichever tripod I take out, I use one of the following excellent ball heads: the Gitzo # 1 (small, lightweight), the Gitzo # 2, (larger), but I mostly use an Arca Swiss # 1; this permits adjusting pressure for easy motion control and accurate panning—following movement —in any direction. The Foba, NPC and Linhof heads all come highly recommended. I personally do not like Bogen tripod heads, they are big and heavy.

Hand-Held Exposure Meters

If your older camera does not have a built-in meter, a hand-held exposure meter is a must. They are also good insurance, in case built-in camera meters fail. What kind of hand held meter should you get?

A flash meter is useful to check an automatic or TTL flash, and essential for all exposures lit by manual flash, indoors or out.

I like all Minolta meters. The model IVF measures flash, daylight and both combined, at all shutter speeds, making manual flash and flash-fill exposures easy to calculate. Sekonic makes the Digilite F, a relatively inexpensive daylight/flash reading meter, which I own. (For more, see Exposure and Flash, in chapter 3.)

Specialist Lenses

When buying telephoto or zoom lenses, take size and weight into account; backpackers especially should not get lenses they can't carry!

Every top camera manufacturer makes very good or excellent lenses, and also superb lenses. These last feature low dispersion (or similar name) apochromatic glass, internal focussing for reduced bulk, super-high speeds, and more. They always carry a special designation, and cost plenty. If you plan to work professionally, they are almost essential today. (See the interview with John Kapriellian in chapter 12.)

Bird specialists probably need the fastest, longest lenses of all. There are 500mm f/4; 600mm f/4, or even 800mm f/5.6 models available. These lenses are big and heavy—the longest require two tripods for stability—and extremely expensive. Top zoom lenses are fast, quite expensive, and mostly heavy, but worth it if you need them, for the precise framing they permit.

Choosing a Camera System

Eventually, almost all serious nature/wildlife photographers settle on a top 35mm SLR camera system, which offers the choice of lenses and many specialist accessories they need. Professionals need the most rugged equipment possible.

What Camera System and Format Should I Choose?

Most professional wildlife photographers shoot with 35mm SLR (single lens reflex) camera systems, for the range of long, fast lenses available, also convience and relatively light weight.

Some nature stock and landscape photographers use a medium format (usually 6x6 or 6x7cm) system.

Many landscapists including fine-art photographers use folding field cameras (4"x5", 5"x7" or even 8"x10" format). Some also use panoramic cameras (or panoramic backs for large-format cameras).

When choosing a system, get familiar with different brands of cameras and lenses. See how they "fit" your hands. Think about carrying them! Are the lenses and accessories you want to own, now or eventually, available for a particular system? Is TTL metering, or simple program operation, or fast autofocus very important to you, or do you prefer to make most decisions about exposure and focusing yourself? Do you need to use a bellows? Wireless remote control, timed interval operation? A microscope? All these things are possible.

Write down what you want now and what you think you will need within the next couple of years. Read about and handle different cameras and lenses before you buy. Ask professional photographers, serious amateurs, or scientific colleagues what they use and what they like or don't like about their equipment. Of course, shop around at dealers, but don't always trust what a camera salesperson recommends. The salesperson's preference may be based on their own experiences as a photographer, their commission, or just long habit! Even with an excellent salesperson, the system they prefer may not be the right one for you.

A good professional outfit, with just a couple of 35mm camera bodies and three or four lenses, plus tubes, extenders and so forth, is a major investment, so don't rush in. Rentals are available from professional stores in most large cities. Consider renting (with the option to buy if possible) a camera and a couple of different lenses from two different systems before investing. Especially, try out expensive long lenses before buying. If your budget is tight, consider buying used equipment, or a midprice camera in a major system with top lenses. Upgrade the camera body later.

Top Professional Systems

Without question, the most popular 35mm SLR systems among professional photographers are Nikon and Canon, both made in Japan. Canon and Nikon cameras and lenses have high resale value. Good used ones are readily available. Both have cameras in different price ranges.

Contax and Leica are also top quality, German-brand SLR systems with superb lenses. They are high priced. Leica of course is most famed for its rangefinder cameras, and makes microscopes too.

If Minolta, Olympus, or Pentax appeal to you, these Japanese systems are also of fine quality. I like Olympus in this range; the cameras are compact. Olympus has many accessories, and also makes microscopes.

Among the "independents" Sigma has just come out with its first 35mm SLR, model SA 300. This is a moderate-price camera with many useful features, and looks very promising. This company's lenses have a fine reputation, and are made with different mounts for major brand cameras.

Tokina is another independent lens brand, with mounts for several brands of camera. I now own two Tokina lenses, which I find excellent.

I recommend buying equipment from a full-service professional dealer, who should expect to keep working with you. I mostly use Ken Hanson in New York. They help with repairs, even emergency loaners, can find esoteric items, and have good used stuff.

When you are ready to commit yourself, pay for purchases with a credit card. Keep all boxes, inner wrappings, and receipts. Try your equipment for a few days. Shoot film. If you like the camera, lenses, and results, complete and mail in all warranties. Otherwise, return the equipment during the period permitted by the dealer (often seven days.)

Be sure and check deep-discounters' reputations, store warranties, and return policies before patronizing them. Some are excellent, like B&H and Adorama in New York, both of which I use (but not by mail). There is no savings with a discounter if you can't return equipment.

The Nikon System

I am a Nikon-system user, and have been for 25 years. Nikon has an unsurpassed range of lenses and professional accessories and it now markets cameras and lenses in all price brackets. Nikon Professional Services are helpful with loaners and expedited repairs for its members, and Nikon continues to add to its line of lenses. I now use N90 and N8008S cameras (marketed as F90 and F801S in Europe).

I currently own several Nikkor lenses. For different types of nature photography I use:

20mm f/2.8 (manual) for sweeping landscapes

28mm f/2 (manual) for gardens, animals in the landscape, etc.

35-70mm 2.8 zoom (autofocus) useful for precisely framing landscapes

55mm f/3.5 macro (manual) flowers, shells, and reversed, with bellows

105mm 3.5 macro (manual) closeups of insects etc., also zoo portraits

70-210mm f/3.5-5.6 zoom (autofocus) This is a budget lens, small and very light as well as sharp; a good first zooms lens.

Top Nikkor telephoto lenses have superb optics, are extremely expensive, and many are very heavy indeed. These fastest, longest Nikkor ED-IF (extra-dispersion glass, internal focussing) lenses are used by a majority of the major wildlife photographers of the world.

I like the 300mm f/4.5 ED-IF, it is an excellent lens. Used with a 1.4X tele-extender it makes a useful 420mm f/6.3 lens, good for many animals, or starting out in serious bird photography. It is not too heavy or expensive.

Nikon has recently introduced three new AF1 lenses, incorporating motors for extremely fast autofocus (pioneered by Canon). They are the 300mm f/2.8D ED-IF, the 400mm f/2.8 ED-IF, and the 600mm f/4D ED-IF.

Nikon heavily promotes its top-of-the-line F4 electronic camera. For me, it's too heavy, too complicated, and too expensive. Their top manual model is the F3. I don't care for it either. The F3 only syncs flash to 1/60, making flash fill in bright light difficult, and the F3 has no hot shoe for on camera flash, which can be useful sometimes.

I now use the Nikon N90, and think it is a great camera. Nikon has fixed a few minor gripes I had about the similar N8008-N8808S models (like having no sync outlet for instance!) Remote wireless operation is possible with the N90, if you need it.

Nikon Accessories

I own all three Nikon automatic extension tubes, which I use a lot with tele as well as macro lenses. I have an old, nonautomatic Nikon bellows, and a highpoint eyepiece for shooting from ground level.

Nikon TTL/dedicated flash units are excellent and make both extreme close-ups with flash and "flash fill" in daylight quite easy. I own both the bounce-head SB 24, and the small SB 23 units. The SB 25 flash has advantages used with the N90. (For more on flash see chapter 3.)

Nikon SB flash units like all dedicated flashes, require a special cable from the hot shoe to the flash, if used off camera.

Electronic Nikons require that you own a dedicated cable release. I have a program back on one of my N8808S cameras, it permits me to set time exposures. The back can also act as an intervalometer. You can now get into the Nikon electronic system relatively inexpensively with the N6006 camera (called the N601 in Europe).

Finally, there are times when a mechanical camera comes in useful, in bad weather conditions for instance. I still have and love four Nikon FM2 cameras, manual except for a very good exposure meter. (Even old Nikon F's and F2s, manual cameras dating from the 1970s, are still around, and might be just the thing for the rain forest or sandstorms, or salty conditions.)

Important note: Nikon lens mounts have remained the same for many years. Virtually all Nikkor lenses fit all Nikon SLR models. (Some old Nikkor lenses require minor adaptations, none are autofocus.)

Nikon also makes microscopes, and accessories for photomicroscopy.

The Legendary Nikon 200-400mm Zoom Lens

This lens was cited to me as their one indispensable lens by four of the world's top wildlife photographers: Leonard Lee Rue III, Len Rue, Jr., Heather Angel, and Art Wolfe. I asked Sam Garcia of Nikon Professional Services why it was no longer made. He said that the lens was very large, very heavy, very expensive, and did not sell well when it first came out. Specialist lenses are made in batches and if they don't sell are discontinued. Sam said that about the time this decision was made, Leonard Lee Rue III wrote in a column how good this lens was and other top photographers picked up on it. Sales went up, but not enough to justify making another batch. Now the lens, which sold for around $3,000 new in the mid-80s, costs about $6,000 used—if you can find it.

A substitute, smaller, lighter and much cheaper, is to use the Nikkor 80-200mm f/2.8 ED zoom lens with a Nikon 2X tele-extender. This makes a very decent 160-400mm f/5.6 optic. This lens does not have a tripod collar and it's too heavy to hand-hold (for me anyway), so I suggest the use of a Kirk Enterprises tripod support with the combination.

Tokina and Sigma Lenses

I traded my old trusty manual Nikkor 80-200mm f/4 zoom for the Nikkor 80-200mm f/2.8 ED autofocus zoom. I wanted the extra speed, but hated two things about the new lens. It was too heavy to me to hand hold and had no tripod collar, meaning the weight of the lens pulled forward. I had problems with unsharp pictures. Herb Zimmerman of Professional Camera Repair told me that the lens was sharp, but that the body of two of my older N8008S cameras had been pulled out of alignment! I didn't want the weight of the Kirk bracket many people use, so traded the lens for my first "independent" lens, a lighter, easier to use Tokina 80-200mm f/2.8 autofocus zoom. This does have a rotating tripod collar. Soon after, I was going to the Galapagos where I knew there would be a lot of climbing over rocks. I replaced a very old 500mm f/8 Nikkor mirror telephoto with a lightweight 400mm f/5.6 Tokina telephoto lens. Both lenses are very sharp, and I am pleased with the results.

I use both Tokina lenses very successfully with Nikon tele-extenders, even though this is not recommended!

The Canon System

If I were starting in photography now, or if I needed very fast autofocus lenses because of poor eyesight, I would carefully consider the Canon EOS system. All Canon EL-UMS lenses for the EOS system (and some independent manufacturers' EOS-compatible lenses) incorporate a motor that interfaces with a motor in the EOS camera bodies, making for extremely fast, selective, and quiet autofocus operation.

The EOS-1 camera with booster, plus EL-UMS lenses, is probably the fastest operating autofocus system on the market at present. The EOS-1 is not as heavy as the Nikon F4, and in my opinion, is much simpler to use. The top Canon lenses are excellent. The EOS-1 is a "hot" camera with photojournalists and fashion photographers today.

Among nature specialists, bird photographers in particular like the EOS-1, and the 300mm f/2.8 lens used with a "doubler" (2X extender).

The EOS Elan camera is an inexpensive way into this system. I recently bought an Elan, with a built-in small flash, and a 50mm f/1.8 lens, to try out the system; I like it very much as a sort of superior point-and-shoot! (Price for both was under $300, here in New York.)

I have used the 300mm f/2.8 Canon lens, it does focus very fast indeed, and it is quite silent in operation, an advantage with wildlife.

The cheapest EOS model, the Rebel, is somewhat flimsy in my opinion.

I am not crazy about the EOS AE model either. This camera lacks an interior light, a major omission for a professional camera.

The Canon complement of lenses and accessories may not be quite as extensive as Nikon's yet, but they are catching up fast.

Important Note: Older Canons (T-90's, etc.) and non-EL Canon lenses have different mounts, and are not compatible with the EOS system.

Other Top 35mm SLR Systems

Minolta, Olympus, and Pentax are other top Japanese 35mm SLR systems; all are used by many serious nature and wildlife photographers and by some professionals, all have extensive lines of lenses and accessories. They are just a notch in price below the first two brands.

In this range, I would probably go with Olympus. Their cameras are beautifully made, smallish, their lenses are highly regarded, and they have a wide range of accessories. Olympus also makes microscopes.

Minolta is noted for fast autofocus cameras; they were pioneers in this field. Their metering is superb, as are Minolta's hand-held meters. Though I do not like the (to me) complicated "program extension" cards used with some Minoltas, you may find them just the thing.

Pentax is the camera of choice for many photo students and photographers on a tight budget. They make a good all-manual camera (rare today). Pentax lenses are fine and the system is quite rugged and extensive. My best friend (a good amateur photographer) took her Pentax Spotmatic around the world a few times and it never failed her. After ten years she has just traded it in for an autofocus model.

I won't discuss the Contax or Leica systems here in detail, because few nature photographers use them. (Leica rangefinder cameras are still beloved by photojournalists, by people who use Leitz microscopes, by a garden photographer friend, and by Bob Rattner in the rain forest!)

Medium-Format Cameras

All else being equal, big negatives are sharper than small negatives when enlarged. Therefore, in today's highly competitive photographic climate, some outdoor photographers are now using medium format. I love nice big negatives, but just don't have the strength to lug those heavy things around. (I also think that one's approach to photography is less spontaneous with big cameras.) For the nature/wildlife photographers who do use medium format, highly reliable cameras are a must.

Hasselblad. All the people I know personally who travel and shoot outdoors with medium format use this time-tested, rugged, extensive 6x6cm system, which has a vast range of lenses and accessories.

The Mamiya RZ67 is a big heavy pretty rugged camera, with a revolving back; 6x7cm is considered an ideal landscape format. This camera is currently used by a few landscape/nature photographers. The rather new Mamiya 6 MF rangefinder 6x6cm camera is suddenly "hot", (used by Curtice Taylor for garden photography—see interview), but does not have too many lenses yet. 6x4.5cm and panoramic 24x54mm pictures are also possible (with adaptors).

The Pentax 6x7 feels like a blown-up 35mm SLR; it's used by a top advertising photographer friend of mine. He swears by the sharp lenses.

Bronicas are well-priced medium-format cameras, often used by students.

All of these systems are quite extensive, but except for Hasselblad, don't have the range of lenses or accessories the major 35mm systems do.

Panoramic Cameras

Panoramic cameras can be 35mm, 120, or large format. The 35mm, and many of the medium format panoramic cameras, do not have interchangeable lenses, or permit perspective correction. Some have lenses that rotate, some use fixed, extremely wide-angle lenses. Some 120 panoramic cameras offer lens and/or back adjustment for perspective control.

Established brands include:

35mm format: Rotoscop; Widelux; Ipan 827.

120 format: Fuji 6x17; Horizon; Noblex Pro 150; Linhof Technorama 617; Widelux.

4"x5" format: Cambo.

Panoramic cameras are built in Germany, Japan, Switzerland, the USA, and Russia. Some are custom-made in relatively small numbers, so getting information on them from manufacturers is not always easy. New York professional dealers Ken Hansen and Lens and Repro specialize in panoramic cameras.

Large-Format Cameras

A few photographers I know use large-format cameras for panoramas, in combination with wide-angle lenses designed to cover the 5"x7" or 8"10 format. Top stock photographer Robert Herko (not a nature specialist) says his Toyo view camera is the only one rugged enough for his needs. He uses it as a panoramic camera, with a 6x12cm back made by Mamiya.

Wooden 4"x5", 5"x7" and 8"x10" flatbed folding field cameras made today still closely resemble the classics of the nineteenth century. Calumet/Cambo, Horseman, Toyo, and Zone Six make popular field cameras.

Antique Deardorff folding cameras are prized. Nathan Farb uses one. (For more on medium and large format, see chapter 6, landscape.)

Backpacks, Bags, and Travel Cases

Whether you hike, drive, fly, or swim to take pictures, most nature and wildlife photographers need something rugged to protect their equipment. Many today use camera backpacks, or fanny packs, even if they don't do much hiking, because it's more comfortable to carry an evenly balanced load than one that drags you down on one side.

Art Wolfe and Galen Rowell have designed camera packs; they would not risk their names on junk, so, their bags must be quality equipment. Lowe-Pro, Tenba, and Tamrac make good packs and tripod bags.

Lightware shipping cases are good; I have one for my Dynalite

Polaroid Cameras, and Backs for Polaroid Film

Professional Polaroid pack cameras (and some Minolta pack cameras that can still be found) come with adjustable lenses and shutters, and are used mainly for tests, especially of lighting. Some landscape and fine-art nature photographers work with large-format Polaroid prints. Polaroid makes filmpack backs for 4"x5" and 8"x10" format cameras, and special cameras for clos-ups photography and photomicroscopy. They will send good brochures on both these subjects.

NPC makes Polaroid backs for most top 35mm SLR's, and some medium format cameras. These are extremely useful for making tests of manual and high-speed flash setups, high-magnification close-ups, and other tricky things. Polaroid's free *Test* magazine will tell you more.

I own a folding Polaroid 110B rangefinder camera, which has an adjustable lens and shutter, and is compact. Originally used with roll film, I had it adapted by Four Seasons Design of Northridge, California to take standard Polaroid 3-1/4"x4-1/4" pack films. The company sells used adapted Polaroid 110A, 110B and 195 folding cameras also.

strobes. Pelican rugged, waterproof cases are used by quite a few people I know. Ammo cases from army/navy stores are water-resistant and cheaper! I favor a lined, water-resistant Domke bag, plus a Domke tripod bag. I use a Japanese leather bag to carry cameras and lenses onto planes. Sometimes I use an old waterproofed NATO pack stuffed with foam, from an army/navy store. Whatever bag I use, I always put in a few black, and white, plastic trash bags to sit on, disguise my tripod, act as a windbreak or reflector, or keep me dry!

Free Specialized Catalogs Worth Sending For—(see Resources, chapter 14): *Cabella's Hunting and Fishing, Calumet Professional Imaging, Connecticut Valley Biological Supply, Edmund Scientific, Helix Underwater, L.L. Rue Enterprises.*

Film and Filters

The more you know about what film can and cannot do, the better your pictures will be. If you plan to market images, you should be aware of the films most picture buyers prefer.

Each color slide film has characteristics that are recognizable by the very experienced. The film you choose for personal work is of course a matter of taste. I will discuss the films I like and use, and that picture editors and buyers prefer. Other professional photographers I know seem fairly united on these films also.

The Films Top Nature and Wildlife Buyers Want to See

Kodachrome Professional Films

For many years, Kodachrome was the standard film used by just about all professional photographers who worked in 35mm format. Kodachrome has been around for over fifty years and is not as popular as it was, but Kodachrome 25 Professional (PKM) is still the sharpest, finest-grain color film made, and it is still used by many nature specialists. Today I use it mostly for landscapes where extremely fine detail must be recorded. It is at its best used in low angle, or bounce sunlight (so are all films). If you must photograph in noon sunlight, this is probably the film to use, but it is contrasty.

Kodachrome 64 Professional (PKR) is used by a majority of the professional nature/wildlife photographers who still favor Kodachrome; they like the extra speed. PKR is a little grainier than PKM and, regrettably, is even more contrasty in bright sunlight. It is at its best, and is excellent, used with flash, when it gives nice crisp details with neutral color.

Kodachrome 200 Professional (PKL) is a moderate-grain film, slightly biassed to magenta, that is useful in low light. It is favored by some underwater photographers. (See interview with Robert Rattner.)

All Kodachrome films look poor when used in bad weather, in my opinion.

Fujichrome Films

A great many top nature and wildlife photographers and buyers today favor slow Fujichrome Professional films. Fujichrome started the vogue for films that slightly exaggerate color; Fuji films are noted for intense blues and greens. When there is enough light, professionals on both the shooting and buying fronts favor Fujichrome Velvia (RVP) above all. This nominally is an ISO 50 film, which has saturated, sometimes almost glowing color, grain almost (not quite) as fine as Kodachrome 25 and 64, and can be pushed a stop or slightly more with almost no color shift. Velvia looks wonderful used in soft sunlight or low light, with subtle color differences in the blues, yellows, and reds. You may or may not like the way it brightens greens. Although Velvia has a rated speed of 50 ISO, I rate it at 40 ISO on the advice of my professional lab, L & I Color, in New York, with excellent results.

Velvia (like all Fuji films) is slightly biassed to red; it "heats up" human skin tones too much to be useful for human portraits in my opinion. Velvia is also very contrasty; I don't recommend using it in strong sunlight. At dusk, Velvia renders blue skies somewhat purple.

Fujichrome 100 Professional (RDP) is also an excellent, fine-grain film. The color is not quite as luminous as Velvia's, but is still very nice. It looks great in soft sun and can cheer up a gray day considerably. The greatest thing about this film is that it can easily be pushed one or even two stops without much color shift, therefore it's useful for wildlife in poor light when the highest possible shutter speeds must be used. RDP does not look bad "pulled" one stop either.

New Kodak Ektachrome Films

Kodak has recently been making a huge effort with its Ektachrome films, with several introduced in the last five years. The newest professional Ektachromes are being marketed under the Lumiere label, and I am sure they will be popular.

Ektachrome Lumiere films are announced to have neutral color balance, and will come in 50, and 100 ISO speeds. Warm-balanced Lumiere X films will initially be available as 50X, and 100X, 200X, 400X and 1600X. I have tested a few rolls of Lumiere 100X, (LPX). I found it to have vibrant color and very fine sharp grain. The rolls I tested were slightly biassed towards yellow (that should take out blue on overcast days). Lumiere films, all made in Rochester, New York, will be marketed in the United Kingdom, Europe, Japan, the Middle East, and Africa under the Panther brand, and in Australia, Latin America, and Asia under the Select name. This apparently is designed to foil gray-marketers!

Other Ektachromes

Ektachrome Plus 100 Professional (EPP) is a current favorite film of mine, especially used at dusk when its rendition of blues is excellent.

Ektachrome 64X Professional (EPX) is fine grain and gives nice skin tones. Ektachrome 100 Professional (EPN) is a neutral-balanced, moderate-grain film that can be pushed or pulled without unpleasant color shift.

Other Films I Like

Scotch-3M markets films made in Italy. Scotch 1000 is a grainy, very blue film, wonderful if you like soft, moody, artistic effects.

Kodak Ektar Professional is the brand of color negative film I like. It comes in 25, 100, and 1000 speeds. Ektar 25 makes great prints.

For black-and-white I mostly use Kodak T-Max 100 and 400 films,

---

"Pushing" and "Pulling" Color Film

You can easily "push", or increase the ISO (speed) rating of Ektachrome, Fujichrome, and other color transparency films that use the E-6 process. Inform your professional lab when pushing film. Slow E-6 films (50, 64, 100 ISO) can be pushed a half, one, or two stops.

Fast E-6 films (400 ISO speed and up) can be pushed three, four, or even five stops for artistic effects, with color shift to brown/yellow.

"Pulling" slow E-6 films one-half, or one stop, can be done if the film was incorrectly exposed. The color shifts somewhat to blue.

Kodachrome films use the K-14 process and were not designed to be pushed. But, for a fairly stiff charge, labs that process Kodachrome can push Kodachrome 200 to 500 ISO with satisfactory results in flat light.

Kodak Professional Ektapress films are the only color negative films I know of that can be successfully pushed. They use the C-41 process.   (Note: Kodak and Fuji do not recommend extreme pushes, or any pulls, of color film. See Professional Film Data Sheets, free from manufacturers.)

---

and sometimes still use Tri-X (400 ISO).

I have also experimented with Ilford XP-1 and XP-2 chromogenic films (developed in C-41 color chemistry). They can produce nice sepia prints.

Filters

Color transparency film does not react to light in the same way the human eye does. We can distinguish detail in bright sunlit highlights and dark shadowed areas at the same time. Our eyes and brain combine to neutralize the actual changes in the color of light that occur at different times of day and year, and in different weather.

Subtle CC (color-compensating) or LB (light-balancing) filters are used to correct color bias on film. Tiffen, Hoya, Kodak, and other makers publish booklets giving information. (Get these at photo dealers.)

Flash fill or reflectors are answers to some high contrast existing light problems, if the subject is within range. Otherwise, you must wait for the light to change or wait for your subject to move into a shaded area. (For more on light, exposure, and filters, see chapter 4.)

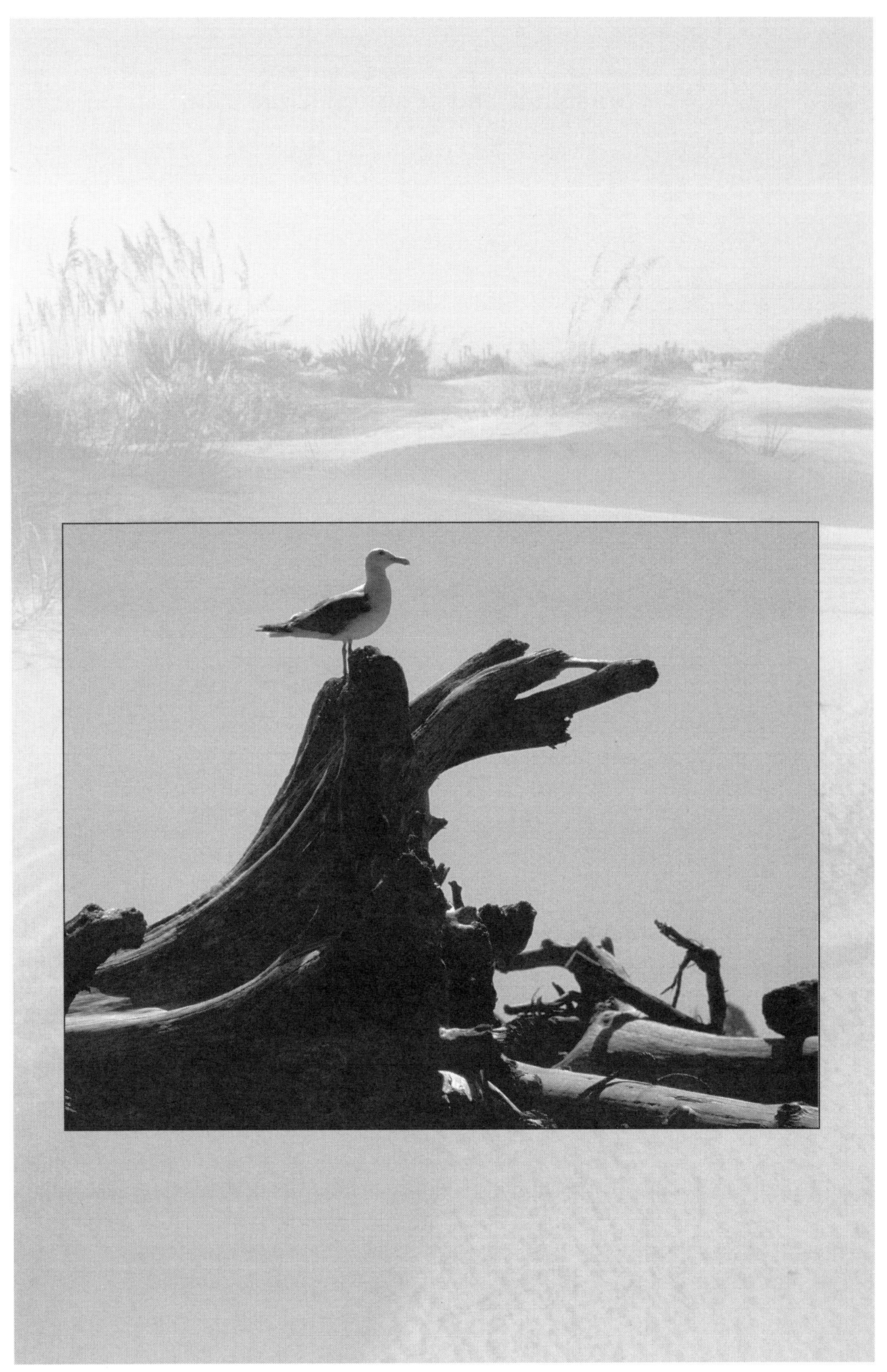

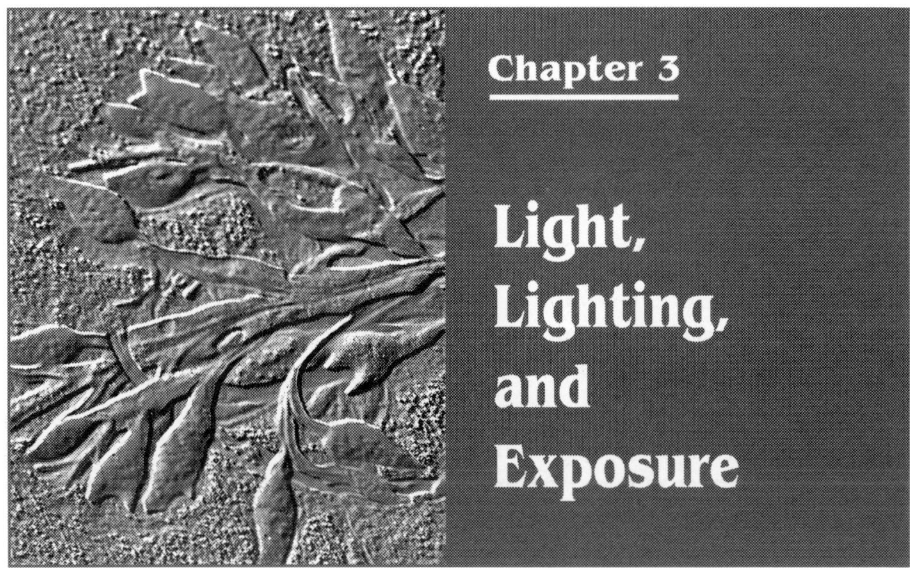

Chapter 3

Light, Lighting, and Exposure

One of the most critical abilities for all outdoor photographers is to "see" and use daylight well. And, nature specialists sometimes must create natural looking light by artificial means. Easily the most practical way to do this anywhere is with small portable flash units.

Light from any single point source is called "specular" light. It produces clearly defined shadows. Bright sun, direct flash, and unshaded clear lightbulbs are all specular forms of light. Multiple specular light sources (like several flash units used close together) can cause confusing shadows if not used with skill.

"Diffuse" light can be of varying quality. Diffused sunlight often looks very pleasant and sparkling when high thin clouds, light mist, or thin fog cover it. Lightly diffused sunlight is soft, with directional shadows. Heavy overcast daylight, with flat low clouds, rainclouds, fog, or snow, is usually boring, dead-looking; it comes from overhead with no shadows.

The sun (or flash) can be diffused through any translucent white material (thin nylon or plastic are often used). Diffused flash can have soft shadows, or be almost shadowless, depending on the density of the diffuser. I will discuss types of light, and how to simulate them with flash.

Sidelight

This directional light from the low-angled sun early and late in the day is beautiful, warm, and my first choice for showing up the contours of landscapes, mountains, and panoramic views. Sidelighting is excellent for revealing textures of fur, feathers, scales, and petals. A flash aimed from the side of the subject produces this quite contrasty effect. Experiment to find the best angle. A diffuser on the flash reduces contrast slightly. A reflector used opposite sunlight or a flash can "bounce" some "fill" light into nearby shadows, reducing contrast.

Backlight

Backlight from directly behind the subject (also called "rim light") is very pretty. It is low morning or evening sunlight, opposite the lens. Long shadows come towards you, animals or birds or flowers may be haloed with sunshine, translucent insects and flowers take on a new beauty, and water glitters when the sun glows low from behind. The low sun itself is often best masked behind a branch or other handy object, unless somewhat diffused by cloud or mist.

Backlight is tricky to produce with flash. You can use an off-camera flash low, (directly behind a subject and masked from the camera) to produce rim light, or hang any flash on a branch or "boom" (overhanging light stand out of lens view) and aim flash down at the subject.

Care must be taken with natural or artificial backlighting to avoid "flare" (unwanted light) bouncing inside the lens and degrading the image. Mask sun flare with your hand or put a "snoot" (long black tube) around flash. Slight flare (little blue blips) carefully placed can be exciting, but avoid orange "spaceships." (Use stop-down preview button to judge effects.) Alter lens angle to light to minimize flare problems.

"Bounce" Light

Light "bounced" onto a shaded subject is one of the loveliest lights of all. Soft bounce light is low sunlight reflected from any nearby large bright, white, or light surface. Create flattering bounce light with portable white, silver, or gold reflectors. Aim a reflector held opposite the sun, until bounce light hits the subject. Use a flash aimed at a reflector to create bounce light also. (Bounce range is about ten feet.)

Flat Light or Front Light

Low sunlight from behind you that hits the subject in front of you is flat light, sometimes called front light. Use this warm light early and late all year everywhere, and most of the day on sunny winter days in northern climates (when it is very yellow). Flat/front light can be very dramatic in a posterish kind of way. It is the way to photograph long reflections on water and is great for dramatizing landscapes with dark clouds just before storms. When the sun is low and frontal, you can underexpose for deep blue skies without the need of polarizing filters.

Direct flash used on camera is a form of flat light. If a flash is too close to the lens "red-eye" (caused by the flash reflecting off the retina) may result if you stand further than about four feet from your subject (it is not normally a problem with extreme close-ups). Shoot down, or use flash high on a bracket or off to the side of the lens to avoid red-eye.

Three-Quarter Light

Old photo manuals recommended shooting with the sun coming over your left shoulder from a three-quarter angle, because it easily defines a subject and is an almost foolproof way of getting good pictures with the simplest camera. A flash used on a bracket at about a 45° angle, aimed slightly down on the subject, produces classic three-quarter light.

Soft Light or Diffuse Light

This can be the low warm light before sunrise or after sunset or sunlight diffused by thin clouds. Mist/fog rising from land or water on dull days give oriental effects of receding planes getting paler. The blue light of dusk is pretty and soft. Sunlight diffused by light mist can be beautiful for photographing wildlife, with no harsh shadows.

Create gentle and flattering diffuse light for flower and butterfly studies on sunny days by holding a white umbrella, or translucent diffuser, over your subject. Diffuse flash for close-ups of tiny subjects in the same way. Or, bounce sublight or flash off an angled relector.

Low Light

You can take pictures as long as you can see, at dawn, twilight, and dusk, when the color of the light can be deep red or deep blue. Use time exposures and a tripod in low light and be aware of possible reciprocity failure for long exposures (see Exposure, below). Low light is not normally created with flash outdoors, but if you need to try, bounce a flash off a large white surface like a sheet, from about six feet away.

Top Light

This harsh light comes from overhead summer, or tropical, sun. It casts hard shadows that record almost black on film and is usually the worst possible light for landscapes, animals, and birds. I make it an (almost) inviolable rule not to shoot if my shadow is shorter than I am.

Contrasty Light

Very contrasty or "spotty" light, where part of a scene or subject is very brightly lit and part is in deep shadow, is normally ugly and to be avoided. Reflectors and flash can help "fill" shadows when used very close. Noon

The Color Temperature,
or Kelvin Temperature, of Light

Daylight films and all small portable flashes (and studio flash or strobe units) are balanced for white, neutral "photographic daylight", which is measured as 5,500 degrees Kelvin (written 5,500°K).

Theoretically, the color of daylight should be white, very close to 5,500°K, between 10:00 A.M. and 2:00 P.M. on sunny days with some clouds in the sky. On overcast days, color temperature is higher, causing a blueish cast on film. Some old or inexpensive flash units may also run blue. (Correct blue with an 81A [or warmer] filter, see chapter 2.)

The color temperature of daylight is lower (warmer) on sunny days from just before dawn to early morning, and from late afternoon to the afterglow of sunset; it will look yellow or pinkish, orange or red on film. Predawn and dusk light are extremely high in color temperature and look blue on film, exact shades range from pale to royal to navy blue. You can see these effects easily with the unaided eye.

sun filtering through foliage or tall grass causes patches of dark shadows and bright highlights, and making the subject hard to see (the principal behind camouflage). Contrasty light can result from unskilled use of several undiffused flash units or hot lights.

Magic Light

Fleeting moments when the natural light is truly extraordinary come rarely. Seize those moments whenever you can. Magic light often comes in conjunction with awful weather. In May 1993, the year of the great floods, I had heavy overcast, rain, snow, hail, sleet, and thunderstorms in Yellowstone National Park for much of my five-day stay. One evening, as I was leaving the park after a deluge, a crack appeared in some clouds and bright sun appeared. A brilliant double rainbow framed mountains against black clouds for a few seconds only. I got two spectacular frames before the rain resumed. Never quit because of awful weather. It will change, and when it does, you will get great light.

Available Light

The photographer who works in zoos, aquariums, and labs is going to have to worry about the color on film of available light from diffused fluorescents (they photograph green and require magenta filtration). Artificial light from photographic and household bulbs are also warmer than daylight, which is why they look orange on daylight film. Use blue filters or Tungsten (Type B) films.

Get better results in zoos and such, (and stop much motion) by using a high sync speed and overpowering the available light with slaved flash units triggered from the camera.

Practical Exposure

The aim of good exposure is either to reproduce a subject as accurately as possible on film, or to express a desired mood, in which case you will probably break some rules.

Color Transparency (Slide) Film Exposure

Accurate exposure is essential for color transparency films. Color transparency films have the capacity to reproduce a range from brightest highlight to darkest shadow of only thirty-two to one, or five f/stops. If you are shooting transparencies that contain both blacks and whites, decide which is more important to you—highlight or shadow detail. Ideally, I like to use color film in soft, hazy, or low sunlight, or on lightly overcast days, where the light to dark ratio is no more than about three f/stops. I like a good "normal" exposure.

Negative (Print) Film Exposure

Color negative and black-and-white films have more latitude than color transparency films (a good negative can record a seven f/stop range, but the prints will only handle about five stops). Color and black-and-white negatives can of course be "dodged" and "burned in" when printing. Accurate exposure is still necessary for quality prints.

**Learn sunlight exposures of your favorite film, and avoid being totally dependent on a meter.
(I also bracket exposures in half-stops.)**

Kodachrome 25 is 1/250 at f/4-5.6 in sunlight.

Kodachrome 64 is 1/250 at f/8 in sunlight.

Kodachrome 200 is 1/250 at f/11-16 (or f/16) in sunlight.

Fuji Velvia is 1/250 at f/6.3 (or a touch less) in sunlight.

100 ISO speed films are exposed at 1/250 at f/8-11 (or f/11) in sun.

Make tests—optimum exposure is to some degree personal taste.

Time Exposures

Time exposures are often used at dusk and at night and when small f/stops are needed for great depth of field (zone of sharp focus). Two problems to consider with time exposures are reciprocity failure and the color shifts in film that may occur. (Subject motion is a third!)

The Law of Reciprocity

At very long exposures (from more than a few seconds up to many minutes or even hours) the correlation between shutter speeds and f/stops no longer exactly applies. A thirty-second exposure is not exactly double a fifteen-second exposure. In practice, I have found that choosing one f/stop and bracketing with the shutter speed works well with time exposures. For instance, I photographed Niagara Falls illuminated at night, with 25 ISO film. I used f/5.6 and shutter speeds of 4, 8, 16, 30, 60 and 90 seconds. All exposures were quite well-exposed and usable, the middle two were best.

Color Shift at Long Exposures

Color "shift" (change) can be interesting. I recently photographed Monument Valley, Arizona, at twilight, using Fuji Velvia rated at 40 ISO, at an f/22 aperture. I used a one-minute exposure, plus brackets of 8, 16 and 30 seconds, and 2 minutes. All pictures were usable, the middle two most pleasing. The color shift was from red to deep purple!

Manufacturers' Professional Data Sheets give filtration data for time exposures and for fluorescent and other artificial light sources. (Kodak and Fuji don't recommend long exposures with most films, because of extreme color shifts.) Try them anyway, the results can be more interesting than "correct" color. Make tests to find effects you prefer.

Reflected-Light Metering
with an 18 Percent Gray Card or Substitute

If you take careful reflected light readings off a standard 18 percent gray card (made by Kodak and others and sold for a few dollars at photo stores) you will get good exposure no matter what the color or tone of the subject. Place the card in the same light as the subject. You can use the palm of your hand as a substitute for a gray card (correlate your palm with the card by testing; skin tones vary). Or, take substitute reflected readings off a midtoned subject, like gray rocks.

Exposing for Backlighting

Backlight (from behind the subject towards the lens) can fool meters. Go in close, or use a long lens in spotmetering mode, or use a spotmeter

Exposure Meters and Metering

All types of meters contain a light-sensitive cell and are designed to give optimum density (exposure) with "average" photographic subjects. In fact, meters are very slightly biased on the side of underexposure, (so as to not overexpose color transparencies). An "average" photographic subject reflects back about 18 percent of the light that falls on it. This has been described as a family snapshot, taken on a sunny day, including a house, green grass and trees, and some people in the middle of the frame. If this scene was painted in oils, and the colors mixed, they would come out as the middle tone called 18 percent gray in photography.

Reflected-Light Meters

All built-in camera meters are reflected-light meters. All reflected-light meters measure the light that reflects off a subject and are normally aimed at the subject from camera position (but from very close-up when the main subject is backlit).

Because the tone of the subject influences the amount of light reflected, compensate when metering light or dark subjects with a reflected-light meter. Close down your lens 1 or 1-1/2 stops (or use a faster shutter speed) when metering reflected light off a dark or black subject, or you will get a tone close to middle gray. Open up lens 1 or 1-1/2 stops (or lower the shutter speed) when metering reflected light off a white subject or extremely light surface, like snow or sand.

Bracket difficult exposures, or have a professional lab make "clip tests" if you can't bracket.

Note: The "middle-gray" rule applies also to automatic and TTL flashes; like meters, they are designed to reproduce "average" subjects.

to take reflected-light meter readings off brightly backlit subjects, or you will get underexposed, even silhouetted, main subjects.

Meter backlit subjects up close, and use the "memory lock" button with program cameras.

Don't totally trust electronic cameras that offer "multipoint", "matrix," or similar name metering, which measures several areas in the picture frame. This gives good exposure for most subjects, but if the backlit subject is small or dark, or the scene high contrast (such as a light-colored bird in a large dark swamp), bracketing is still advised. Some high-end cameras offer automatic bracketing, built-in or optional.

Quick Tips for Good Exposure

- Dead meters can't read exposures. Always carry spare batteries!
- Bracket exposures if subject is light, dark, contrasty, or backlit.
- Take care to align dome or disc of incident meters correctly.
- Avoid photographing anything partly in sun and partly in deep shadow.
- Mechanical camera shutter speeds should be checked every few months.
- Trust electronic shutters unless exposures are obviously way off.
- Have your camera or meter checked out if you drop it or bang it hard.
- Set film speed on hand-held meters, manual cameras, and flash units!
- Use the same film outdoors consistently; learn exposure for sunlight.
- Choose identical ISO speeds when shooting two types of film together!
- Use the old "sunny-sixteen" rule of exposure in sunshine if desperate. *(Set the lens at f/16 and use shutter speed as close as possible to film speed. With 100 ISO film, exposure is f/16 at 1/125.)*
- Read your camera, meter, and flash manuals, and carry them

Incident-Light Meters

Incident-light meters are hand-held and can be identified by their opaque white dome (or a white disc used with flat subjects). This meter is normally aimed from the subject position to the camera position. Incident meters measure the light that falls on a subject and are not influenced by the tone of the subject. Care must be taken to align an incident meter correctly. When metering a landscape, overexposure will result if the dome is aimed down, reducing light from the sky; the film will be underexposed if the dome is aimed to include too much light from the sky. An incident-light meter cannot give an accurate reading if in shadow when the subject is in sunlight (or vice versa).

Flash Meters

Flash meters measure the intense short burst of light from any small flash (or large strobe or studio flash unit).

Incident flash meters measure both flash and available light. The most versatile incident flashmeters measure flash at all shutter speeds, less expensive models at only two shutter speeds—1/60 and 1/250 of a second—the most common shutter "sync" speeds on 35mm SLR cameras.

Depending on the features of the flash meter you choose, they can be used with or without a sync cord to the camera, and measure available light, flash/strobe light, or both combined. Any flash meter is useful to measure light from two small flashes used together close to the subject on a bracket. (See chapter 2 for my choice of flashmeters.)

Spotmeters

High-end TTL cameras have built-in meters with a spot option for narrow-angle measurement. Hand-held spot meters are useful for accurate exposures of distant wildlife when not using longest telephoto lenses.

Portable Flash and the Nature/Wildlife Photographer

Space permits only a brief guide to using flash here.

The camera shutter must always be fully open when a flash "peaks" or part of the image will be blacked-out. Learn and use the "sync-speed" setting (usually marked with an X on older cameras) or any speed below sync to ensure this. (Sync speed is set automatically on TTL/dedicated cameras when used with dedicated flash unless you choose S [shutter priority] mode, which permits low sync speeds and recording backgrounds in low light [see camera and flash manuals].)

- Older SLR cameras almost all "sync" with flash at 1/60 of a second.

- Most modern SLR cameras sync at 1/250 (making flash "fill" easier).

- Most cameras with leaf-type shutters sync at 1/500 of a second.

Using Flash Sucessfully

The most important thing to remember when lighting with a single flash is that the light falls off very quickly (according to the square of the distance from the subject). Therefore, you cannot successfully light a scene in-depth with one flash. If the subject in the center of your picture frame is a gray birds' nest four feet from the flash, branches on the left two feet from the flash will look almost white, overexposed on film, and the tree trunk eight feet from the flash will look almost black, underexposed in your picture. (Either frame the nest with a longer lens so that foreground and background are eliminated, or use several slaved flashes spaced out, to evenly expose the larger area.)

Flash "Fill"

To "fill" with light means to lighten small, close, dark-shadowed areas of a picture, but not to overpower the overall existing light. Any tiny, inexpensive manual flash can be used to "open up" close shadows in sunlit scenes, or to put a highlight into a creature's eye if it is within range (about ten to twenty feet from flash). Simply use the highest possible sync speed and appropriate f/stop, then add flash.

To fill with a tiny flash on gray days (or with backlit subjects) use sync speed (or any speed below sync) and choose an f/stop to give a half-stop under exposure to the backround. Then add flash within range. You may have to experiment a little with your distance from the subject.

Advantages of TTL/Dedicated and Automatic Flash

I strongly recommend investing in a TTL/dedicated flash and camera that measures the light off the film plane. Thyristorized TTL/dedicated flash units cut off when there is enough light for a correct exposure. Dedicated cords permitting the use of one or more flashes up to a distance of about six feet from the camera are available. (Soon, we are promised multiple dedicated-flash use without cords with top-of-the-line cameras.) TTL combined daylight/flash metering off the film plane makes using flash fill in bright sun or low light easy to do. It also considerably simplifies making close-ups with externally focussing macro lenses, extension tubes, or bellows (all reduce light reaching the lens), eliminating the use of tables (supplied by manufacturers; and which vary according to the primary lens being used).

Good dedicated flash units can be used on manual full-power or reduced-power levels. Get one of these as you become expert; manual exposures give you creative control and the option of high flash speeds.

Automatic flashes work with a sensor on the flash or can be used with a remote cord that attaches to camera hot shoe. The flash cuts off when the sensor has received enough light. You select a distance range, choose an f/stop, and the flash does the rest. Automatic flash works well for fill in daylight in my experience. The Vivitar 283 and 285 models are popular, relatively inexpensive bounce-head flashes of this type, used by many professionals, with manual variable power options.

Macro Flash Use

Two small TTL/dedicated flash units mounted on a bracket close together and joined with dedicated cords are often used today for macro flash photography in daylight. If your small flashes are manual, you will have to meter the light. In either case, use a very small f/stop for maximum depth of field. Make your own macro flash bracket or use the popular Lepp bracket. (For more on close-ups, see chapter 8.)

Using Automatic Flash Units

Automatic, thyristorized flash units with swivel heads for bouncing light are quite easy to use. The photographer sets the film speed, chooses a lens aperture and distance range from a scale, and the flash cuts off when enough light has reached the subject. Used close, the flash peak is of short duration, stopping much motion. **Vivitar, Sunpak,** and **Metz** are three popular automatic flash brands.

A Basic Flash Outfit

❏ A bounce flash unit (dedicated to your TTL camera if you have one). Or get an automatic variable power flash like a Vivitar 283 or 285.

❏ A remote flash cord (for TTL or automatic units off-camera) or a standard sync/ PC cord (for manual flash units used off-camera).

❏ A cable/shutter release (or a TTL/dedicated shutter release).

❏ A thirty-six-inch round white translucent reflector for diffusing and bouncing daylight or flash light into close, shadowed areas.

❏ A hand-held, incident, flash/available light meter (see chapter 2).

❏ A few filters (see chapter 2 for my basic filter kit).

❏ A flash bracket (I use a Stroboframe, "flippable" for verticals).

TTL/Dedicated Flash Units

Computerized TTL/dedicated flash units, used with compatible dedicated cameras, are capable of sophisticated lighting effects. They make using "flash fill" simple (once you have learned how to use the flash— the manuals can be a bit technical). TTL/dedicated cameras and flash units used together measure and control all the light reaching the camera's film plane, saving much calculation with macro lenses, extension tubes, bellows, and so forth. Dedicated flashes are made by camera manufacturers, and independents, notably Metz/Mecablitz.

Manual Flash Exposure

Manual exposures are consistent and infinitely repeatable, which is why most professional photographers use them. (This applies to exposures with automatic or TTL/dedicated flash in manual mode also.) I recommend using a flash meter, but if you don't, manual exposures are determined by using a distance scale on the back of the flash or the guide number.

The Formula for Using Guide Numbers:

The guide number is determined by a combination of the power of a flash and the film speed used (see flash manuals for guide numbers).

To find the f/stop, divide the the desired distance from flash to subject into the guide number. With a guide number of 56 (common with one-piece flashes and 100 ISO film) at seven feet, you must use f/8 for instance.

To get the distance from flash to subject needed for correct exposure, divide the f/stop you must use into the guide number (for correct exposure for flash fill for instance). With a guide number of 120 (a powerful small flash unit used with 100 ISO film) at fifteen feet away, you must use f/8 for instance.

When two flashes are used close together on a macro bracket make tests using one stop less from guide numbers, as basis.

Testing, consistent flash to subject distances, and experience will eventually ensure excellent manual flash exposures. A flash meter helps!

Thyristorized Flash Units

Automatic thyristorized flashes have a sensor on the flash unit (they can also be used off-camera attached by a remote sensor cord). After the film speed is set on the flash and the camera, a lens aperture and distance range are chosen from a scale on the flash. Within those limits, flash exposure is automatic, the flash cutting off when the sensor has received enough light for a good exposure. Automatic flashes work well for fill light in daylight in my experience.

TTL/dedicated, thyristorized flashes meter light through the lens and use a sensor on the camera film plane. They take all light factors into consideration before cutting off the flash. They can be used on the camera hot shoe, or off-camera with a dedicated cord. (Soon, remote TTL/dedicate flash units will be available.)

Thyristorized flashes cut off the flash when enough light for correct exposure has reached the sensor. At close distances this produces very bursts of light, extremely useful for stopping motion. (Thyristors conserve batteries also.)

High-Speed Flash Exposures, "Ghosts," and More

The speed of the light from a small flash unit used on full power is quite high, about 1/350th of a second. If you combine flash and low available light (by using a wide f/stop and choosing a slow shutter speed, say 1/15 of a second), the background exposure also registers in your frame. Essentially, you are taking two pictures at the same time, a time exposure and a flash exposure. If your subject is moving fast, you may get "ghost" images (where the daylight and flash exposures overlap). You generally need to take quite a few exposures to get good effects; some are too confusing. To make sure "ghosts" fall behind your subject, choose rear shutter curtain sync if you camera permits this (see camera manual). Minimize ghosts, too, by panning (moving the camera in the direction of the motion).

I like Vivitar flash units. The Vivitar 283 automatic flash has an optional Varipower attachment (the VP-1) from full to 1/32 power, which costs about $25. The Vivitar 285 has a similar but built-in Varipower module; it costs about $25 more than the 283. This flash unit is bigger and not so easy to modify as the 283, but does have a built-in Fresnel lens that can somewhat extend its range.

Many better automatic or TTL flash units have variable power options permitting exposures from manual full power to 1/2, 1/4, 1/8, 1/16, and even 1/32 power. This permits bracketing flash exposures (useful with contrasty subjects) and the use of relatively high-speed flash.

Turning flash power down reduces light, but increases the speed of the burst of light. Quite high-speed action, like bird or butterfly wings in motion, can be stopped (recorded without blur on film). The flash

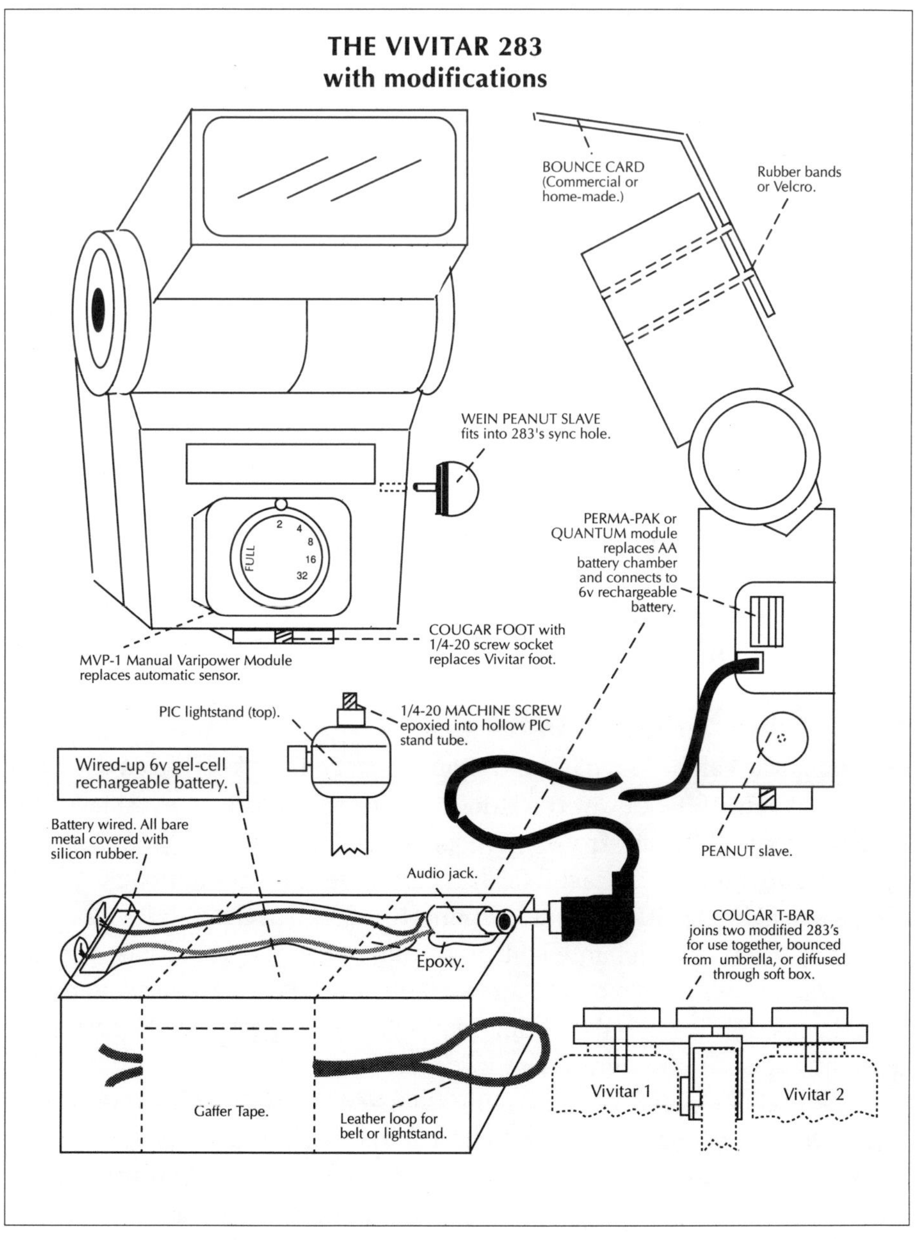

must be used very close to the subject, because light output is low.

High Speeds with Small Flash

The speed of a Vivitar 283 flash turned down with an VP-1 Varipower module has been measured photographically by Phillip Leonian using a circular saw and markings of a specific length. (The inexpensive VP-1 module is hard to set accurately, so precise speeds are not repeatable.)

On full power, 283 flash duration is about 1/350th of a second.

On half-power, duration is about 1/1,200.

On quarter-power, duration is about 1/4,000.

On 1/16-power, flash duration is about 1/6,000 of a second (this speed will stop an average bird's wings, but not a hummingbird's wings).

Set up slaved, turned-down flash units very close to a bird feeding station; stop much action by using slow film and a high sync speed.

S.A.I. Industries of Moorestown, New Jersey, makes the NVS 1 unit, a double-powered Vivitar 283 modification, and sells a Wild Bird Lighting Kit. The NVS 1 has a full to 1/256 power variator that produces repeatable flash output. Used close, flash speeds on lower settings are high and f/stops reasonable. (For information on this unit in use see chapter 5).

Measure the "stopping power" of any flash by making a five-inch diameter cardboard wheel with colored pie segments and different size letters on it. Tape this to a buffing device on an electric drill and photograph the wheel in motion (or mark a power saw as basis for your tests). Most home power tools rotate at about 2,000 rpm. When you can read quarter-inch or eighth-inch high letters whirling at that speed, you have stopped much action.

I have tested a Vivitar 283 placed thirty inches from a wheel and stopped motion at 1/32 power, with an f/11 aperture and 100 ISO film.

"Slave" and "Trigger" Units

Portable flash can be "slaved", and then "triggered" (set off) from the camera up to about 100'-500' away outdoors, using various devices. A slave unit fires a remote flash or strobe by responding to a trigger signal from the camera. Any number of slaved flashes can be set off simultaneously. Most slaves are light sensitive. Some respond to any small flash, others only to an infrared light. Multichannel infrared trigger/slave combinations or radio trigger/slaves are used when others are setting off flashes nearby. Radio or sound activated trigger/slave combinations are used for special purposes, including remote photography of wildlife.

I like Wein trigger and slave units. I use a WP SSR IR Trigger Model XT. The infrared signal does not show in pictures. I use Wein Peanut or infrared slaves on my Vivitar 283s (and strobes). Wein's infrared Pro Sync combination comes with two or four channels and has a long range.

Sunpak is a good flash, the company also makes reliable slaves.

Quantum, a company known for reliable battery packs, makes radio-controlled slaves and triggers used by scientists and outdoor photographers.

External Flash Battery Packs

Disposable batteries have a short life, don't recycle flash fast, and soon become expensive. Realistically, allow about one battery set per roll of film. Rechargeable battery packs will save you money in the long run. They shorten recycle times and permit a couple of hundred flashes per charge (more if flash power is reduced). Manufacturers like Quantum, Perma-Pak, and Jackrabbitpack offer proven six-volt rechargeable packs, or, wire up your own.

For directions on how to wire rechargeable six-volt batteries, and more information on Vivitar 283s and modifications, see my previous book, *Travel Photography: A Complete Guide to How to Shoot and Sell.*

Custom Made, High Voltage, Ultra High Speed Flash Units

I know of two makers: Kenneth Olson, an electrical engineer and fine avocational nature photographer (FPSA), from St. Paul, Minnesota, makes two high-voltage portable units, both with four light heads. His Lightweight unit gives 1/10,000-of-a-second flash duration used at full power, or 1/18,000 at half-power, with exposures of f/32 at four feet or f/16 at four feet. His Ultra Hi Speed Unit gives 1/20,000 at full power, and 1/33,000 at half-power, with exposures of f/32 at 5-1/2 feet, or f/32 at 3-1/2 feet, respectively. They currently cost $1,275 and $1,850. (Units are powered outdoors by twelve-volt motorcycle batteries. Twelve-volt AC adaptors for studio use, and twelve-volt chargers are also available.)

The Prestoflash Ultra High Speed Flash Units come in two versions, giving 1/30,000 and 1/100,000-of-a-second flash durations respectively. Prices start at around $4,000. For more information, contact coinventors and builders Dr. John Cooke in Dutch Flats, California, or Tony Tilford in Norwich, England. Dr. Cooke is a former director of Oxford Scientific Films, famous as makers of TV nature documentaries. He has a Ph.D. in biology and is a top scientific nature photographer and author. Mr. Tilford is an electrical engineer and published nature photographer. Both serve as high-speed lighting consultants to TV, films, big still shoots, and come complete with lighting equipment.

The best book I know on small flash in general is *Electronic Flash,* by Lester Lefkowitz, one of the useful Kodak Workbook series. (For all manufacturers' addresses and phone numbers, see Resources. chapter 14.)

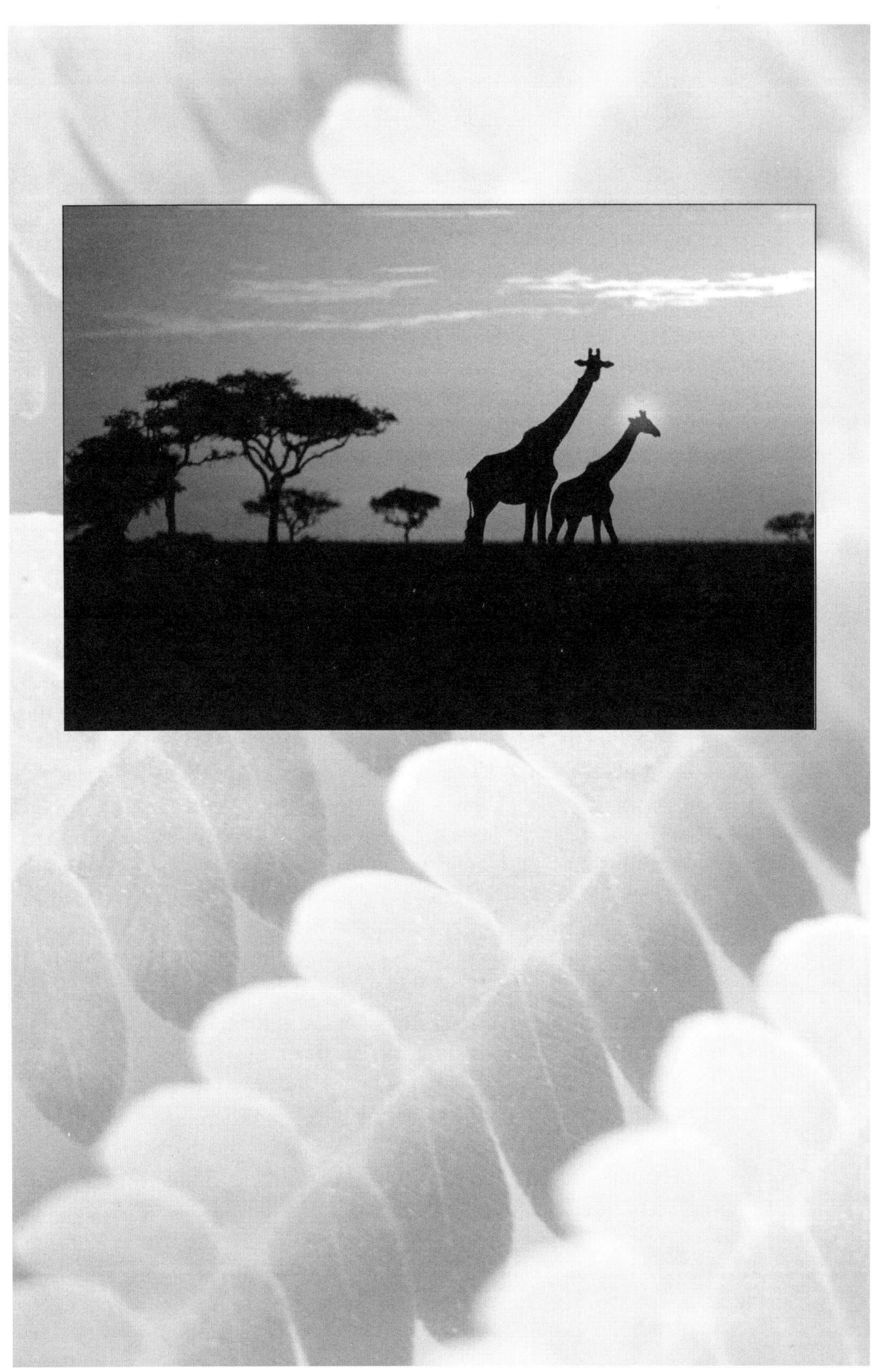

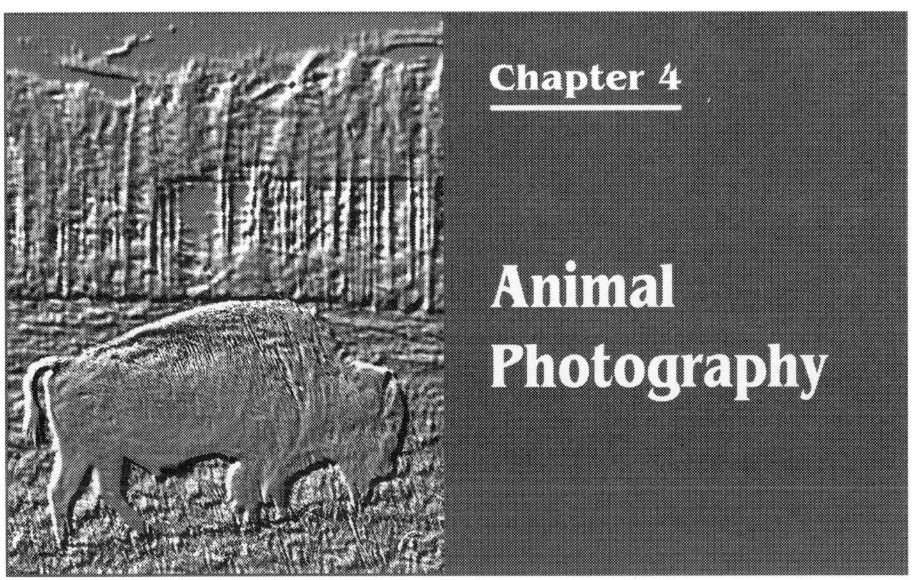

The largest land mammals are my favorite nature subjects (and a great many other peoples' too). Just to observe magnificent creatures in the wild is a thrill. Big animals' habitats are almost always grand, and traveling to them can be an adventure. To photograph great beasts in great places for me has the inherent challenge of getting something more on film than routine likenesses and landscapes. Fine pictures of lions and elephants, bears, moose, and others sell well as stock, and unlike some stock, the pictures don't go out of date! All of this for me adds up to making the time I spend photographing big animals extremely satisfying.

Large Animals

I am not going to write at great length about basic techniques for animal photography, as there are many excellent books on the subject by some of the greatest nature photographers in the world. (My favorite books are listed in the bibliography.) But, I have done quite a bit of animal photography and think my observations may be of value to you.

First and foremost, to photograph the largest animals in the wild, you must plan where and when to go to find the beasts you seek. In North America, by far the easiest places to spot bears, moose, elk, mountain sheep, and caribou are in national parks in Colorado, Montana, Washington, Wyoming, and Alaska, and in Canadian parks in Alberta and British Columbia. Hunting is not allowed in these parks, so the animals in many cases may easily be approached to within the seventy-five yards permitted by regulations, and extremely long lenses are not needed to get good-sized images. If you photograph from a vehicle in Yellowstone National Park in spring, fall, or winter, you can often get elk and bison very close to the road. A 200mm lens is more than long enough to fill the frame then. I normally carry a 400mm lens, an 80-200mm zoom lens and two tele-extenders when photographing mammals. If there are likely to be some cute small ones like chipmunks around also, I take my 105mm macro lens. With these lenses I can get herds, groups, and individual animals, and some portraits, and I can carry the lenses easily in a backpack. I usually carry a wide-angle lens or two also, they weigh little, and I use them for photographing animals in a sweeping landscape.

Although some of the largest mammals can also be found in national wildlife refuges, state and provincial parks and in national forests, national grasslands, and national recreation areas, seasonal hunting is allowed in most of these places, (and in big state parks like Baxter in Maine), so the animals are shyer and harder to photograph, and locating them may take considerable time. This is fine if your primary goal is being close to nature, but if you want (almost!) guaranteed big mammals, you will have to go where they congregate in fair numbers. Most of the best places and times of year to photograph wildlife in the U.S. and Canada are widely known among serious nature photographers (and nowadays are often quite crowded). Prime location in the U.S. lower 48 is Yellowstone National Park, in Wyoming and Montana, the place for bison, elk, occasional bears, and many smaller animals like antelopes, deer, beaver, coyotes, and marmot. Denali National Park, Alaska, is famous for grizzly bears and caribou. Everglades National Park, Florida, is where to go to photograph alligators, snakes, frogs and other creatures of the swamp, (and many large wading birds also).

There are still good animal habitats that are relatively uncrowded. On a recent visit to the Great Plains, I enjoyed the vast empty rolling grasslands and enormous skies of Custer State Park, South Dakota, which adjoins Wind Cave National Park, close to Mount Rushmore. Custer has pronghorn antelope, a few elk, hundreds of reintroduced bison, wild burros, and many prairie dogs. Eastern Wyoming has large herds of pronghorn antelope, rare elsewhere, that can be photographed close to Interstate 90 with a 400mm lens. There are also relatively uncrowded parks in northern Montana, eastern Idaho, Washington State, and central and western Canada where elk, moose, mountain sheep, and more can quite easily be seen.

The Nebraska sandhills are famed for prairie life, especially around the pleasant small town of Valentine. Close by is the Fort Niobrara

National Wildlife Refuge, which has a great many prairie dogs, plus elk, bison, and deer. The great nature photographer Jim Brandenburg told me that he recently photographed bison and pronghorn at the Blue Mounds State Park, near his hometown of Luverne, Minnesota, for a National Geographic story on the Great Plains.

To help you find the best places to photograph wildlife at home or overseas there are now a number of excellent, very specific nature guidebooks to refer to. (Also see chapter 11, and the bibliography.)

The second most important thing to do to make good pictures is to spend enough time in one place and on one species. My favorite way of working anywhere is to concentrate on a small likely, area until I feel I have all that can be got from it. In late May, in Yellowstone National Park, I stayed outside the north entrance. Len Rue, Jr., recommends this area for elk, especially mothers and young. I drove around on arrival and spotted two good views where elk were grazing in the distance. On my second day I got up around 5:30 a.m., drove into the park for a couple of miles, and stopped to take a few shots of one of the fine views. Very casually I glanced down. Beneath me was an elk who had just given birth to what I later learned was the first fawn of the season. I stood for three hours watching and photographing as the mother cleaned the newborn fawn, and expelled and ate the afterbirth. No other photographer or tourist was there. Periodically, the fawn took a few wobbly steps, slept, nursed, stood up, wobbled, and slept again. Mother kept licking, cleaning everything up, and from time to time nudging the fawn to walk. Finally, the fawn's legs were strong enough for mother to usher him out of sight. Time, good information, and a measure of luck had led me to the event. Most of those pictures are somewhat bloody, the mother elk was matted with a late winter coat, the scene was never pretty or "cute". But the experience was authentic and I wouldn't have missed it for the world. At dawn the next day I saw mother and fawn doing fine on a high hillside. Late that day, I found several young buck elks with antlers in velvet and made some good portraits of them. I then felt I had all the spring elk pictures I wanted and drove further down in the park, where bison feed, and spent two good days with them.

What Makes A Good Animal Photographer?

It is my sincere opinion that you don't have to be a great photographer, only a hard-working one, to take very good animal pictures indeed.

Great animal pictures require more than time and effort, they come only with an eye for a picture, passion, dedication, and often physical hardship; years of practice for anticipation and timing; a good knowledge of animal behavior, and, not least, the kind of luck that you make for yourself by being out there often!

Basic Equipment for Large Animal Photography

- You will need as a minimum:
- Two identical camera bodies of the kind you prefer, to shoot with.
- A spare camera body for emergencies is wise insurance.
- A 400 or 500mm lens - get one no slower than f/5.6.
- An 80-200mm zoom lens; I like f/2.8 in this range (so it can be "doubled" with a 2X tele-extender, becoming a useful 160-400mm f/5.6 lens).
- Or, get a fast 75-300mm zoom as a first large animal lens.

Increase the focal length of telephotos and zooms of over 100mm with 1.4X and/or 2X tele-extenders, get one the prime lens manufacturer makes. Good extenders do not much affect lens resolution; they do reduce light, by the factor of the extender.

I often use wide-angle lenses for photographing animals in a landscape, and like both 28 and 20mm lenses for this. You may prefer a 24mm lens.

A tripod is a must with a lens of 200mm or over for consistently sharp pictures, and a good ball head mounted on it will make following motion easier

Basic filters, a portable flash unit with remote or PC cord for use off- camera, plus cable release or dedicated release, and for wise insurance also, a hand-held flash meter that also reads daylight, complete a good outfit

Carry spare batteries, "gaffer" tape, a Swiss Army knife, a tiny screwdriver, a notebook and pen, and a marker and labels for film cassettes.

Load this gear in a favorite camera bag, or a water and dust resistant plastic case (or use a balanced camera backpack if you hike any distance).

(See chapter 2 for brands and types of equipment I suggest.)

Wild antelope, bears, caribou, deer, elk, moose, mountain goats, sheep and others don't just stand about waiting for their picture to be taken. Not only must you go to the general area where there are known concentrations of the species you seek, but you must be in those places at the right time of year (or you may get absolutely nothing). Then, you must know the specific areas within the often very large parks, refuges and so on, where the animals are most likely to be seen. Asking rangers, wardens, and locals on arrival is a good bet. Some helpful, quite specific local guide booklets are available only on the spot.

You may find it well worth your while to hire a professional nature guide or backcountry outfitter who specializes in wildlife. Locate guides through ads they run in the free promotional books you can get from state, provincial, and local tourism organizations. These are usually subdivided by region, so finding someone close to where you plan to go should not be too hard. If you have spent a lot of money to get to a specific location, the extra dollars spent for a guide may be wise picture insurance. Guides can drive, leaving you free to look, and they can carry heavy equipment too, if you have to hike!

Before making any expensive journey, practice basic animal photography skills locally. You can do this quite well in zoos where animals have space. Get used to setting up the camera and tripod quickly, then concentrate on keeping beasts in sharp focus as they move. The eye is the critical point of focus with any animal, but the more of a scene you can keep in sharp focus the better the picture as a rule.

If you have the time to hike and like wilderness areas, but grew up in a city or suburb like me, try to persuade a country-born person, off-duty park ranger, or a hunter or trapper to accompany you on at least one photographic expedition to a convenient woodland near home. Wear comfortable footgear and clothes that don't rustle (see outdoor and hunting catalogs). Have your mentor show you basic stalking and tracking skills, such as walking slowly and very quietly from cover to cover, all the while keeping downwind so that your scent does not alarm the animal.

Ask your guide to point out any hoof- or pawprints, animal droppings, and other signs that beavers, deer, foxes, muskrats, raccoons, porcupines, or rabbits, might be in the vicinity. Skilled hunters know a lot about wildlife habits and can be terrific teachers. And, who knows? You might persuade someone to trade in a telephoto sight for a telephoto lens. (Locate hunters if you don't know one, through rod and gun clubs, or even taxidermists, listed in local phone books, or by asking at sporting goods stores.)

Photographing Animals in Zoos, Safari Parks, and Commercial Game Reserves

In any park or zoo, first and foremost choose an angle to avoid showing bars, wire, or any barriers at all if possible. To eliminate/minimize these intrusions, use long lenses at wide apertures and throw backgrounds out of focus (check effects with the stop-down preview button on good cameras). Vary compositions. Make some pictures with the animal looking into the camera and some with it looking right and left. Watch out for shadows (use flash fill if needed). People may show up in backgrounds if you photograph animals in the largest enclosures of crowded zoos. Avoid them if possible, or wait for the space to clear. But, if the feeling is pleasant and not too crowded, take a few frames to record the scene. (Shots showing people enjoying modern zoos are needed for stock.)

Practical Large Wild-Animal Photography

The way to solve problems photographing big animals is first to define them:

- There aren't any large animals around here.
- There are large animals around here but they run off when they see you.
- It's hard to get close to large animals.
- Large animals don't do anything interesting.
- It's often cold/hot/wet out in the open.
- It's very expensive to travel to where the biggest animals are.

Here are some solutions:

- Photograph at first in zoos, wildlife parks, local nature reserves
- Travel to national parks, and other places where animals live in the wild.
- Learn the best times of year as well as best places to see wild animals.
- Learn stalking skills to approach nondangerous animals up close.
- Photograph from inside a car in National Parks, many animals ignore cars.
- Use a telephoto lens of at least 200mm focal length to start.
- Use a fast lens, a high shutter speed, and always use a tripod.
- Photograph at dawn and dusk, when many large animals feed.
- Great patience is often required to get good action and behavioral pictures.

Small and Midsized Wild-Animal Photography

The way to solve problems is first to define them:

- There are animals around here, but it's hard to get close.
- Small animals look too small in the picture area.
- Small animals don't do anything interesting.
- It's often cold/hot/wet out in the open.
- It's too dark to photograph when small animals are active.
- All the good small animal pictures have already been taken.

Here are some solutions:

- There are small animals almost everywhere.
- Look for them at dawn and dusk.
- Ask local outdoor people to help you locate habitats.
- You can stalk or track them (but not in woods during hunting season)
- You can set up a "blind" or hide to photograph from.
- Sit quietly in the blind and wait patiently for something to happen.
- Dress for the climate, in layers you can add or remove.
- Use a lens of at least 300mm, plus 1.4X or even 2X tele-extenders
- Use a flash, or teleflash on a light stand off-camera, placed near the subject and triggered from the camera.
- There is always a demand for good new stock images of "cute" small animals.
- Nature magazines, childrens' books, science textbooks, even calendars and greeting cards use behavioral pictures showing how animals live.

Early and late are the least-crowded zoo times; outdoor light is best at those times too. Feeding times (often posted on cages) can make for fine action pictures. Most zoo animals are fed from about 11:00 A.M. to 2:00 P.M. (obviously for the convenience of the keepers; the harsh overhead light is not the greatest at those times on sunny days in summer). It may be better to choose a lightly overcast day for your zoo photography at that season. The giant panda in the National Zoo in Washington, D.C., snoozes most of the time, but he is fed at 11:00 A.M. and puts on a show ripping up and chomping down large bamboo fronds (and an occasional carrot) for an hour or more daily. Many of the best stock panda pictures have been taken at this spot. (Use a 400mm lens with an extender, or a 500mm, or 600mm lens for frame-filling images; the enclosure is rather large and the panda is not actually gigantic.)

Tigers, leopards, and rare and endangered creatures are also mostly photographed in zoos. You can go a long way and spend a great deal of money to see elusive creatures in the wild, and not succeed if you have only limited time. Some zoos are particularly noted for one type of animal. (See interview with Norman Owen Tomalin in chapter 10, Stock, also check the AAZPA directory in good libraries. (See Resources, chapter 14).

Among my favorites zoo creatures are a colony of Japanese macaques (snow monkeys) in New York's Central Park Zoo. These little monkeys inhabit a spacious environment open to the sky, with rocks and pools that quite closely approximates their natural habitat in Hokkaido. The macaques constantly groom, play, nurse their children, tease, squabble, and make love. I have spent days taking pictures of them (with a 400mm lens plus 1.4X tele-extender). The monkeys are in families, but each individual has a distinctive face and personality; all the macaques, from babies to seniors, express a wide gamut of emotions, from tenderness to skepticism to rage.

When you get some very good pictures at your local zoo, show them to the administrators. If you offer picture usage at a reduced fee (if professional) or for expenses if (so far) an amateur, you may get the privilege of early admission, or a late stay, or even be allowed access inside cages. Volunteering in zoos is also a way to gain access. Authorities almost always react favorably to a sincere interest and willingness to help!

Photographing Animal Models

Two top commercial game reserves in Montana, Wild Eyes and Triple D, (in Columbia Falls and Kalispell, respectively) have fine collections of American wild cats, and authentic settings carefully designed for film makers and still photographers. Animal handlers are on hand to help you get just the "posoe" you want. One of my students took a week-long workshop at Triple D, led by a well-known nature photographer. He got excellent close-ups of bobcats, mountain lions, lynx, puma, and more, which would be very expensive, time consuming and even dangerous to get in the wild. The cost was quite high, a couple of thousand dollars for the week, but the pictures were of saleable quality. For this reason, photographing in such places has been popular with professional nature photographers for years, especially in spring when animal babies are available. On an individual basis, I was told by Wild Eyes that in 1994 they will charge $300 per day, for a session with a big cat, and an additional session with a "secondary" animal.

A less expensive place that I have been to, where you have good access to small mammals, owls, and more, is Northern Trek, a popular private nature reserve near Tacoma, Washington. You can ride around in an electric tram with other passengers to photograph elk, bison, mountain goats, and sheep (at some distance) for about $7 per hour. The tram has open windows. Get up close to some individual species in enclosures for a fee of about $50 per hour.

There are quite a few private nature and game parks. In some you may be able to arrange close-up photography of a species you want, for a fee. Inquire locally.

Using Flash For Animal Photography

When a beast is within fifteen to twenty feet of a camera, backlit by low sun, or its head is in shadow, a small flash can highlight eyes, lighten shadowed dark fur, emphasize claws and whiskers and even individual hairs, all of which will improve pictures. There is no need in sunlight to alter basic exposure for flash fill, as long as the shutter is at sync speed or below. Just expose for the brightest area, and add flash, which will affect dark shadows only. (For more on using flash, and flash fill, and a design for an inexpensive teleflash attachment that carries light to distances up to about fifty to sixty feet, see chapter 5.)

What Do Animal Picture Buyers Want?

A great many picture buyers want everything in the frame to be tack sharp, which often calls for using a rock-solid tripod, a very fast lens, fine-grain film, and sometimes, flash under controlled conditions. Of course buyers also want good composition, lovely color, and, often, interesting action. So, decent weather and light, expert camera-handling skills, and fast reflexes are also needed. Most of all what is needed is that indefinable "great eye" for a picture. Develop your own by practising constantly and looking at great pictures of all kinds.

Getting the Best Possible Pictures

What almost every animal photographer wants to record most, and every buyer wants to see, is action. Good pictures that show feeding, fighting, hunting, courting, playing, mating, nursing, and animals with young are highly saleable. The sharpness of individual hairs is not quite so important as capturing a fleeting moment on film, which is far from easy. But, for salability, some part of the image must be sharp, even if a blurred-motion effect was sought for artistic reasons.

To make the best possible images of big beasts anywhere usually requires local scouting, and considerable waiting about or driving around. You must allow for enough time in the place, because even the hottest of hot spots can be without animals sometimes, or the animals can be doing nothing much. Wait. As long as animals are in sight, there is always a chance of action. When you have found an interesting animal or group, keep photographing for as long as it or they are around. By waiting, you will outlast all distracting tourists and many other photographers. The best shots of all may come after several hours at one spot.

Photographing Wildlife Overseas

Quite a few nations today have established national parks, including Australia, Belize, Botswana, Brazil, Britain, Chile, Costa Rica, Ecuador, France, India, Indonesia, Israel, Kenya, Rwanda, South Africa, Spain, and Zimbabwe. You can get details from national tourist offices or consulates, and sometimes from national airlines, in New York and other big U.S. cities.

Migrations of large number of animals (wildebeests and zebras in East Africa, caribou in Alaska, polar bears in Manitoba) are more or less constant, but at certain times and places are more accessible to viewing and photography than others.

Animals in Africa

The dream of most wildlife photographers is to go to East Africa, one of the last places in the world that teems with large amounts of easily visible wildlife. Evermore are going to southern Africa, Botswana, Zambia and Zimbabwe. Even in Africa though, you must go to specific wildlife reserves/national parks and be there at the right time to see the greatest possible number of animals. Perhaps the most spectacular migrations are of wildebeests and zebras. Look out for the carnivores that prey on them that follow along behind.

Many animals can inhabit the same space because no two species earns its living in the same way. Carnivores have a hierachy, with lions at the top, as they kill the biggest game. Lions live in groups called prides and hunt buffalo, wildebeestes and zebras mostly; females do the hunting. When not hunting, which is most of the time, lions lie around panting and switching their tails at the flies that annoy them. They don't look very glamorous then! At a kill, lions gorge, in strict order of their pride.

Leopards hunt alone and have become quite rare. They drag their prey up trees to feast undisturbed, so look up and you may get lucky. I enjoy the challenge of following cheetahs, the fastest animal on earth, through my lens. They mostly hunt the smallest, swiftest antelopes. Stick around a kill, the hunter is only the first to eat. Hyenas and jackals eat the leftovers and crunch on bones left by the big cats. Vultures and marabou storks have beaks designed to tear flesh and pick off the small scraps of flesh left on skin and bones by even the hyenas and jackals. Small birds, beetles, and other insects digest the rest.

The vegetable-eating (herbivore) inhabitants of the African plains are similarly divided in their feeding habits and can share the same area. Giraffes eat leaves from the tops of the tallest trees. Elephants like the middle leaves and can pull down a tree if need be (releasing plenty of insects for birds and reptiles to feed on). Larger deer eat lower leaves of trees and bushes, smaller ones the lowest leaves plus grass. Rhino like bark as well as grass shoots, zebras eat the tops of tall grasses, and wildebeest the midheight grasses. Hippos eat aquatic plants in rivers, ponds, and lakes, and spend much time up to their nostrils in water, but they venture on land sometimes too.

Acquiring behavioral information is a key to photographing wild creatures, which are concerned always with survival. Avoiding enemies, feeding and drinking, searching for and attracting a mate, or battling for mates, and mating and rearing young, governs existence. To do these things animals may migrate seasonally in search of food, water, or a warmer climate, or to return to ancestral breeding grounds. At the beginning of each mating season some males fight others to establish dominance and mate with the largest possible group of females. Leaders of herds sometimes fight to protect territory. Many species engage in elaborate courtship rituals. Some animals pair for life, others for a season, still others for a few hours or minutes. Some creatures construct dens, lairs, or burrows. Much activity of female mammals surrounds gestation, birth, and the feeding, training, and protection of young.

Birth is a time of great peril. The youngest members of all species have enemies always ready to pounce, seize, and swallow. The young and their parent(s) require a readily available source of suitable food, which may be affected by weather or other factors. A high percentage of newborns mammals are killed or starve in their first minutes or hours of existence. Some may be killed by the mother if frightened by humans, others by jealous fathers. Nature often does not look like a Walt Disney movie.

After they have survived the first dangerous period of life, young animals must learn the skills of survival and then the whole cycle begins again.

Approaching Animals in the Wild

Whether you drive, and spot your subjects from a vehicle (which is the way many professional nature photographers work), or, you go on foot to track or stalk your subjects, always, as the Boy Scout motto has it: "Be Prepared." Keep camera loaded with film and exposure set for the prevailing light.

With automatic or electronic systems, relative novices can use the camera on P (program) setting but you don't have much creative control, except in framing the shot. I normally prefer to use S (shutter-priority) setting and choose high shutter speeds to stop animal motion. Sometimes A (aperture-priority) setting is needed with a slow shutter speed for maximum depth of field or to show motion with blur. Whatever setting you choose, with lenses longer than 200mm (and with them too where possible), keep the camera attached to a tripod, legs extended full-length, ready to use quickly if action occurs (you can fold extended tripod legs together while walking or driving).

When driving, if you see something you want to photograph, quickly and quietly pull off the road and turn off the vehicle engine. You may get out or not, depending on circumstances. If hiking, set down your pack. Move as quietly as possible. Spread tripod legs, focus, and compose as fast as you can. When working close, be sensitive to the signs animals send. Flicking or laid-back ears, raised hackles, and bared teeth mean anger; if an animal stares hard at you, that too usually means it's mad! Back off slowly if that happens; even if the beast isn't big enough to hurt you much, you are stressing it! Be extremely cautious with the animals that can hurt you. In Yellowstone Park recently, I saw a tourist with a point-and-shoot camera risk death by going to within ten feet of a bison for a close-up. The man was very, very foolish. Luckily, the bison was in a good mood that day.

Financing Wildlife Shooting

Except for *National Geographic,* no publication that I am aware of can afford to finance any still-photography assignment of more than a very few weeks. Most magazines today give assignments measured in days. However, if you really want to get someplace and stay there to do ex-

Photographing Animals in the Landscape

When animals are very close, you can photograph them with a wide-angle lens for both a good-sized image of a beast and an expansive landscape, all in sharp focus. I use both 28mm and 20mm lenses on 35mm cameras for such shots.

A picture that I took with a 20mm lens of a fine male lion with females behind him in the Ngorongoro Crater of Tanzania, is my all-time animal bestseller; it has appeared in *National Geographic,* German *Geo,* a story in the old *Signature* magazine, in two *Scholastic* publications and on the covers of several safari brochures, to date. That single picture has (so far) earned me as much as I was originally paid for a four-week African tourism assignment! (I have now had the picture duplicated for safety!) Another bestseller from the same trip, with the same lens, is of a fine young elephant, with gleaming tusks, just emerging from a bath. (The lower half of his body is wet, dark gray; exactly halfway up, there is a precise demarcation line above which he is pale and dry!)

Do not neglect to take wide angle-lenses on animal/wildlife shoots!

If you stay in a top wildlife location, like Yellowstone or the Serengeti, for several days or weeks at the optimum times of year, probably you will photograph everything in sight at first, however distant. Those first images of bison or elk, zebra or lion, are irresistible! But soon you will hardly bother to photograph a single animal, unless it is very close or doing something exceptional, but will react only to families, groups, or the herds of beasts present during mass migrations. When you find such situations, of course, shoot your heart out.

tensive wildlife coverage, you will find a way if you persist. You might find part-time work to pay expenses; perhaps family would help. There are seasonal opportunities working in hotels in some places, notably the U.S. national parks. (Apply in December or January for those jobs.) Perhaps you can volunteer with a research expedition or project. Many top people start small. When you show desire and talent and don't quit, sooner or later, someone or something will help. (See the interviews with Jim Brandenburg and Frans Lanting in chapter 13.)

If you take very fine animal pictures over quite a period of time, you will almost certainly be able to make some income from stock photography. Just how much will depend on how hard you work and how many pictures you produce. Art Wolfe told me that stock has freed him to do exactly what he wants. See the interview with him in chapter 13; also see chapter 10 which covers stock.

Selling Animal Pictures

To market animal picture stories, or stock, be aware of today's high technical standards. Wildlife pictures should normally be sharp; there is probably no such thing as a nature picture that is too sharp for most purposes. Most importantly, the creature's eye should be in sharp focus in almost any picture. A highlight in the eye brings sparkle and life to any animal portrait; train yourself to look for this and to focus on it. In very dull, overcast weather or in undergrowth, there may not be any highlight visible, but the eye should still be what you train yourself to focus on.

To sell pictures, another "market fact" you should be keenly aware of is that some animals are more popular than others, most especially for stock purposes. Good picture stories detailing the life of almost any species will probably be of interest to nature and scientific publications. For mass-market uses (advertising, greeting cards and the like), the animal must have mass appeal.

Think about it. How often do you see pictures of African warthogs or jackals, compared to those of lions and elephants? While the first two animals may be marketable to humorous greeting cards, the stately lion, the king of beasts, has broad market applications. (Lionesses are beautiful too, and powerful, and queenly!) The African elephant, the world's largest land mammal, also represents power, and is a symbol both of memory and longevity.

The most popular North American mammals today are among the rarest and hardest to photograph—bears of all types (even grizzlies somehow manage to look cuddly most of the time) and wolves. They symbolize the wilderness and freedom. Stags of all deer species and bull moose, with fine racks of horns, are much admired, and sell well too— do they represent the male psyche perhaps? (Curiously, pictures of female deer and related species, except with young, are not so popular; probably because most don't have horns.)

Come up regularly with good shots of the perennial best stock sellers and any nature stock agent will love you! (For more about what animals and other natural subjects symbolize, animal-model agencies, and the business of stock see chapter 10.)

Photographing Small Animals

Perhaps you are thinking, "This stuff about travel to far places is all well and good. It obviously costs a lot of money, which I don't have."

Or, perhaps photographing animals in zoos or faraway places is not your idea of what nature photography is all about. How do you start to photograph small wild animals and are such images saleable?

To start, research locally and concentrate on places where small creatures are likely be found within a day's drive of your area. Woods, riverbanks, hedges, ponds, and city and suburban parks all shelter a surprising amount of small animals. Beavers, deer, foxes, hares, marmots, mice, muskrats, otters, rabbits, porcupines, skunks, squirrels, and prairie dogs are all cute, interesting, and/or appealing creatures (though some some people consider some of them as pests). Tiny chipmunks, ground squirrels, moles, and pikas may be photographed easily in some places. Good picture stories showing the lives of these species sell to childrens' books and magazines, and science textbooks. Striking individual shots sell as stock, as well as to magazines and to calendar and greeting-card publishers.

The very fine nature photographer Dwight Kuhn specializes in photographing "nothing bigger than a robin" and makes a very good living, though it took him a while to get there. (See the interview with him in chapter 13.)

Small animals sometimes live in unexpected places. I recently visited the Devil's Tower National Monument, an isolated rock formation close to the town of Sundance, Wyoming. (The monument was featured in the movie *Close Encounters of the Third Kind.*) A road runs round the base of the tower and there is a huge prairie dog town right next to the road. Hundreds of the cute, noisy, mustard-colored little creatures inhabit the place. They seem accustomed to people, and are easy to approach. I spent several hours there, getting close enough for good photographs. In other places noted for prairie dogs, like the wildlife refuges in La Creek, South Dakota, and Fort Niobrara near Valentine, Nebraska, they were much more timid.

Photographing Animals in Cities and Suburbs

Big cities have big parks that shelter a variety of animal life; by no means all of it is brown rats, stray cats, other pests, or escaped pets! Many city parks (like Central Park in New York) are rest stops for migrating birds (see chapter 5, birds).

Central Park, like many city parks, has resident squirrels, field mice, muskrats and rabbits. Some suburban parks have deer. These creatures are good to photograph when you can't get far out of town. Stock agents have found that there is a demand for urban wildlife pictures, especially for textbooks. (Also see interviews with John Kaprellian and Norman Owen Tomalin, following chapter 13, stock.)

Quite a few species of small animals flourish in suburban areas (some are not beloved by vegetable gardeners!) and more than a few deer inhabit large farms and deep woods fairly close to suburbs. They can often be seen at dawn and dusk, especially in winter and spring.

Fall of course is hunting season; smart deer lie as low as possible. Smart photographers are very careful not to be in the woods at that time either. Early in my career, in big-city-dweller ignorance, I was photographing for a new edition of the Readers' Digest *Beautiful America* book. Included on my list of places to go was the Allegheny National Forest in Pennsylvania. It was October. I was working with an assistant, hiking through the woods. While I was focussing on a special mixtures of greens and fall colors, some hunter, evidently thinking we were a deer, took a potshot in our direction. Luckily his marksmanship was as poor as his judgement! We heard a bullet thunk into a tree, and yelled. The rest, thankfully, was silence, but I finished the assignment on the edge of the forest!

Animals in Wildlife and Nature Reserves

The largest number of animals are to be found in protected areas of course; usually national, state, and county parks, and wildlife preserves. Some also inhabit large private landholdings (where you must get permission to photograph). Since animals living outside national parks are frequently hunted, trapped or sometimes poisoned by man, plus pursued by their natural enemies, they are almost always very timid. Many are nocturnal, but some feed at dawn and dusk. Animals often live in places inhospitable to humans: thorny hedges, rocky hills and mountainous areas, the deepest woodlands, and swamps. Since they need water, most prefer habitats near lakes, ponds, rivers, and streams.

Inquire from your state, province, or county fish and game, or wildlife management department (or similar name) to find out about nearby possibilities. There are over 500 national wildlife refuges in the United States alone. One or more is within a day's drive of almost everyone in the U.S. The species to be found near you will obviously depend on where you live.

Getting Close to Small Wild Animals

If you live in suburb or city, the wildlife you see when looking casually may just be an occasional white flick of a doe's tail as she bounds off into a field by a highway, or a glimpse of a chipmunk or woodchuck scuttling to shelter in a park. For picture taking, that's no good even for practice.

What should you do to get close to animals in suburbs or cities? First study up a bit. Buy a basic nature guide to the region where you live or, buy the pocket-sized and interesting Golden Guide *Mammals of North America.* This costs less than $5, is well illustrated in color and has range maps. Then, ask people who are likely to know exactly where creatures live. To start, photograph the most common diurnal (daylight active) creatures, like squirrels. As they are very fast, getting sharp pictures of them can be a real challenge. (Carry a bag of hazelnuts in their shell to help.)

Spring and fall, times of birth and mating, are when there is often animal activity to be seen. Pictures of mothers and young are always top sellers, but of course don't do anything that would frighten the parents to get pictures. Sometimes even drawing attention to a den or litter in a populated area may put animal babies at risk; people or predator animals or birds may follow you. No photograph, in my opinion, is worth the risk of killing young creatures. In winter, animals are hungry and come close to people for food; you may get some good wildlife pictures by putting out food.

(Note: It is illegal to feed any creatures in national parks and national wildlife reserves and in some other places too, because some animals are considered pests. If you have doubts, check local ordnances.)

Never be afraid to ask for help in locating animals. In cities, make friends with park employees, they can tell you which old tree has squirrels living in it; a farmer who is not too far from an outer suburb will know where in his fields the rabbit warren or badger sett is; a dedicated fisherman probably knows which bankside houses a muskrat den, and the ranger or game warden in a lakeland region can most likely locate a beaver dam.

When you get more advanced, you may want to try to photograph at dawn and dusk, these are most timid small animals' feeding times and you will see deer most easily at the edges of woods then.

Set up equipment before dawn or before dusk and be prepared to spend time. You may need to sit in a blind. Use a long lens (300mm or 400mm is good on a 35mm SLR) with the camera on a tripod, prefocussed and ready at a likely spot, until a creature emerges. Set up a slaved flash close to a lair or den, and trigger the flash from the camera when an animal appears. For a description of how to set up small flashes to light a small area, see chapter 5, Birds. The general technique is the same for birds and small animals, except that working with animals, who have an acute sense of smell, you must be extremely careful not to leave your scent around: on clothes, shoes, camera, or flash. (Hunters' catalogs market odor masks, and super cleaning, odor-free soap.)

Reptiles, Amphibians, and Bats

Frogs are not too hard to photograph in the early morning when it's cool, and they are not too active. Many people catch them, put them in aquarium tank set ups to photograph, and release them later of course. **Caution:** Knowledge is especially essential when photographing snakes. Some types of lizards or tortoises can be found just about everywhere. Shyness is a problem; finding these creatures is often the hardest part of the excercise. A macro lens, or close up extension rings used on a telephoto lens, are sometimes helpful. So are one or two small flashes used on a bracket. (For more on that subject, see chapter 8.)

Two fine books that go into handling techniques for reptiles and amphibians in detail are by Patricia Caulfield and Leonard Lee Rue III. They are listed in the "how-to" section of the bibliography. Pat Caulfield has much experience with these creatures: she discusses it in the interview in chapter 13.

To locate bat habitats, inquire locally. They mostly are photographed at dawn and dusk, or hanging in caves. Flash is a must. Dr. Merlin D. Tuttle talks about his superb bat pictures, also in chapter 13.

Remote Camera Operation

Early animal and wildlife photographers often used remote photography (not controlled by the operator) to capture action. Edweard Muybridge made the first animal motion studies by having a running horse break a dozen trip lines that were attached to separate cameras equipped with high-speed shutters. He went on to make thousands of motion studies and to invent the forerunner of the motion-picture camera.

George Shiras III made night pictures of deer in the Minnesota wilderness by placing taut strings across narrow deer trails, the shutter was connected by a circuit to a magnesium flash pan. The lens was focussed on the string, with the shutter left open. Deer passing along the trail broke the string, closed the circuit, and triggered the flash. Not all the pictures were in focus and unless Shiras went without sleep, only one picture a night could be made. But by working like this for years, he did get very some good pictures.

Theoretically, trip lines could still be used to trigger camera and flash. In fact, remote photography today is virtually all done electronically, with light beams. I talked to a few photographers who have used the beams and got a mixed response. Ivan Eberle of Pacific Grove, California, is an enthusiast. He custom makes beams from Radio Shack parts and uses two crossed beams at known animal dens at night. He says his units are sensitive enough for any large and most small animals, though not for insects or small birds. (His beam-triggers are for sale. See resources, chapter 14.) Patricia Caulfield says that when she tried to use a beam, she got pictures of just about everything except what she needed (including a troop of Boy Scouts) and wasted a great deal of film because beams do not discriminate.

Bernard Furnival, a nature photographer and technical expert who works for dealer Ken Hanson in New York, invented a light beam that he uses in a studio for insect photography. He says that there are two problems using light beams outdoors with animals. The first is that you will probably leave scent or otherwise alert an animal to the camera/ flash presence when you set up the beam. The second is that unless you know exactly where the animal must go, and it does go exactly where you expect it to, you are likely to have a great many poorly composed pictures, with the animal not completely in the frame, or out of focus (or both). Even two beams crossed do not guarantee good shots, because the animal may never hit the exact spot where the beams cross. Bernard also said that a problem with all specialized remote and ultra-high-speed equipment is that there is not a great demand for it, so companies tend to go in and out of business. Nor is it easy to get accurate information on the whole subject. I can verify that. I had to make a lot of phone calls and talk to quite a few people to learn this much.

All the photographers and stores I talked to agree that the most widely used light trigger today is the Dale Beam. You can buy one, or two, from Protech, in Alexandria, Viginia.(See resources.) The units are not cheap, must be special ordered, and delivery can take a long time.

Several people I talked to, including Heather Angel, said that light-beam triggers are most helpful when taking flash pictures of tiny, very fast-moving creatures in studio setups with carefully planned backgrounds. They can also be used at birds nests. Birds have little sense of smell and birds feeding young come back to the exact same spot frequently.

Dr. John Cooke, coinventor of the Prestoflash ultra-high-speed unit, uses a trigger for his scientific animal-locomotion photography. You may be able to get a beam trigger from his company.

Dr. Merlin D. Tuttle, famed for high-speed photography of bats, does not use a beam trigger. Dr. Tuttle says he judges the moment to release the shutter by eye.

Photographing Small Animals
Under Controlled Conditions

Studio setups for small-animal photography must be carefully lit and "propped" (correct vegetation, stones and the like selected, and the setting designed) authentically. The scene can be lit with small flash units like Vivitar 283s. If the flash power is turned down and placed close, much motion stopping is possible (see earlier in this chapter, and chapters 3, 5 and 8, for more about using flash, and high-speed flash). Polaroid testing of lighting setups is a very good idea, especially if you use small flash units, which unlike studio strobes do not have modelling lights to assist you in placing flash for best effect. You can use a small household lamp or even a flashlight at flash positions to help you place lights though. A diffused flash unit used at a high three-quarter angle can be used as a main light. Place it slightly above a small box or aquarium used to house the field mouse, frog, snake, or any small creature being photographed. A weaker "fill" light (or a reflector) is placed lower, opposite the main light to reduce contrast and deep shade. Read up on still-life photography to help you light small moving subjects too, then experiment and make tests until you get pleasing results.

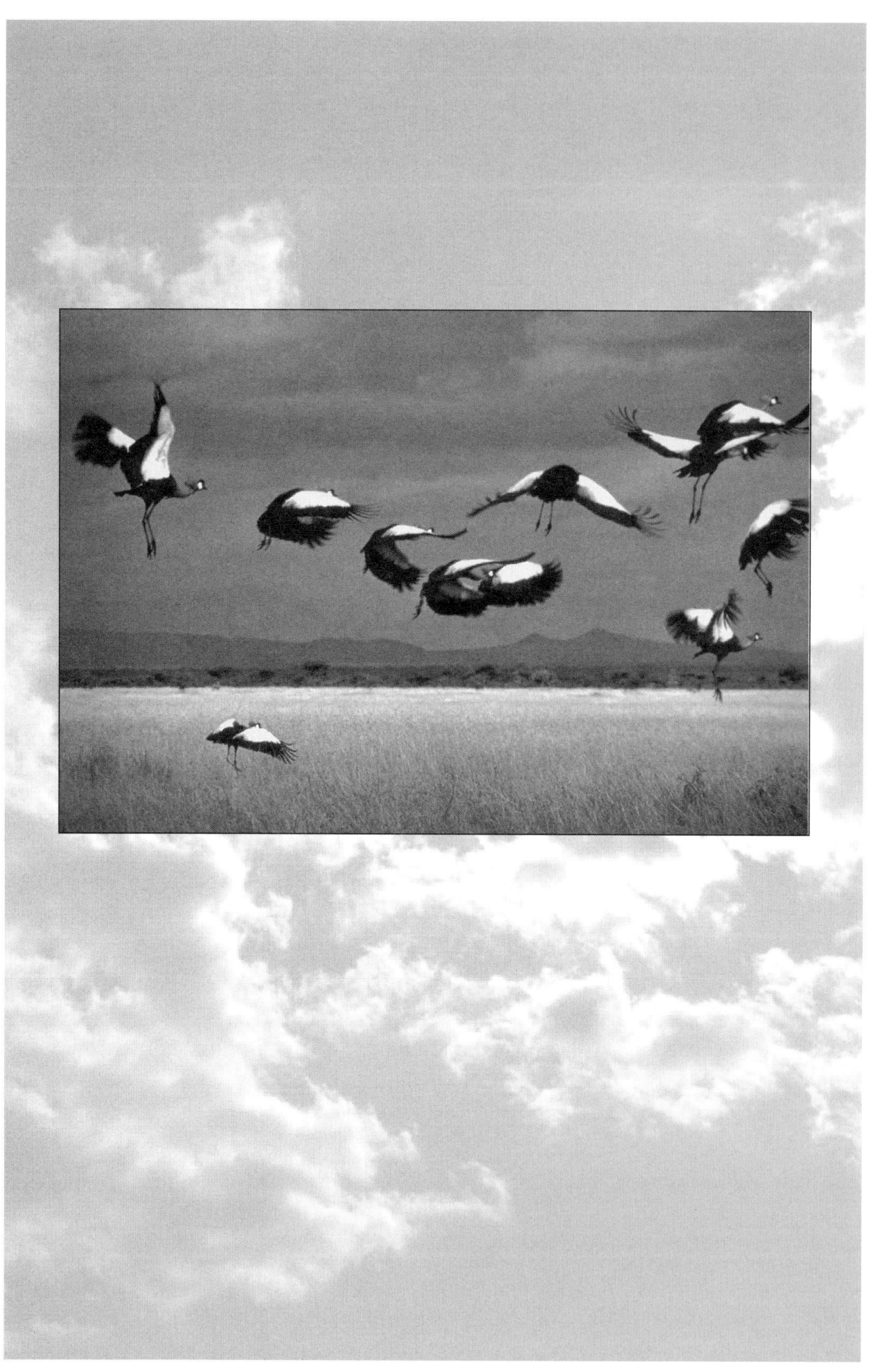

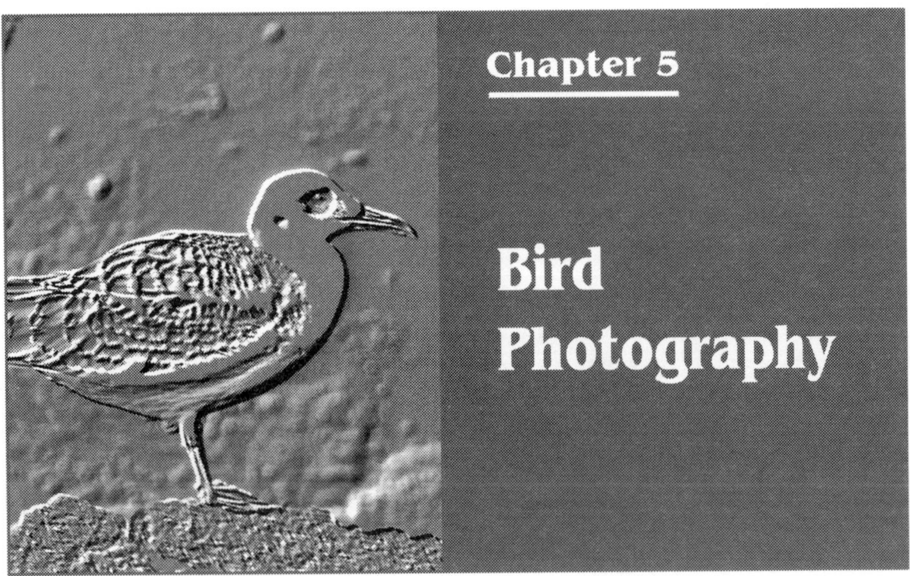

Birding is one of the most popular forms of outdoor recreation in the U.S. and Canada; the British, who don't have many large animals to enjoy, do have large colonies of resident and migratory land and sea birds, and may be the most passionate bird-lovers in the world.

Starting Out

Good bird photography is technically quite demanding. You will need a 300mm telephoto lens and a good tripod as absolute minimum equipment. Some books say you always need a "blind" to photograph birds. A portable blind is a camouflaged, tentlike structure, sometimes just a car with camouflage netting taped on the side windows. Permanent blinds exist at some bird sanctuaries, and you can construct one on your own property.

Blinds are essential to photograph shy birds in open areas like prairies, marshes, and lakes, and to photograph birds on nests, but in my experience there are plenty of bird pictures you can get without a blind. You can get pictures at home feeders with a 400mm lens, if birds are fed and given water regularly, and if you sit sheltered by a tree or bush, waiting patiently, camera on tripod. Or, you can black out a window inside your house and photograph from there. It is also possible to get many bird pictures without a blind in city parks, where birds are accustomed to people, again by sitting quietly and patiently. Prefocus on feeders or on branches where birds land to go to a feeder.

Photographing exotic birds in zoos is fairly easy, if you can get the lens close enough to enclosure wires or mesh to throw them out of focus.

Lenses for Bird Photography

If you are at all serious as a bird photographer you will need a long telephoto lens. McCartney's Law for bird photography says that no lens is too long or too fast for birds, provided you are able to carry it!

I have settled on a 400mm f/5.6 Tokina lens for bird photography. It has fluorite glass, is eight inches long, weighs 2 lbs. 2-1/2 oz., and focusses to a minimum of eight feet. I can hand hold it at 1/250 of a second if I must, but normally use it with a tripod. I use this lens with 1.4X and 2X Nikon tele-extenders without any loss of quality that I can discern through a loupe.

Nikon and Canon both make superb telephoto lenses; if you want one of those, I recommend buying a 300mm f/2.8 autofocus of either make. Use it with 1.4X and 2X extenders, for convenience, and light weight.

Basic Bird Photography

The easiest way I know to get good bird pictures is by going to a known birding "hot spot" at the right season, when breeding or migrating birds are present in great numbers. Breeding seabirds especially are not shy. (Use a tripod with any lens longer than 200mm, accidentally blurry pictures are almost never good!)

Small birds can be elusive. But, with patience, a long lens, and luck, you can get pictures of these too without a blind. Last May, using a 400mm lens, I stood for half an hour and made two rolls of frame-filling close-ups of a house wren singing its heart out in a cherry tree in the middle of downtown Washington, D.C.!

Most excellent pictures of the very smallest birds are made under controlled conditions, in a yard or garden, with portable flash units placed around a feeder, waterbath, or both.

Photographing Birds With Flash

If you want the sharpest possible pictures of small birds, you must light a place that they frequent. Use two or more flash units close up, with flash power reduced for short flash durations. Use highest possible sync speed for your camera and small f/stops. Meter the light. This method excludes daylight from influencing the scene and, carefully done, looks very natural. You will have to experiment with placing the lights, so that the background does not look black.

Practical Bird Photography

The way to solve bird photography problems is first to define them:

- Most birds are small and shy.
- Birds have superb eyesight, move quickly, and fly off when disturbed.
- Many birds look very small in the picture "frame."
- It is difficult to focus on flying birds.
- Pictures of moving birds often come out blurred.
- Pictures of white and dark birds are often poorly exposed.

Here are some answers:

- Birds that are fed, or otherwise used to people, are not so shy.
- Birds that live on and around water may be more tolerant, if you move towards them slowly, or get set up in one spot and wait there.
- Seabirds that live in island colonies are normally not shy at all.
- You can photograph birds from inside windows so they don't see you.
- You can carry and set up a portable "blind" to photograph from.
- At some places and times migrating birds gather in very large numbers.
- Long telephoto lenses make birds look bigger in the camera frame.
- Use a good autofocus camera and lens, and practice, to help you focus.
- Tripods and ballheads keep long lenses steady, help following flight.
- You can prefocus on a spot where you know birds will come for food.
- Flash permits small f/stops for great depth of field, and can stop motion.
- Don't meter off a light or dark bird, but off "average" tone in scene.

Ultra-High-Speed Flash and Bird Photography

According to Dr. Mike Hill and Gordon Langsbury, in their excellent *Field Guide to Photographing Birds in Britain and Europe,* the late Eric Hosking, considered one of the greatest of all bird photographers, did his work with a portable flash with a speed of about 1/5000 of second, about the equivalent of today's Vivitar 283, turned down to 1/16th power.

But, to stop wing motion of the fastest birds like hummingbirds (and to get smaller f/stops than is possible with a Vivitar) a custom-built ultra-high-speed flash is normally used. These can have light speeds as short as 1/100,000 of a second. They are often are used with a light-beam trigger. Sometimes special high-speed shutters may supplement or replace standard shutters, and other accessories may be needed also. High-speed flash units currently available are discussed in chapter 8.

Making a Habitat to Photograph Small Birds

A flash setup, ready to go, is S.A.I. Photo Products' Wild Bird Lighting Kit, which uses two NVS-1 custom Vivitar 283 flash conversions. The Wild Bird outfit comes with bare bulb-flash heads, parabolic reflectors, flash mounting brackets, a Jackrabbit two-outlet six-volt power pack with six-foot cords and a charger, Wein infrared slaves and trigger, and instructions. S.A.I.'s Norman Stuessy suggests placing the two flashes about thirty inches on either side of the "set" being photographed. (The light must be metered, using 64 ISO film, and 1/32 flash power f/8 is an average aperture. The flash duration short enough to stop water drops in the air and much wing motion.) I have tried the S.A.I. kit, at a landscaped watersplash constructed by bird photographer Gerard Bailey of New Jersey. I used Velvia rated at 40 ISO at the ground-level bath. The short flash duration at 1/32 power stopped water droplets splashed by bathing catbirds in midair, and wing motion too.

Gerry Bailey loves warblers in particular, and spends many patient hours in this blind every week, about eight feet from the splash. With a 300mm Nikon ED IF lens plus 1.4X extender, he has made great close-ups of bathing yellow warblers.

Wild Bird magazine runs articles telling you just how to attract birds to feeders and how to construct water splashes for photography.)

Constructing a Blind

A blind can be anything that hides you from birds and permits you to poke a lens out. It can be be a garden shed with a blacked-out window, or holes cut in the sides for the lens. Construct a homemade portable blind inexpensively out of artists' canvas stretchers hooked together, or use PVC pipe frame. Use opaque fabric stretched over any frame. Disguise lens holes with flaps of camouflage netting (from sporting goods stores). About four by four feet, and six inches taller than you are, is a good size for a blind.

Flash does not seem to disturb birds, nor does the click of a shutter. What does disturb birds is movement, however slight. So, be sure that your blind does not flap or rattle, and that it is opaque. I have seen blinds made out of waterproof camouflage fabric (available from hunting stores or catalogs), old army blankets, tarpaulin, artists' canvas, and green tent nylon (waterproof fabric is best, for obvious reasons).

Permanent blinds can be made from plywood, wooden fencing, brushwood, even corrugated iron nailed to a frame. Improve your chances when using a car as a blind in a national wildlife refuge where you can photograph birds from the vehicle, by cutting camouflage netting to shape and gaffer-taping "curtains" over the side windows.

L.L. Rue's ready-made pop-up blind is convenient, but should not be left exposed in all weathers. I do not care for the portable blinds you wear over a hat; they are hot. A couple of ponchos snapped together can be a temporary ground blind.

Photographing Nesting Birds

Nests first have to be located, and then a blind on a platform must be constructed, or set up and moved within range of the nest, gradually, when parent birds are absent. If a nest is high, the brave photographer may want to climb to get pictures. Climbing aids, platforms, and portable towers are used by hunters and can be used for photography; (they are available from catalogs listed at the end of the book).

No photograph of birds in nests is worth killing them for! All the bird experts I have talked to agree that great prudence and patience are needed to photograph nesting birds. Move "dummy" flash setups into place over several days, putting them a little closer to the nest each time the parents are absent. But, if at any time the parent birds are obviously so distressed that they will soon abandon the nest, you must make the decision to stop, remove any construction, and abandon that project. If all is okay, when the "look like" flashes are within about four to six feet of the nest, and the parents are accustomed to them, substitute real flash units mounted with infrared slaves. (Protect the units from weather with clear plastic bags tied round them.) Settle yourself into the blind when parent birds are absent, and once in the blind, use an infra red flash trigger and a long telephoto lens. Prefocus on the nest and photograph whenever parent birds comes to the nest. The camera and flash can also be triggered by a long sync/P.C. cord from the camera to the flash, or automatically by using a light- beam setup. A bird breaks the beam by crossing it, and fires the camera and flash. (For more on the use of light beams, see chapters 4 and 8.)

Photographing Birds at Feeders From the House

For best results, place your feeder(s) about ten feet from a smallish, unimportant window, that can be temporarily or permanently blacked-out by an opaque curtain or dark window blind taped taut, or hardboard. (Cut a crossed slit, or sew a sleeve into fabric, or cut an opening in hardboard a bit larger than your lens, so you can move the lens around). The window should open quietly. The feeder(s) should have bushes nearby, as shelter, safety, and waiting spots for the feeding birds. When the birds perch on branches near the feeder, you will get natural-looking backgrounds and some "wild" bird pictures. There is demand for pictures of birds at feeders too.

If you put seed and water out regularly soon birds will come to rely on the feeder. The type of bird you get will depend on locale, season, and what kind of food you put out.

Set your camera with a long lens on a sturdy tripod. Prefocus on your feeder. Try to catch birds alighting, so heads are not obscured inside the feeder. Pictures of pretty-colored small birds (cardinals, blue jays, orioles, and goldfinches for instance) outsell brown, black, and gray species by a large margin! To begin with, be happy with well-exposed, sharp pictures of small birds of any color.

Try using a flash to "stop" birds in motion. Use the technique noted earlier in the chapter, with any flash. Flash may momentarily startle birds, but they soon become accustomed to it. (One theory is that birds equate flash with lightning.) When using a flash at the feeder watch for ugly reflections on glass or plastic; to avoid or minimize reflections, you may have to put "slaved" flashes outside the house close to the feeder, and "trigger" them from the camera inside. Wein infrared triggers and slaves work well for this, and there is no unwanted light.

In a city park, you are guaranteed sparrows and pigeons if you take corn or, better, birdseed. Don't scorn these humble birds, both are hard to photograph with the details showing and are fine for practice. In parks with ponds there are often ducks and sometimes geese too. During spring and fall migration seasons, between March-May and October-November, many unusual birds are temporary visitors to city parks.

Photographing Birds in Central Park

Central Park in New York City is a "hot" birding spot, especially at the Ramble, a wilderness area. Near a small pond there, New York City Audubon Society members fill feeders with seed of different types, plus suet, apples, and pineapple slices. A former student of mine, Deborah Allen, has been photographing there for five years, and now has over 150 species in her collection, some rare. Her pictures of a pair of red-tailed hawks nesting on a Fifth Avenue building next to the park were recently published by *The New York Times Magazine.*

One fine April afternoon, I photographed at the Ramble, using a 400mm lens; no blind was needed. This was what I got in two hours:

American robin, a black-and-white warbler, a black-capped chickadee, a blue jay, a common grackle, a downy woodpecker, some European starlings, a few house sparrows, a pair of mallards, a northern cardinal, several red-bellied woodpeckers, a red-tailed hawk , two red-winged blackbirds, and a lot of rock doves (better known as pigeons)!

Photographing Large Birds

Many birds that live on or near water are larger than average land birds. If you live on or close the ocean, a river or marsh or big pond, you can spot egrets and herons and other wading birds if you wait patiently in a blind.

You will need the longest, fastest possible lens you can afford (a 400mm f/5.6 lens on a 35mm camera is a good, not too expensive minimum focal length. You will also need a very sturdy tripod, preferably with a good ball head so you can follow flight easily. Serious nature photographers who want the best possible bird pictures routinely use 500mm, 600mm and even 800mm lenses, plus tele-extenders, for maximum image size of birds at a distance. (See the interview with Art Wolfe in chapter 13.) Although blinds can be elaborate, anything that hides you from the birds is okay. Make or buy a portable blind, (see earlier in the chapter).

Photographing in National Wildlife Refuges

In some refuges you can photograph from a car. In others like Jamaica Bay, in Queens, New York, a birding "hotspot", you must hike (there are some permanent blinds there). Call refuge superintendents ahead for details of conditions, what birds are there when, best times to visit, and whether a permit for a blind is needed to get close. If you are at any major wildlife/bird refuge during the right two or three weeks during spring or fall migration, or during the breed season, you will probably see very large concentrations of birds.

The three major migratory bird routes between North and South America are the Atlantic flyway on the East Coast, the central, or Mississippi flyway, which starts and ends in Arctic Canada, runs through Ontario or Saskatchewan, and roughly follows the river on its journey from the source in Minnesota down to Mexico and points south; and the Pacific flyway which runs down the West Coast from Alaska to Baja California and then Central and South America.

I have visited quite a few refuges. One of the most beautiful I have seen is the remote La Creek National Wildlife Refuge in South Dakota. La Creek is noted for its colony of American white pelicans, where they nest on an island in the center of the refuge. When the birds are laying or sitting on eggs, the superintendent of the refuge worries that a visit from a photographer at that critical time might cause the birds to stay away, allowing eggs to overheat. Photographers must wait until the chicks have feathers, and then a visit to the island, very early in the day, might be possible according to the superintendent.

Pelicans can be seen flying around the refuge, and feeding peacefully in a stream. Be very still, they are wary. It is a good idea to camouflage car windows. Also look for raccoons, the huge prairie dog town, ducks, geese, cormorants, and moorhens in this lovely place.

In the State of Washington, I visited the Nisqually Wildlife Refuge one very rainy day last August; not many birds were about. I moved on and found quite a few varieties of shorebirds during several days at Kalaloch, Ruby, and Rialto beaches in Olympic National Park. Nisqually is best in spring and fall.

Photographing Large Birds in Flight

This requires considerable practice. Getting and keeping fast moving birds in focus is not at all easy. A "gun-stock" shoulder lens support may help you to swing a long lens smoothly. Fast autofocus is often helpful (if there are not too many birds flying in different directions, when autofocus mechanisms tend to get confused, and whirr back and forth). When photographing flying birds, you must keep aiming slighly ahead of them, to allow for the delay in your reflexes releasing the shutter. Try fast and moderate shutter speeds for different effects. Gliding birds are much easier to capture on film than flying ones. Study patterns of flight: a lot of birds have a moment when there is a pause in the movement and they hold wings steady. Just before landing, birds extend their legs, especially waterbirds with webbed feet.

Photographing Seabirds

The birds that appeal to me most are the seabirds that come to small offshore islands only to breed, spending the rest of the year on the ocean. Some, like the Arctic tern, make long voyages annually; others, like the Atlantic puffin, never stray far from their breeding grounds.

Puffins can easily be photographed off Newfoundland, New Brunswick, and Maine in North America, and the northern islands around Britain and Ireland. I went recently from Jonesport, in northern Maine to Machias Seal Island, New Brunswick, twenty miles from the coast. This breeding ground has thousand of puffins, plus hundreds of murres, razorbills, terns, and eider ducks among its summer residents. Blinds are set up, and you can often fill the frame with puffins using a 300mm lens.

Seabirds are perhaps the easiest of all birds to photograph if you can go where they nest. One of the best places in the world to photograph many of them is the Galapagos National Park, in the Pacific, about 600 miles due west of Ecuador. Boobies, albatrosses, frigate birds, and gulls permit you to approach within feet, without fear. You can get Galapagos hawks and migrant shorebirds, plus seals, sea lions, giant tortoises, and iguanas there too. For more on the Galapagos and other great destinations, see chapter 12.

Birds of Prey

Rehabilitation centers, zoos, and wildlife parks offer possibilities to photograph these best-selling birds. To photograph them in the wild, raptors are virtually everywhere; ask locals about their haunts. You can sometimes attract birds of prey with calls mimicing their own kind, or small birds, or with carrion as a lure (see the interview with Pat Caulfield.) To photograph bald eagles, go to one of the places where they congregate each year. Haines, Alaska, and vicinity is known for these magnificent birds, and large numbers can be seen there in November. Spring Creek, in northern Oregon, is for nesting great gray owls in spring, and for other predators too. I have seen ospreys and kestrels nesting on poles on Long Island, and around the fishing harbor at Cape Charles, Virginia. (For more, see books recommended in the Bibliography).

Exotic Birds

If you go to the Amazon rainforest, or to New Guinea, or to Australian national parks, you may be lucky and spot exotic birds in the wild. Using a teleflash attachment on your lens may be helpful under trees; they concentrate the flash giving an exposure increase of about two f/stops and extend the flash range to about sixty feet. Buy one from L.L. Rue's catalog or make a lightweight one inexpensively, using a plastic Fresnel magnifier. (For directions, see diagram at the end of this chapter.)

Zoos are most reliable places to find exotic birds. A famous exotic bird collection is the Jurong Bird Park, a reservation in Singapore. Commercial "parrot jungles" (there is one in Miami) offer some opportunities to photograph birds flying free.

Bird Pictures That Sell Best:

Birds of prey, including eagles, hawks, falcons, ospreys, kestrels.
Owls—they are predators, plus, they represent wisdom.
Bald eagles, the symbol of the United States.
Colorful birds on home feeders or bushes, especially in snow.
Robins with bright red breasts, pulling up worms, building nests.
All species sitting on eggs or feeding young in nests.
Migrating birds in V-shaped flights (symbolic of leadership, teams).
Ducks in general (many of these are sold to hunting magazines).
Game birds, grouse, or wild turkeys (they sell to hunting magazines).
Woodpeckers pecking, especially species with bright tufts (industry).
Colorful parrots, macaws, toucans, especially in the rainforest/wild.
Penguins, all types, en masse and couples (they symbolize humans).
Exotics, like peacocks and mynahs, displaying magnificent feathers.

Ethical Guidelines and Regulations for Bird Photography

Nesting birds are usually photographed by someone hidden in a blind using a long lens. Do not approach nests too closely. Never frighten parents sitting on eggs, cut back concealing vegetation, or draw attention to occupied nests. It is against the law to harass or get closer than senty-five yards to any species in U.S. national parks, or to photograph endangered nesting birds in Britain. While these regulations are not always strictly enforced, you run a risk by breaking them.

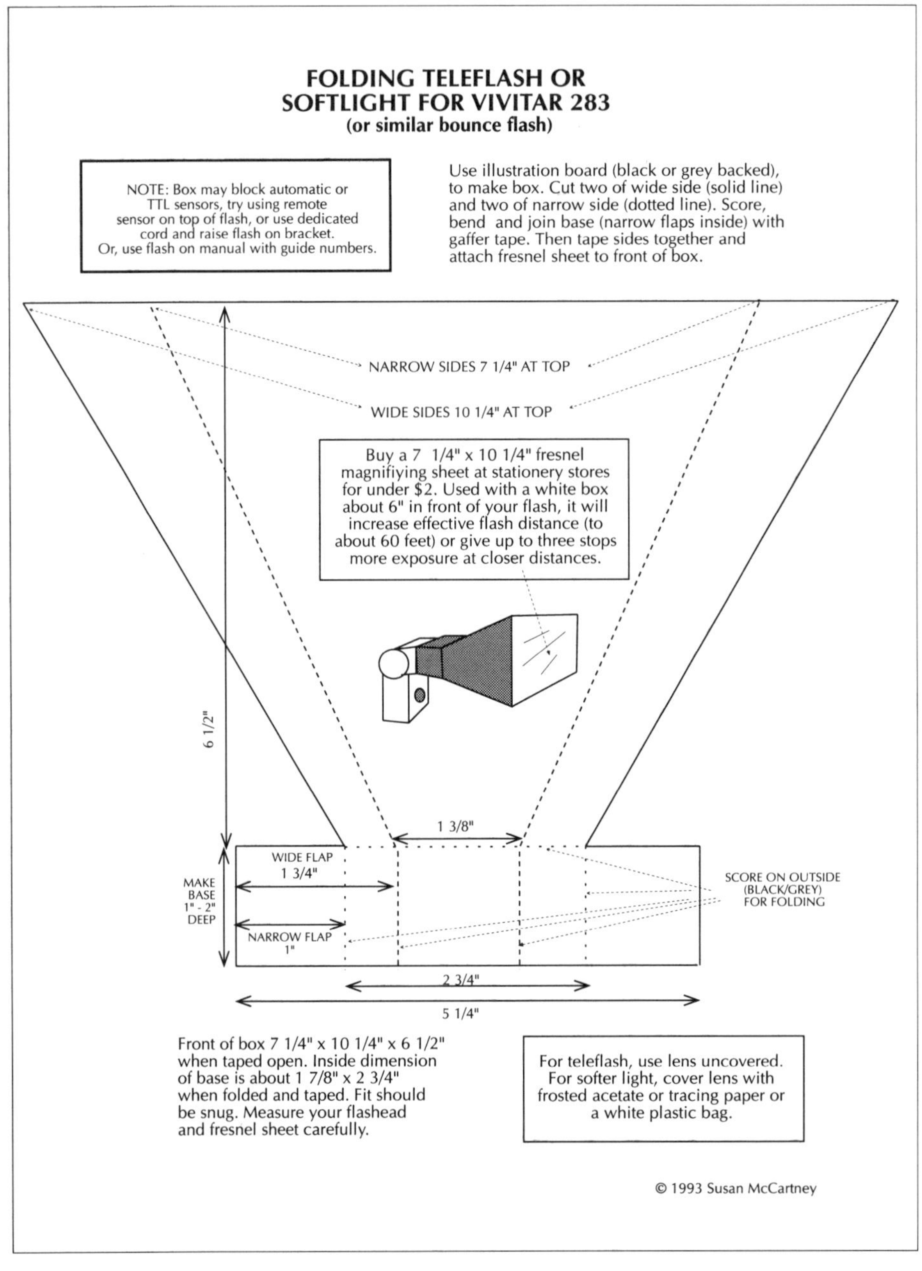

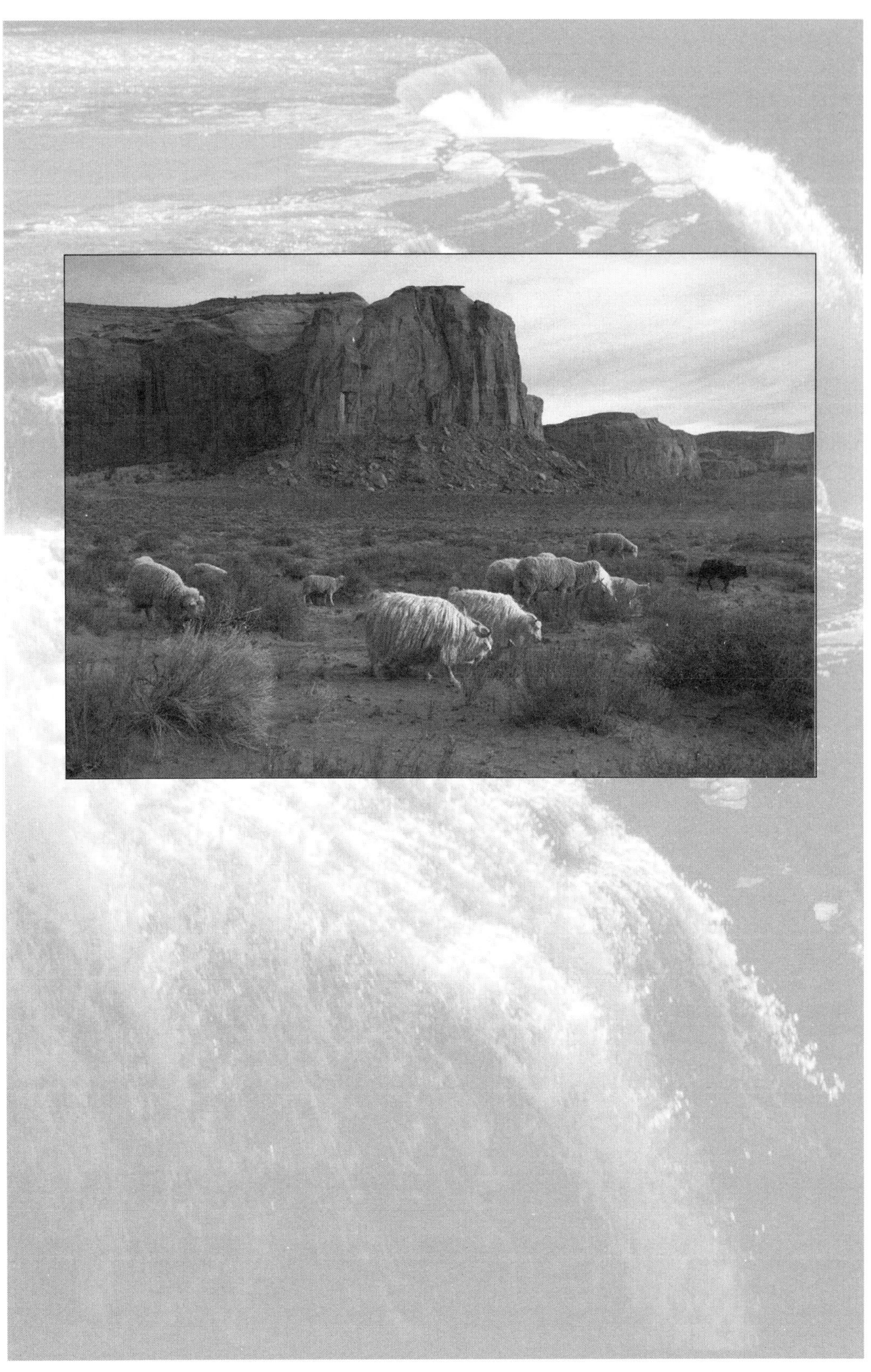

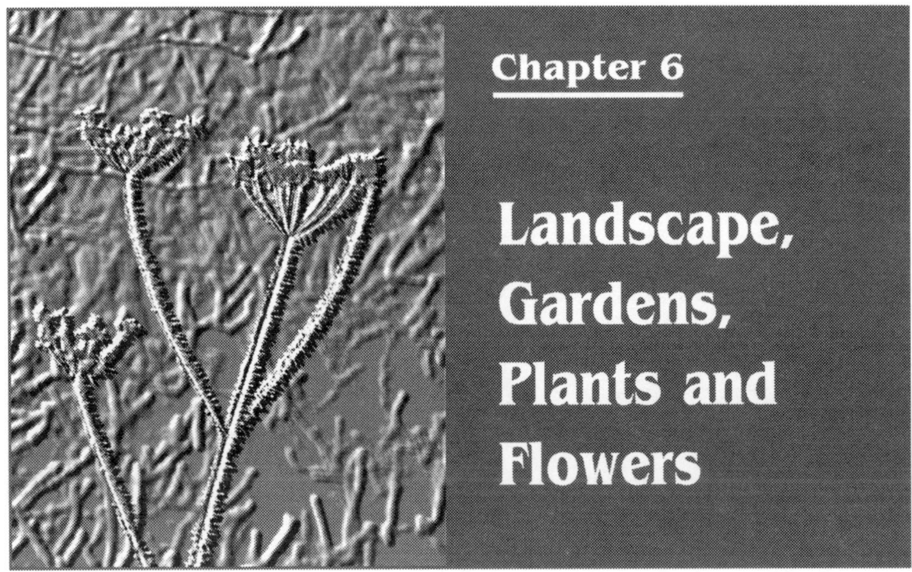

Landscape photography is at the same time easy and difficult. A person with no knowledge of photography can get good landscapes with the simplest camera, if they are in a marvellous place when the light is right. My 81-year-old-cousin Betty Thompson has a natural "eye" and has taken great Instamatic snaps of Willoughby Lake, Vermont. If you get a bad picture of a bear, you've got something to recall that special moment. But if you miss the essence of a landscape, you've got nothing.

My challenge to a great landscape photographer would be to capture South Dakota on film. I have fallen in love with its space and emptiness. Driving across South Dakota, you don't seem to move at 80 miles an hour, because it rolls on unchanging, hypnotically green and flattish for about 500 miles until you get to the western extremity of the state, when the Badlands erupt, and then the sharp, Black Hills. Expressing this vastness in a photograph is no mean feat. The sky is almost always essential to a landscape, never more so than in the Dakotas.

Landscape photography calls for a photographer's highest skills and subtlest judgement. Unless you specialize in mountains like Galen Rowell (whose work I much admire), there is nothing inherently dramatic in most landscapes, and unless animal life is present, there is no action to record except the movement of the light. Pure landscape photography shows nothing man-made. It is the art of choosing, isolating, and distilling significant elements, arranging them within a two-dimensional picture area, in an arresting composition, at a time when natural light makes them look most interesting. Some great landscape painters and photographers have returned to a favorite place for a lifetime, trying to capture its elusive moods in different light, weather, and season.

When I was twelve, a cousin gave me a little book of Cezanne reproductions. It took me years to understand the collection of watercolors of Mont Sainte Victoire, painted over and over again.

Quite a few clichés are written about landscape composition. Framing a landscape with the branch of a tree may or may not improve it. Placing a horizon line one-third from the top or bottom of a scene may look excellent, or it may not. Perhaps a center of interest should be placed one-third from the left or right side of the picture area, but, then again, perhaps it should not. I don't believe in rules of thirds or anything else, and think that there are only two practical ways to improve compositional skills. These very largely are intuitive and artistic. The first step is to look at as many great landscape paintings and photographs as possible, and let them soak into your unconscious mind and eye.

I refer you back to chapter 1 for some of the landscape photographers I admire; you will find their work, and will develop your own favorites, by going to art museums and top galleries.

The second practical way to learn to compose is to get out with a 35mm SLR camera, early and late when light is usually beautiful. Walk around looking at the landscape and light with the camera glued to your eye like a Cyclops. I suggest starting out using a 35mm camera, because you don't need to use a tripod at first and the lightweight format makes it easy to move around a lot to vary your viewpoint.

Choice of lens makes a great difference also, because landscape-element relationships are altered with different focal-length lenses. Use a 20mm and a 200mm lens on the same view to see what I mean.

Some Approaches to Recording Sweeping Views

Always select the best portion of a view while looking through the lens. Try crouching down, standing on something high, revolving to right and left. Frame distant scenes with zoom lenses, or lenses of different focal lengths for a different point of view. I most often shoot 35mm landscapes with 28 or 20mm lenses. I also find an 80-200mm zoom lens to be just the right length for framing hilly or mountain views, compressing them slightly, and making them more dramatic.

Often several very different landscape images can be made from the same viewpoint, by altering the focal length of the lens, by shifting the horizon line, by varying the placement of foreground objects within the frame, and of course, by waiting for the light to change.

Practical Landscape Photography

The way to solve landscape photography problems is first to define them:
- What is a landscape anyway?
- Landscape pictures often look boring.
- Landscapes often look too blue.
- Landscapes are often marred by man.
- It is difficult to keep landscape horizon lines straight.
- It is difficult to keep both foregrounds and backgrounds in focus.
- It is difficult to get the whole scene into the picture.
- Pictures of sunsets and sunrises are often not well exposed.

Here are some answers:
- The usual definition is a sweeping view of a natural scene.
- Try placing the horizon high or low, not in the center of the frame.
- Shoot from a low angle or a high viewpoint, not always from eye-level.
- Try including rocks, trees, flowers, or water in the foreground.
- Shoot early/late when light is warm and long shadows reveal texture.
- Block ugly things with out-of-focus leaves or flowers near the lens.
- Use both hands to consciously level the camera, or use a tripod.
- Use a tripod, shoot at f/11, or smaller aperture, and choose a slow shutter speed to maximize depth of field.
- Meter off the nearby sky, not the sun itself, at sunset/sunrise.
- Use a sturdy tripod whenever you can, even with a 35mm camera (they are essential when using medium, large format, and panoramic cameras)
- Choose your viewpoint looking through the lens always!

If you go back to one favorite spot and record it in different weather and different seasons, as many great landscape painters and photographers have done, you will find almost an infinity of possibilities, especially when clouds are present.

Weather

The effects of weather on the quality of light is important when shooting landscapes. Lightly overcast days are shadowless and with today's good 100 and 200 ISO films, and fast lenses, some very beautiful pictures, especially of flowers and foliage, can be made. Mist, fog, light rain, and softly falling snow make for moody landscapes. Just before it rains, mountains and distant views are usually a sharply delineated deep blue. You can easily photograph in rain or snow (protect your camera with a clear plastic bag): use 1/60 of a second or higher to record snowflakes, 1/250 for a blizzard (or use flash fill to "stop" nearby snowflakes or raindrops). Blue dusk is a great time to shoot mountain vistas.

Of course, the light in many of the above situations is low, requiring exposures far too long for hand-held shooting. A stable tripod with an adjustable head is an absolute must.

Time of Year in Landscape Photography

Some landscapes are not just "morning shots" or sunset scenes, they are summer, fall, winter, or spring shots. The difference between cool, clear air and humid, hazy, or misty air quality, and the position of the sun on the horizon at different times of year, all profoundly affect landscape pictures. The spectacular cloudscapes of New Mexico are at their peak in August, in Alaska it gets dark at around 4:00 P.M. in October, most mountain ranges look very blue and hazy in midsummer, and rainy seasons are to be avoided everywhere.

Spring and fall have the most beautiful, clear, angled light almost everywhere. In spring, there many still be snow at higher altitudes, but wildflowers may be blooming lower down. Acid-green leaves in spring and early summer are spectacular against dark blue skies with big white clouds (you may want to try a polarizing filter if shooting color, or yellow-green as well as yellow, orange, or even red filters in taking black-and-white pictures). I hardly need to talk about the advantages of fall color, which varies from being soft and mellow in England, brilliantly red and gold and world famous in New England, yellow in Colorado. Some fall color happens in all regions with deciduous trees. Overcast days are good for shooting glowing fall colors.

Crisp, clear, sunny winter days have sparkling light; snow on the ground acts as "fill" and reduces contrast. **Caution:** Meter off gray rocks!

Photographing Sunsets, Sunrises, and Dusk

Sunsets usually last longer and are more colorful than sunrises. Some effects last just a few seconds, others half an hour or longer. The number-one rule is to get to your chosen viewpoint well before the rise or fall of the sun, which may mean getting up very early in the summer in temperate latitudes. In summer, in the extreme north or south, it hardly gets dark at all, above the Arctic Circle the sun doesn't set at all in midsummer. This of course is also true in the Antarctic.

Use slow- or medium-speed film to photograph sunsets and sunrises. Always meter off the sky around the sun, not the sun itself, or you will get a correctly exposed sun, but a very dark to almost black sky. I always bracket sunset/sunrise pictures. The best sunsets are usually when there is a lot of pollution or haze, making the sun deep orange or red. Some places where the sunsets are fantastic are Arizona, New Mexico, Bermuda, and the west coast of Scotland.

On extremely clear days, light is too contrasty for great sunsets or sunrises. Photographs of sunsets are disappointing if shot with a normal 55mm, or wide-angle, lens. (The sun will look like a pinhole in the frame). Sunsets can be boring clichés and are not worth doing in my opinion unless the overall scene is also worth recording, or the color or cloud effects especially good. Try placing interesting silhouettes of rocks, trees, or mountains in your sunset. If any animals or birds are close, get down low and include their silhouettes against the sky.

Take some big low suns alone also. Big pictures of the sun can be useful for sandwiching or scanning into landscapes with dull skies, or combined with animal or bird silhouettes if your taste runs that way, and nature does not cooperate and let you get what you want on one frame. To get a reasonable-sized image of the sun rising or setting you will need at least a 200mm lens; a 300, 400, or 500mm lens is better, because they make the sun appear large in the frame. If you use a 2X tele-extender with a 400 or 500mm lens, also, you can make a very nice large sun with the 800 or 1000mm focal length that results.

(**Caution:** Never look through the lens directly into even low sun for more than a few seconds.)

Flash Fill For Landscapes

Use a flash to "fill" and record foreground detail of any rocks, trees, flowers, animals, or birds silhouetted within about twenty feet of the flash. Set your camera to expose for the background, and move in close enough, or adjust the flash so the fill value is within one stop of background exposure. (Be sure the shutter speed is set at sync or slower.) You can also use flash fill in bright sun to "open up" small dark shadows within camera range, by exposing for the brightest area, and just adding flash. (See also chapter 3.)

Twilight and Night Photography

My favorite "night" pictures are usually made at deep blue twilight. Totally black night skies record as greenish, brownish, or purplish on film, depending on film brand you choose. With film rated at 40, 50, or 64 ISO, try f/5.6 and eight, fifteen and thirty seconds as a starting basis for night pictures. You will have to make tests before seriously shooting night skies. If you use a slow film at f/22 or f/32, you can make exposures of stars anywhere that artificial light won't interfere. Exposures are six or seven hours, and the stars record as circular streaks of light.

Photographing the Moon

To shoot the full moon with 100 ISO film, I used an old 500mm f/8 mirror telephoto lens and a 2X tele-extender for maximum moon size, this gave me an aperture of f/16. I measured the light with the in-camera meter, and shot a wide variety of exposures. The best were 1/30 and 1/60. With 400 ISO film the best exposures were 1/125 and 1/250 of a second. Make your own tests, because the brilliance of the moon varies. Remember you want good exposures of the surface of the moon itself, not the surrounding sky (which may vary from pale blue to black). Don't use the slowest films to photograph the moon unless you have a very fast long telephoto lens, because the moon moves during long exposures!

Large moon (or sun) images (about the size of a dime in a 35mm frame) can be duped or scanned via computer disc into the backgrounds of landscapes, if you like that effect.

Advantages of 35mm Format in Landscape Photography

I happen to think that 35mm is a superb format for landscapes, if the finest grain films, like Kodachrome 25 and Fuji Velvia, are used. You can work with the camera on a tripod and use very long exposures for great depth of field and interesting color shifts, and you have a great range of lens options available to you. 35mm film is relatively inexpensive, so extensive bracketing of time exposures will not wreck your budget. I have had great enlargements made (of up to 6x9 feet) from 35mm slides, so don't let anyone say that the format is not sharp.

Medium- and Large-Format and Panoramic Photography

Although I am a 35mm equipment fan, a majority of specialist and fine-art landscape photographers use large-format cameras, because, given the same film, image resolution is higher the larger the film area, and because the swings and tilts of view cameras can be used to maximize depth of field. A not inconsiderable factor is that some large-format specialists like working in the way that the early photographers did with folding field cameras. (Some photographers prefer modern technical cameras.) Also, commercial and private buyers of landscape photography tend to be artistically conservative.

The fact of using a heavy camera makes one approach a scene very deliberately, and the high cost of large format usually means that a photographer is extremely selective in choosing views. Small apertures are often used for great depth of field. The choice of lenses and film stock is personal, the photography straightforward. The one "must-have" accessory for serious medium- or large-format landscape photography is an excellent tripod. Some graduated filters are useful.

Many stock-picture buyers today like big chromes or negatives, and some agencies feel they have a commercial advantage with big pictures, but some stock photographers don't want to carry heavy view cameras. Instead they use medium format, especially 6x7cm (the so-called ideal landscape format). There are no special problems with using medium format for landscapes. Choose a model that has lenses available in the range that that you want. Again, a good tripod is a must.

Panoramic photography

This is extremely popular for both stock and fine- art photography today. Panoramic photography requires skill and the careful use of a spirit level (if one or more is not built into the camera). Viewing is normally through a special rangefinder, which may be hard to get used to at first. Bob Herko, a top stock photographer, uses a 4"x5" view camera with a panoramic roll-film back. He can view and compose easily, and use the camera's swings and tilts too.

Note: Disposable and "point-and-shoot" 35mm cameras advertised as panoramic have 25-28mm lenses, the film plane is masked so that only one-third of the image is used, and the central strip of each negative only is printed, double-sized for a panoramic "look." Removable masks for a panoramic effect with some interchangeable lens program 35mm SLR's are just coming into use. In either case, only one-third of a 35mm image is being used, and resolution is not good enough for huge enlargements.

Where to Go

My favorite place to shoot landscapes in the whole wide world are still in the American Southwest. Monument Valley and the Saguaro National Monument are both great. Arches National Park, Utah, comes close. In the Pacific Northwest, I love the marine section of Olympic National Park, Washington. Jasper and Banff national parks in Alberta are pretty spectacular also.

What Sells

Lush green landscapes; high, cool blue mountains; forests, waterfalls and wildflowers, preferably all in the same picture, sell extremely well as stock photographs, and never go out of date. Photographers who live in Colorado, Wyoming, Montana, Washington, the Canadian Rockies, or Swiss Alps, etc. have a huge advantage here! Pristine beach scenes, with palm trees, are perennial best-sellers also.

Go Where You Like

One of the finest landscape photographers working today is Nathan Farb. Unlike many modern masters, who work in the western United States, Nathan has claimed the Adirondack region of New York State as his own, and is commercially as well as artistically successful. See the interview with Nathan Farb in chapter 13, and look for his book *The Adirondacks*.

Photographing Gardens

Being English does not automatically make one an expert on gardens, but it doesn't hurt. Gardens are the national passion in England, from postage-stamp-sized ones in front of cottages or council houses, to elaborate estates where mountains have been moved, rivers diverted, lakes created, and exotic trees and plants imported. In London, there are elaborate gardens in the Royal Parks, on many apartment house roofs, in subway stations, in front of pubs, even on a department store roof, and there are lots of minigardens in front yards and window boxes. There are great gardens at stately homes throughout Britain and Ireland. I have seen and photographed many, many beautiful gardens in the course of travels there, as well as fine ones in the rest of Europe, the U.S. and Japan.

To me, the wide-angle lens is the key to garden photography. I use 28 and 20mm lenses almost exclusively, rarely use a tripod, and search for definitive angles. I often exploit the wide-angle's quality of making foregrounds look large in relation to backgrounds, enhancing the feeling of space. I like to use a reasonably small f/stop, put flowers in the foreground close to the lens so they look large, and use optimal focus so that the whole garden is sharp, though smaller, in the background. If there are paths, trellises, ornaments or sculpture, pools, and even gardeners, I make pictures including them too. Don't show dead flowers. Try photographing a garden from ground level looking up, or from a high viewpoint looking down.

One of the most famous gardens in England is Sissinghurst, created in the 1930s and 40s by the writer V. Sackville-West and her husband Sir Harold Nicholson. To photograph it, I went in June, and first took overall views down from the ancient high tower on the site. I then photographed some rather casual parts of the garden, which is divided into sections by the ancient walls of a manor house. Most parts of Sissinghurst have predominantly blue and pink flowers, but I especially focussed on the celebrated white garden. Here every bloom of flower or tree is white, and many of the leaves are silver. I worked in the evening, when light was low, and there were not too many visitors (the place can get very crowded). Other superb gardens are Monet's garden at Giverny, France, the Keukenhof Gardens at Lisse, Holland (open in spring only), the temple gardens in Kyoto, Japan, and the water garden at Tivoli, outside Rome. In the U.S. a few places to enjoy are: Longwood Gardens, Pennsylvania, and some fine, not huge, desert gardens around private homes in the Camelback Mountain area close to Phoenix, Arizona.

There are gardens to enjoy, practice on, and follow through the seasons everywhere. Check local botanic gardens and tourism offices.

Photographing Wildflowers

Again, people who live near western mountains or other high ranges have an advantage, because spring and early summer alpine plants are spectacular. Some places to go are central California for orange poppies, Washington and Montana for mixed flowers, the area round Austin, Texas, for bluebonnets, and Tuscany, Italy, for red poppies. Read nature newsletters and outdoor magazines for more. Your own area too undoubtedly has meadows of wildflowers in spring and summer, so do some parks. Look for wildflowers to photograph close-up, just about anywhere.

Photographing Flowers and Plants in Cities

Botanic gardens in big cities offer opportunities to practice exotic flower photography. Most parks and many zoos have flower plantings several times a year. Commercial greenhouses offer opportunities too.

How to Photograph Plants

To do this seriously, you have two main problems: plant movement caused by outdoor breezes and the shallow depth of field inhetrent in close-ups. You may also have a problem getting low enough, unless your tripod has legs that extend to almost ground level.

I prefer flowers photographed in natural light, just before they come to full bloom, and like to work early, when plants look dewy and cool and the breeze is normally low. Evening light is pleasant too, but often warm, so be careful if accurate color rendition of a plant is needed for horticultural purposes. You can, if needed, stake sheets of clear plastic as windbreaks around plants if you must photograph them when it's breezy.

Wildflowers should never be picked unless they are abundant, and very sparingly then. Cleaning the area around wildflowers is considered okay. Nature stock agent John Kapriellian says that photographers should include leaves with some wildflower pictures, and ask locally for names, as identification of some species is difficult.

Selling Flower and Plant Pictures

It is not extremely difficult to take good flower or plant pictures, so competition is keen. There is a market for fine-art flower pictures. Black-and-white flower studies by the late Robert Mapplethorp are considered some of his finest work.

The textbook market always needs scientific information, so be sure to photograph the surroundings of a rare plant, as well as close-ups of the bloom. Get scientific plant names wherever possible. Pictures of roots and plant reproductive organs are needed too, as are shots showing how the plant reproduces and how it is distributed.

Practical Garden, Flower, and Plant Photography

The way to solve garden, flower, and plant photography problems is first to define them:

- It is difficult to show a whole garden in one picture.
- Some public gardens are very crowded.
- There is a design in most gardens, but it is hard to bring out.
- Gardens and plants only look their best for short periods of time.
- Flower and plant close-ups can blur or go out of focus in a breeze.
- White/light flowers, dark plants, and/or foliage, are hard to expose.
- Are garden, flower, and plant pictures saleable?

Here are some solutions:

- Show an overall garden view from up high, perhaps use a stepladder.
- Use a wide-angle lens; 28, 24, or 20mm (or wider) on a 35mm camera.
- For public gardens, try to arrive before visitors, or at opening time.
- True. Be flexible and be prepared to shoot just before blooms peak.
- Use apertures of f/11 or less, a slow shutter speed, camera on tripod.
- Use fast film, high shutter speeds, wait for calm, shield plants.
- Bracket exposures when light flowers and dark foliage exist together
- Use flash, or flash fill, to photograph plants when there is a breeze or high contrast. To exclude daylight use highest possible sync speed.
- Get down to plant height, use telephoto lenses with extension tubes to isolate plants, use macro lens plus tubes to show tiny details.
- Wait for breeze to stop, protect plant with a windbreak, stake plant.
- If not rare, cut plant and photograph it in a controlled setting.
- Garden and outdoor and travel magazines, book, calendar, and greeting. card publishers all buy garden and domestic and wildflower pictures.
- Wildflowers and exotic plants are increasingly popular. Textbooks buy pictures of rare plants, photos showing plant structure, and the like.

Flowers and Greeting Cards

Stephanie Bruzemas, a former student of mine, works as an assistant to a fashion photographer. She photographs bouquets of flowers left over after shoots, as well as flowers in gardens in New Jersey, the Brooklyn Botanic Garden, and even in Manhattan's Greenmarket. She sells her flower studies for good prices to greeting-card companies. She finds the companies whose cards she likes by browsing in card shops.

Perennial greeting-card bestsellers (I couldn't resist the pun) are:

Bouquets of lilies, snowdrops, and delicate white flowers of all kinds, all year (used for weddings, birthdays and sympathy)

Violets and red roses (Valentine's Day and love in general)

Bluebells (happiness)
Hyacinths and lilies at Easter
Red poinsettias, holly, and mistletoe at Christmas
Fields of gorgeous wildflowers

Calendars

Calendars are quite an important market for nature photographers. Check good book and paper goods stores to see the styles used. Query calendar printers (commercial and those put out by conservation organizations) with a stamped self-addressed envelope to see how to submit. See also chapter 10 which covers stock.

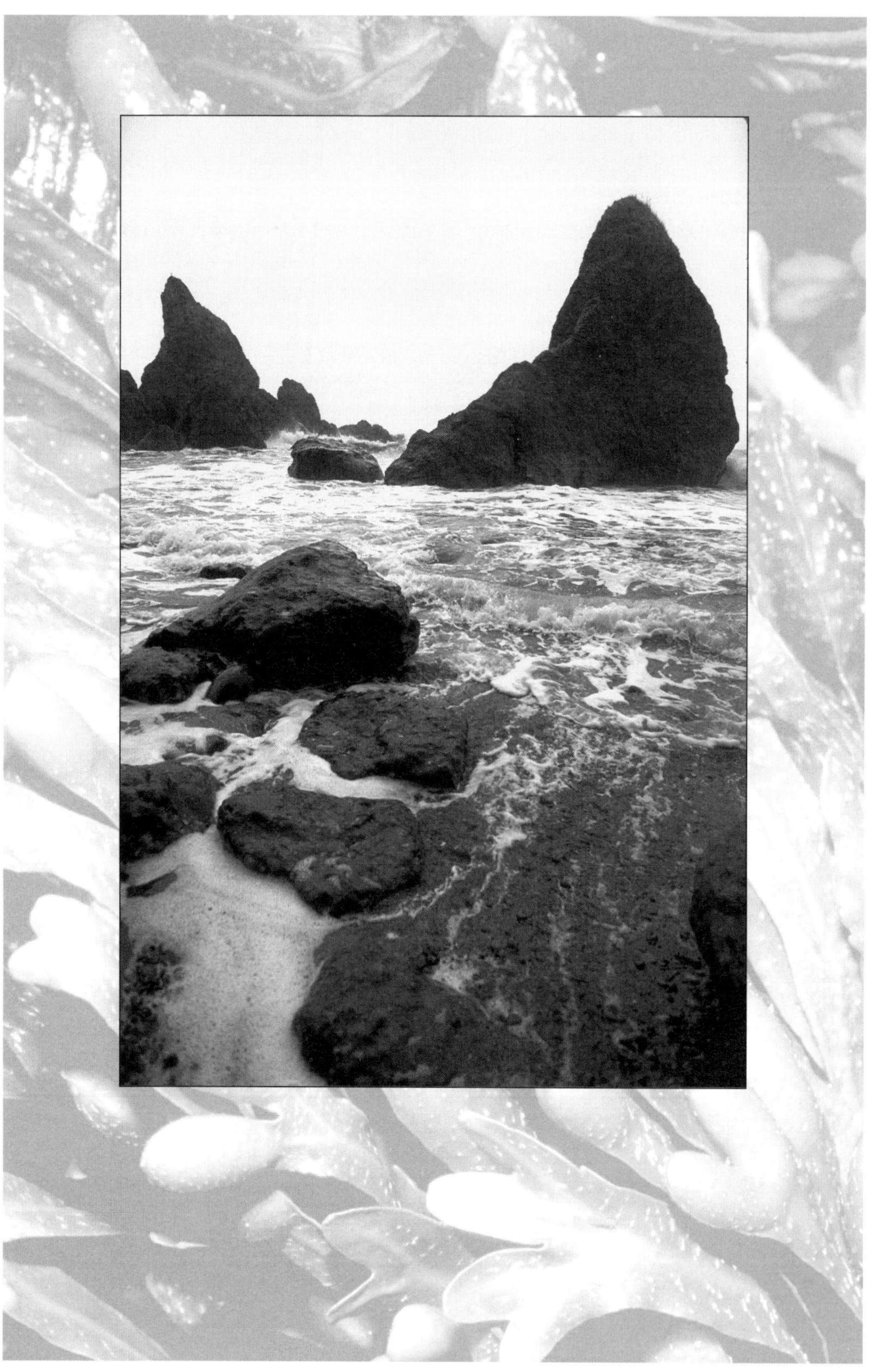

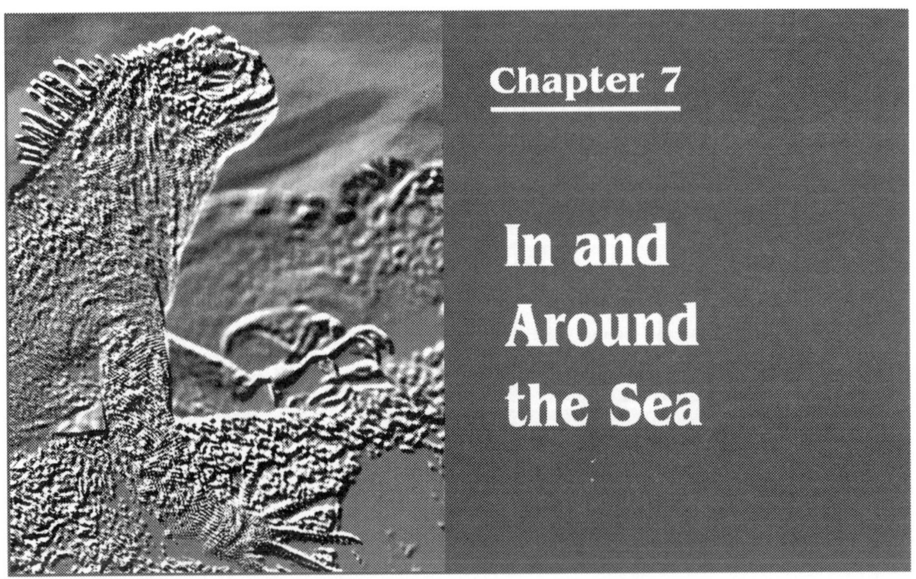

I spent my earliest years in a house high on chalk cliffs above the English Channel in Sussex. A nearby winding path led down to a shingle beach. My mother loved to swim, my sister and I were taught early, and we would spend long fine days in and around the very cold water, splashing and building sandcastles. Many later school vacations were taken at the seaside. I have always loved swimming, listening to surf booming, slithering on seaweed looking for crabs and starfish, clambering on cliffs, and taking long walks along strands of sand, shingle, or rocks. When I first came to America, in my teens, I lived on the New Jersey shore, which has some great sandy beaches. Since then, I have spent time on Long Island Sound in New York and Connecticut, on Block Island, at Cape Cod, and at the Assateague and Cumberland Island national seashores. I've recently explored the rocky coast of Maine, and last summer I went to wonderful Olympic National Park in Washington State. I've made four visits to the spectacular Ile d'Ouessant, part of the Armorique National Park in northwestern France, and I've snorkeled in the Bahamas, Bermuda, the Virgin Islands National Underwater Park and the Galapagos, as well as taken pictures of aquariums. So, though I'm no marine biologist, this advice should get you started with photographing life along the shore and underwater.

Photographing at the Beach and Along the Shore

On any beach, sunny day or not, wear a long-peaked cap, plenty of greaseless waterproof sunblock, shorts, and a long sleeve white shirt over a bathing suit. You can get a bad burn if you don't. Rocks and shells are sharp, seaweed is slippery, cliffs are crumbly and often have thistles or gorse growing on them. Wear sneakers or slip-ons with good treads. Nylon, rubber-soled "reef walkers" made for divers are great.

Salt and spray are bad for cameras, most especially expensive electronic ones, so on the beach I carry an old Nikon FM2 mechanical camera, plus Nikon 55 and 105mm macro lenses which focus to one-half lifesize. I also carry a set of three Nikon automatic extension tubes, in 27.5, 14, and 8mm lengths. (Nikon now makes 60mm and 105mm macro lenses that focus to lifesize without tubes, and a 200mm macro that focuses to one-half lifesize without tubes.) I sometimes use an inexpensive Nikon f/3.5-5.6 80-200mm zoom lens with the tubes. I also carry a polarizing filter, a small Nikon SB23 flash, a flash meter, a modified Stroboframe bracket, an infrared trigger and slave, a remote flash cord, batteries, and film. I put these in a water-resistant NATO backpack (from army-navy stores) to leave myself balanced and hands free. A pair of garden gloves is useful if you must get down low to scramble over sharp barnacle-covered rocks or over cliffs.

I don't use a monopod, though many people like them. I do carry a light Gitzo tripod. Usually it's in the bottom of my pack, but I can use it legs extended and folded together as a hiking support or as a probe to test depth of water or seaweed. (I unscrew the legs and wash them well in fresh water as soon as I get home.) Of course I use it as a tripod when needed, or it can support a flash or reflector. I carry Gaffer tape, a few clear Ziploc bags to store exposed film and any interesting finds, and a collapsible round white diffuser/reflector. Big white plastic bags are handy to sit on, and can reflect light. Put over tripod legs (rubber banded or taped tight), they protect legs from extended immersion in salt water. Spread under tripod legs, they help prevent them sinking into sand (or use a poncho). A towel and poncho complete my "beachcomber" kit.

When photographing on busy beaches, walk along the shore as far away as you can get from parking areas. You will soon find you have plenty of beach to yourself. Of course, take careful note of tide times wherever cliffs or rocks behind a beach could block your escape route on a rising tide. Start out an hour or two before dead low tide to give yourself maximum time at low tidepools in rocky areas like Maine or Scotland, or where there are cliffs and huge dead trees on the beach, in the State of Washington for instance. The lowest tidepools are the places you are most likely to find crabs, sea anemones, starfish, and more. Great places for tidepools include Mount Desert Island, in Acadia National

Practical Beach, Tidepool, Whale-Watching, and Snorkeling Photography

The way to solve problems around/in water is first to define them:

- Salt, sand, and spray are bad for all cameras and lenses and tripods.
- Reflections and glare are a problem on sunny beaches.
- Extreme contrast between dark and light is a problem in tidepools.
- It is hard to focus on subjects that are covered in water.
- Crabs and other marine creatures move very quickly - so do whales.
- Small and large fish that swim near the surface are very fast.
- Direct flash reflects off water above or below the surface, it can also cause unwanted glints from suspended particles in the water.
- Underwater pictures, even taken at shallow depths, come out very blue.

Here are some solutions:

- Clean everything with moist towel and brush after use; have cameras professionally cleaned after extended use in sand or spray.
- Use a plastic underwater housing for a good camera even above water.
- Use an underwater camera in or above water, some lenses work in air.
- Focus manually on objects below water surface if you are above it.
- Use a polarizing filter to reduce glare from water.
- For close-ups, use flash on a bracket, angled to avoid reflections.
- Feed small fish with pet fish food; that will keep some around.
- When whale watching, carry wide-angle as well as telephoto lenses, in case the big mammals come close; shoot at high shutter speeds.

Park, Maine, the remote Queen Charlotte Islands, British Columbia and the rocky peninsulas off southwest Scotland.

Sanibel Island, Florida, is a world mecca of shelling.

What will you find to photograph on the average beach? Living seaweed or kelp, snails and whelks, and burrowing crabs. Look too for empty shells, bird tracks in the sand (they show up in low sidelighting early and late), driftwood, feathers, stones, and patterns, texture, and color.

Crashing waves against rocks make great pictures anywhere.

In tidepools, look for living marine species like crabs, starfish, and more. Big crabs and shells can be photographed with a normal 55mm lens plus an extension tube. Smaller creatures and tiny shells will require the use of a macro lens, and possibly one or more extension tubes. Practice at home on a souvenir shell or coins to see how much magnification you can get with the equipment you own. If you need another tube or two, or a macro lens, buy them before you take off for a distant beach. For moving subjects, using flash close-up may be needed. (For more on close-up photography see chapter 8.)

Whale Watching

This can be done on a day-trip basis on both the Atlantic and Pacific coasts, as well as Hawaii and Alaska, and can be entertaining to exciting from spring to fall, depending on whether the whales co-operate and how near you get to them. Humpbacks are the great performers, lifting their tails and breaching (jumping out of the water). The waters off Provincetown on Cape Cod, and Hawaii are well known as humpback viewing sites. Use a long focus lens. I like a 400mm lens, but since you can't use a tripod on a boat, use a high shutter speed.

Baja California is the place to get very close to a lot of whales, specifically gray whales. Heather Angel, who leads photography tours to Baja for Biological Journeys, keeps a 20mm lens handy there because the whales are sometimes are so close. (See the interview with her in chapter 13).

Photographing Aquarium Tanks

Most tanks are best lit from directly above, as they are in big aquariums. Since fish are fast moving, use flash, a high sync speed, and small aperture to overpower daylight. Light a small tank with one flash diffused through white opal plastic, plastic, or fabric sheeting, the light should be centered over the tank from a stand. A big tank may need to be lit with two or four flashes. Collapsible fabric light boxes, like those made by Chimera, do the job very well. Two Vivitar 283s joined with a Cougar T-Bar, fit neatly into rings for Chimera fabric light boxes, which come in all sizes. Angled outwards, two flashes produce a nice even light over an average aquarium. Light fish tanks from the sides too, with one flash and a reflector, or two flashes. The only way to shoot an aquarium with on-camera flash is by putting the lens flat on the glass: use a rubber lens shade folded back as a cushion. (You will get reflections from shiny fish and bubbles and particles in water.) For more on using flash in a studio setup, see chapter 8.

Photographing in Shallow Water and Snorkeling

Use an underwater camera or housing (which can be an inexpensive plastic one; check stores and underwater catalogs). For very casual use, try a water-resistant "single use" camera. Better are point-and-shoot camera that can safely be taken down to ten to twenty feet. At or just below the surface, you can have fun with either. The resolution with disposables is not good enough for anything other than album-sized prints.

My neat little Nikon Action Touch underwater point and shoot has made fine slides in the rain and at the surface, but the lack of a sports finder is frustrating underwater. When wearing a mask, the small rangefinder eyepiece is about three inches from the eye, and it is extremely difficult to compose and judge focus. I suggest getting a used Nikonos, or a basic underwater camera with a sports finder if you are just starting snorkeling and aren't yet sure how serious you are about taking pictures underwater. (This camera will be a useful backup if you get serious; buy a posh underwater camera or housing later.)

With a camera that has a sports finder, you can frame quite easily. There are then two problems to deal with that you don't get on land. One is that motion underwater can cause blurred pictures because waves bounce you about (to compensate, use medium-speed or high-speed film and a shutter speed of at least 1/125 when there are underwater swells). For exposure, use an underwater meter, the Sekonic Marine is recommended. or, open up one stop from surface exposure at ten feet of depth in clear water in bright sunlight.

The biggest problem with underwater photography is guessing focus. Focussing is not easy for the inexperienced underwater photographer, because, due to refraction, everything looks about 25 percent bigger, and there are none of the usual reference points (except other snorkelers or divers) to help you judge distance. To start, with a medium-speed film, use an aperture of f/11, and set focus at six feet. You will then be safe from about four to fifteen feet. For close-ups, stretch out your arm to judge distance. My arm is 26 inches from shoulder to fingertips. Set your exposure at 2-1/2 feet for close work; at f/11, you should be in focus from about two to four feet.

For true underwater close-ups, supplementary lenses and wire frames are used, permitting accurate focus as close as two inches from the subject.

Flash Underwater

Point-and-shoots with built-in flash do not work too well underwater, because a lot of light blips are reflected directly back into into the lens from sand and bubbles. Underwater photographer Bob Rattner says that for best results a flash should be aimed from about two feet from the side, and down onto most subjects. (See Interview.)

Caution: Do not believe everything you hear about underwater flash. Recently, I overheard a camera salesman assuring a customer that using two flashes is the only way to light underwater. In fact, Bob Rattner says this often results in flat uninteresting underwater pictures (just as using two evenly spaced flash units does on the surface).

Other Underwater Equipment

The mask you get is crucial. Buy a good one and carry it with you. Masks should be selected to fit the shape of your face. Tusa masks are good.

Don't rely on rented masks; they never fit properly and so leak, which is always miserable and interferes with photography. Rent flippers on the spot if you wish. They are not crucial, but lightweight plastic ones will help you to swim faster and longer without feeling tired.

You are taking a chance anywhere if you rent an underwater camera.

Dunk any new or repaired underwater camera in a tub or the deep end of a swimming pool for a couple of hours, to check it out for leaks!

Basic Underwater Photography

Practice underwater photography in the deep end of a swimming pool near home before traveling to a great snorkeling location. Put a few small heavy object on the bottom of the pool, try to get them in focus, nicely framed, and correctly exposed. Have the film developed, and see if your technique needs further work before you go.

Try the new Ektachrome underwater film (UW; 64 ISO) and see how it compares with traditional underwater favorites like Kodachrome 200.

When snorkeling in calm clear water near the surface, keep pet fish food in a few plastic film containers in a pouch around your waist, and feed harmless fish periodically to encourage them to stay around.

Look for interesting compositions underwater just as you do on the surface. Bigger subjects are easier to photograph than small ones! You can get a terrible sunburn on your back and legs while surface snorkeling if you don't use plenty of waterproof sunblock. Do not touch coral unless it is absolutely unavoidable, because contact kills it. Coral scrapes are painful and take forever to heal. Inquire locally about jellyfish and other things that can hurt.

Read the manuals on how to use and care for underwater equipment. Carry spare O-rings and ring grease for your cameras. Do not let sand get on O-rings, or inside cameras. Wash your underwater equipment under a running faucet, or better, soak it in fresh water after each use. Do not open anything up until all the crevices are dry.

Learning to Scuba Dive

Jacques-Yves Cousteau invented self-contained underwater breathing apparatus (scuba), in the 1950s, as well as the Calypso underwater camera (forerunner of the Nikonos 1, first of the famous underwater cameras). To scuba dive safely, which provides the foundation you need to be able to photograph better in deep water than is possible with snorkeling, and to stay underwater for long periods, you must take a good scuba course, which takes about one month, to be certified. (You cannot rent air tanks without proof of certification.) After you are certified, you must practice as often as you can. Dive courses are offered in even the most landlocked places nowadays. Check classified phone books, ask around.

Just as you are not a great driver when you have first passed your road test, it will take time for you to be comfortable in diving gear. Zvi (Ziggy) Livnat, an Israeli underwater photographer and former student of mine who learned his skills working for a dive shop in Eilat on the Red Sea, says that it took him about 200 hours underwater before he felt comfortable enough to concentrate entirely on photography, and not on diving technique alone. Ziggy says that the water in Eilat is so clear, you can sometimes see clouds above the water from sixty feet down, and that you can take good fish pictures at Eilat without getting wet, in the underwater aquarium, from glass-bottom boats, and from a Yellow Submarine.

Catamarans, and better, glass-bottom boats offer possibilities for underwater photography above the surface in many locations, including the Australian Great Barrier Reef, and the Virgin Islands.

Marine Pictures that Sell

- Brightly colored tropical fish
- Colorful coral reefs
- Dolphins leaping
- Large schools of silver fish
- Salmon migrating up to breeding grounds
- Sharks, especially looking fierces
- Shells on clean beaches
- Starfish with bright colors
- Waves, alone and crashing on rocks
- Whales, breaching the surface and underwater

To learn a great deal about top class underwater photography see the interview with Robert Rattner in chapter 13.

Helix of Chicago publishes an underwater catalog, and an underwater Book catalog. *Underwater Photography*, by Charles Seabourn, is a good, well-illustrated book on the whole subject.

Nikon offers courses in underwater photography for Nikonos-camera owners. Some dive-tour operators also run photography courses, and advertise in diving magazines. See also the resources section, in chapter 14.

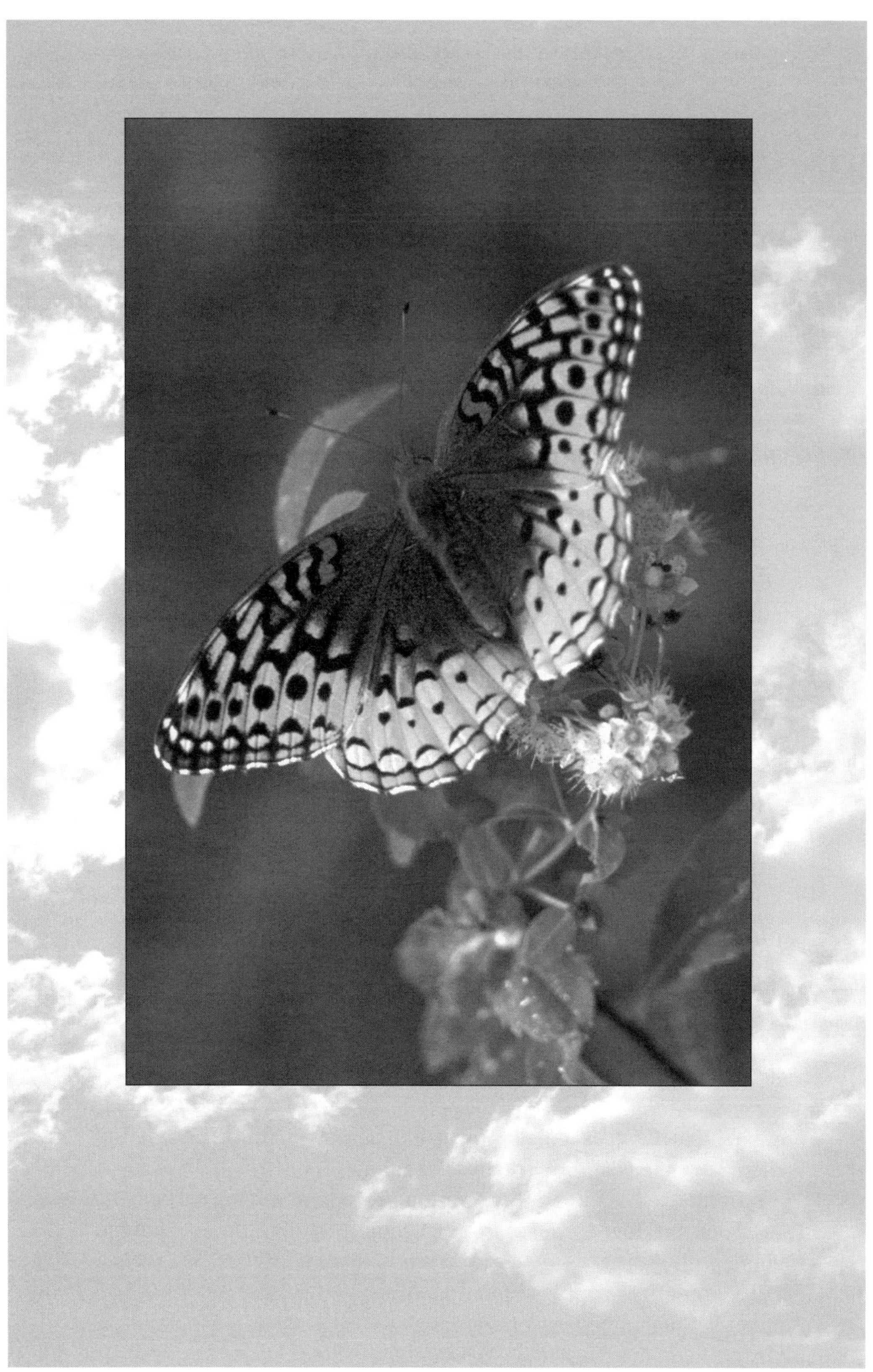

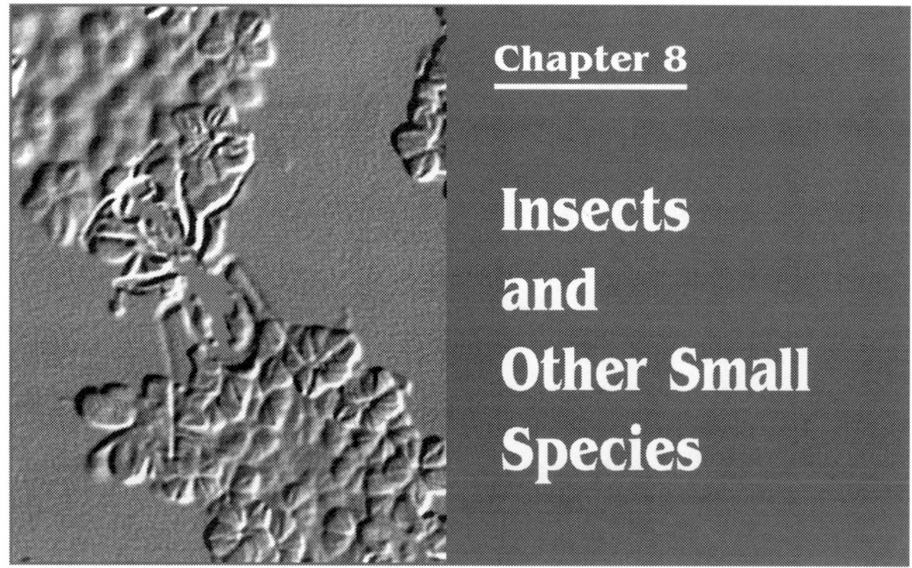

Stalking bright butterflies in a field of wildflowers, or mysterious, soft secropia moths with a lamp outdoors at night, hunting for spiders lying in wait for their prey, or chasing dragonflies flitting around dewy morning ponds are some of the pleasures of photographing insects.

Photographing Insects

Technically, not everything small that flies or scuttles is an insect. All creatures without a spinal column are classified as invertebrates, but only those with six legs are insects. Spiders and their relatives have eight, so technically are arachnids. Bugs with many legs are centipedes or millipedes. There are a few small bugs with plated shells that are members of the crustacean family.

To photograph fast-flying insects outdoors is not easy; you will need telephoto and macro lenses, plus a couple of extension tubes and a tripod as minimum. If you add a small flash on a bracket that can be easily adjusted to a good position for close-ups, you will be able to stop fast motion. The big problems with small subjects are the shallow depth of field at close working distances, and an insect's tendency to move off just as you have it nicely framed. It's probably a good idea to get technique under control by first attempting close-ups of things that don't move fast, like caterpillars and spiders, before attempting things that are almost never still, like bees and butterflies.

I learned after some frustration that the easiest way to photograph butterflies is with a telephoto lens plus extension tube. I now use a camera on a light tripod and a 400mm lens plus 15mm tube (which represents only about one-quarter of a stop in light loss) to stalk butterflies. I watch and note the flowers the butterflies prefer, and then prefocus on a pretty flower, to be ready to shoot, and hope a butterfly alights. Usually it does; that way I catch it and the image is large enough in the frame for a good picture.

I like daylight for airy-looking pictures of butterflies, spiders, dragonflies, and such, and look for low backlight (on spiderwebs especially) to bring out the fragility and structure of wings and webs.

Some people always photograph butterflies with a flash on bracket, once mastered, the technique is a sure way of getting sharp pictures, but the quality of the light usually leaves something to be desired. For me, creatures lit that way often look too solid.

It is reasonably easy to get pictures of tiny insects up to two or three times life-size with a macro lens plus extension tunes or bellows. At these magnifications, depth of field is very shallow indeed, and controlled conditions are best. This means catching the insect with a net or bug bottle and taking it (with suitable vegetation and moisture) into a studio, lighting it with flash, photographing, then releasing it. Some people use fish tanks covered with fine mesh as temporary or permanent insect habitats, some construct small, shallow-depth glass-box ministudios, to make focussing on tiny creatures easier.

Dwight Kuhn is one master of close-up and macro photography. He makes images of insects and marine organisms at magnifications of up to 20X life-size, using a custom-made long bellows, the shortest focal length macro lenses, high-intensity lighting equipment to view images, and high-speed flash to record them on film. Dwight of course has his trade secrets, but I saw his "studio," which is only about eight feet square. Some of his equipment is homemade, and some can be purchased from biological supply houses. Study Dwight Kuhn's excellent childrens' nature-picture books in libraries.

Some highly technical insect photography is done inside tunnel-shaped black boxes in virtual darkness, with the camera shutter open, or special fast-acting shutters used. The box is designed so the insect flies towards a finely tuned infrared beam or crossed beams, where the lens is prefocussed. When bug hits beam, it sets off high-speed flash units. To master such skills takes years of patient experimentation.

Briton Stephen Dalton is world-renowned for artistic, scientifically impeccable photographs of insects, amphibians, and other tiny creatures in their environment, some taken with repetitive ultra-high-speed flash. His *At the Water's Edge* is a lovely book.

Closer than about 20X life-size, a microscope is needed. Photomicroscopist Len Lessin recommends reading *Using the Microscope, a Guide for Naturalists*, by Eric V. Gravé, to get you started looking at and photographing the tiniest species. Kodak's *Photography Through the Microscope*, by John Gustav Delly, is a technical book on microscopy.

Practical Close-Up Photography

The way to solve close-up photography problems is first to define them:
- It is difficult to keep a close-up picture in overall sharp focus.
- It is hard to get close to butterflies, dragonflies or bees.
- Many insects move fast and close-up pictures come out blurred.
- Many insects don't stay in one place long enough to photograph them.
- Macro lenses alone do not permit enlargements bigger than lifesize.
- Dark shadows spoil many sunlit close-ups.

Here are some answers:
- Close-up extension tubes are inexpensive, and can be used with any lens.
- Wait before you photograph for an insect to settle, a breeze to stop.
- Choose flat subjects to focus on at first; look for color or pattern.
- A 300 or 400mm telephoto lens plus an extension tube can capture shy butterflies and bugs from a distance, large in the frame.
- Use macro lenses with two or three extension tubes for close-ups of up to about 3X life size, or, use a bellows and a reversed 55mm macro lens.
- Spiders and moths are slow moving, so are other insects when it's cool.
- Stop insect motion with flash, used off-camera on a bracket or stand.
- Hunt for insects early, in wildflower fields, damp or swampy areas.
- Put sugar water or diluted honey on flowers to keep bees feeding.
- Use a translucent white diffuser over subject to even out light.

You will find insects everywhere; they are the largest order of living things by far. There is a new interest in planting gardens to attract butterflies. Buddleia is called the "butterfly bush" and one of those in your yard will attract some specimens.

Exotic butterflies and other insects can be raised in cages under the proper conditions. There are now several exotic butterfly exhibits in the United States, including Butterfly World in Coconut Creek, Florida.

The annual migration of the monarch butterfly is famous. The brave orange insects fly between northern breeding grounds to California and Mexico, where thousands can be seen each spring, usually in April.

Places noted for large resident populations of butterflies are Brazil, Costa Rica, Indonesia, Madagascar, and Papua New Guinea.

There are literally millions of insect species in the Amazon rain forest. A couple I know who went to Amazonian Ecuador to see tropical birds, were impressed most by the variety of insect life.

Selling Pictures of Insects, Spiders, and More

Close-ups pictures of the prettiest, most colorful butterflies (the rarer the better) and jolly insects like ladybugs sell best for calendars, greeting cards, and general stock. To illustrate nature books for children, photograph caterpillars, insect eggs, larvae, and pupae. Pictures of spiders in webs, bees, and ants are popular for this market too. For high school and college books, and of course to illustrate scientific research and texts, a good series of pictures showing the life cycle of any insect, bug, worm, or other tiny species however insignificant, can be valuable.

Insect Repellent

When photographing insects, especially in damp places, you want to keep the obnoxious ones off you, as far as possible. Use a greaseless insect repellent, or, you will soon have oil on lenses and other undesirable places. Deet is effective.

Avon's Skin So Soft was originally marketed as a bath oil. It has a flowery smell. It has been found to be a terrific insect repellent, issued to, among others, U.S. Marines in tropical locations! If diluted 1:1, and put in a pump bottle, clothes can be sprayed with it. Get it from your Avon lady, and now, some drugstores.

Using Macro Lenses and Extension Tubes

Macro lenses have longer tubes than regular lenses, and are designed to focus continuously from infinity to either 1/2 life-size or life-size. Thirty-five-mm macros come in 55 or 60mm, 90, 105, and 200mm focal lengths, depending on manufacturer, and can be used with extension tubes, or bellows units, or both, between camera and lens for greater magnifications. I like the 105mm macro lens, and also have a 60mm macro lens, which, when used reversed on tubes or bellows (attached with a double-threaded lens-reversing ring) permits extremely close focussing.

Extension tubes are literally metal tubes that are used between any focal-length lens and the camera body to permit closer focussing. You cannot focus on infinity when using these tubes. Automatic tubes stop down lenses from maximum viewing aperture automatically, a convenience. Autofocus tubes are now available from many manufacturers, but like anything else automatic, may not produce the most creative results. (See the interview with Heather Angel.)

Short-focus macro lenses (of about 20mm focal length) are used with 35mm equipment for magnifications of up to about 20X life-size with long bellows. (See the interview with Dwight Kuhn.)

Hasselblad has a macro lens, most medium-format camera manufacturers offer extension tubes, and closeups can be made with any view camera with a long bellows draw and an appropriate lens.

Light Reduction When Photographing Close-Ups

Macro lenses used focussed close (distance depends on lens) and extension tubes and bellows all reduce the amount of light reaching the film by varying amounts. Manufacturers' supply tables (and light loss varies) with different lens/tube combinations. There are standard mathematical formulas that can be used to determine closeup exposure factors. These are listed in *Closeup Photography*, one of the excellent Kodak Workbook series, that I suggest reading as a general background to the subject even if you don't need all the technical information it contains.

Exposing for Close-Ups

Cameras with built-in TTL metering take all light-reducing factors (macro extension, tubes or bellows, filter) into consideration when exposing. TTL would is the perfect solution to all close-up exposure problems, except for the fact that automatic, program, dedicated and TTL daylight and flash exposures are designed to reproduce average, mid-toned subjects, and average exposure isn't always best. But, if you manually adjust the film-speed index, you can bracket daylight TTL exposure. Here's how:

To decrease light output (for a darker exposure) using 100 ISO film, set ISO speed on 125, 160, and 200, for a 1/4-, 1/2- and 1-stop exposure reduction.

To increase exposure, rate film at 80, 64, and 50.

How to Get Accurate Close-Up Flash Exposure

To expose flash close-ups well, you must use manual flash settings. If you practice with a small flash, the same film speed, and work at about the same distance all the time, you will soon learn the settings that work for you.

To start, use your favorite macro lens and set ISO speed on camera and shutter at highest possible sync speed. Focus the lens on infinity, and meter exposure off a gray card. Note exposure on an index card. Then, focus lens as close as possible, and note the light loss (in all likelihood, you will get one f/stop less light for 1:2 lenses).

Then, focus lens at 1/4, 1/2 and 3/4 extensions (some macro lenses have these marked on them). Note these exposures. If you use the macro lens with extension tubes, measure exposures with one, two, and three tubes. (If you use a bellows, meter it at different extensions also.)

Meter flash exposure, then deduct the light loss caused by the lens extension (and filter if used) for the close-up exposure.

For instance, with a 105mm macro lens fully extended, plus a 27.5mm tube, the light reduction is 1-1/2 stops.

With flash exposure determined by meter to be f/22 at eighteen inches, less 1-1/2 stops, the adjusted exposure would be f/11-16 (for a midtoned subject).

Note: For a white or dark subject, compensate additionally by closing lens down or opening it up slightly.

Flash Brackets for Close-Ups

With flash close-ups, it's tricky to get the flash aimed at the subject just where you want it. Top nature photographer George Lepp designed a double macro flash bracket that is popular with many people, and now marketed by Stroboframe. When using two flashes with any double bracket, put a diffuser over one of them so the light is less flat.

I like to light close-ups with one flash, sometimes with a small white or silver reflector opposite it for fill. I had a standard Stroboframe bracket modified so that it is a little more flexible, and use a small Hama ball head under my flash; it works well for me (see diagram.)

Ultra-High-Speed Electronic Flash

Any portable flash used with the power turned down (like the Vivitar 283 or 285) produces quite short flash durations (see chapter 5.)

It is not easy to get information about using true ultra-high-speed flash, for specialized nature subjects. Not many people use the equipment and some experts who do use it keep techniques to themselves.

Dr. Merlin Tuttle, a world-class scientific photographer, told me some of his methods for getting beautiful bat photographs (see the interview in chapter 13.) He very generously, told me about the lighting he uses. This is custom-made by an electrical engineer and nature photographer, Ken Olson, (a Fellow of the Photographic Society of America) who originally wanted high-speed flash for his own use. Mr Olson makes two different units to special order, the faster has a light speed of 1/33,000 of a second. The units are quite moderately priced.

Dr. John Cooke is not at all reticent. He has a Ph.D. in biology from Oxford, is a former director of Oxford Scientific Films (the makers of many nature documentaries seen on TV) and is an authority on animal locomotion and high-speed flash photography. Dr. Cooke is a long time ASMP member who has authored a beautiful scientific book, *The Restless Kingdom,* on animal locomotion, and took many of the phoptographs. Dr. Cooke told me he is currently working on a "how-to" book on high speed flash photography.

With electronic engineer and nature-photographer Tony Tilford, Dr. Cooke is is coinventor and builder of the Prestoflash. There are two models, one producing speeds of up to 1/100,00 of a second. I am told (not by Dr. Cooke) that this is the fastest unit available in the world. The Prestoflash company also markets infrared motion sensors, and fast reacting shutter controls and delays, all available on special-order.

To contact Mr. Olson, Dr. Cooke, and Mr. Tilford, see Resources, chapter 14. For more on flash, and flash in practical use, see chapters 2, 4, and 5.

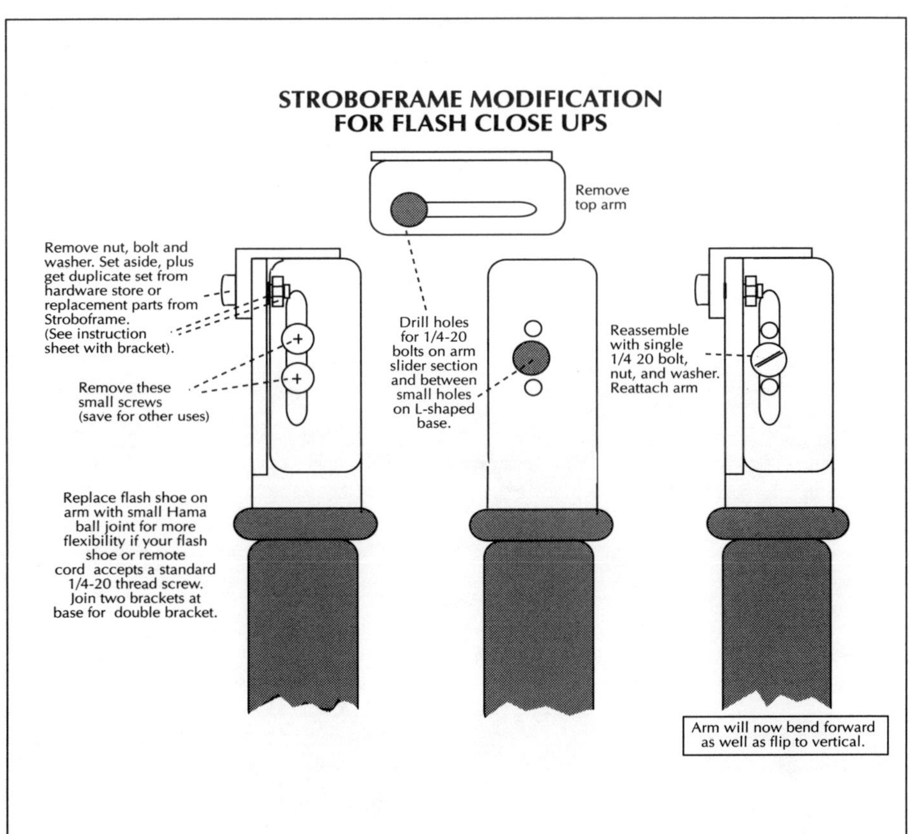

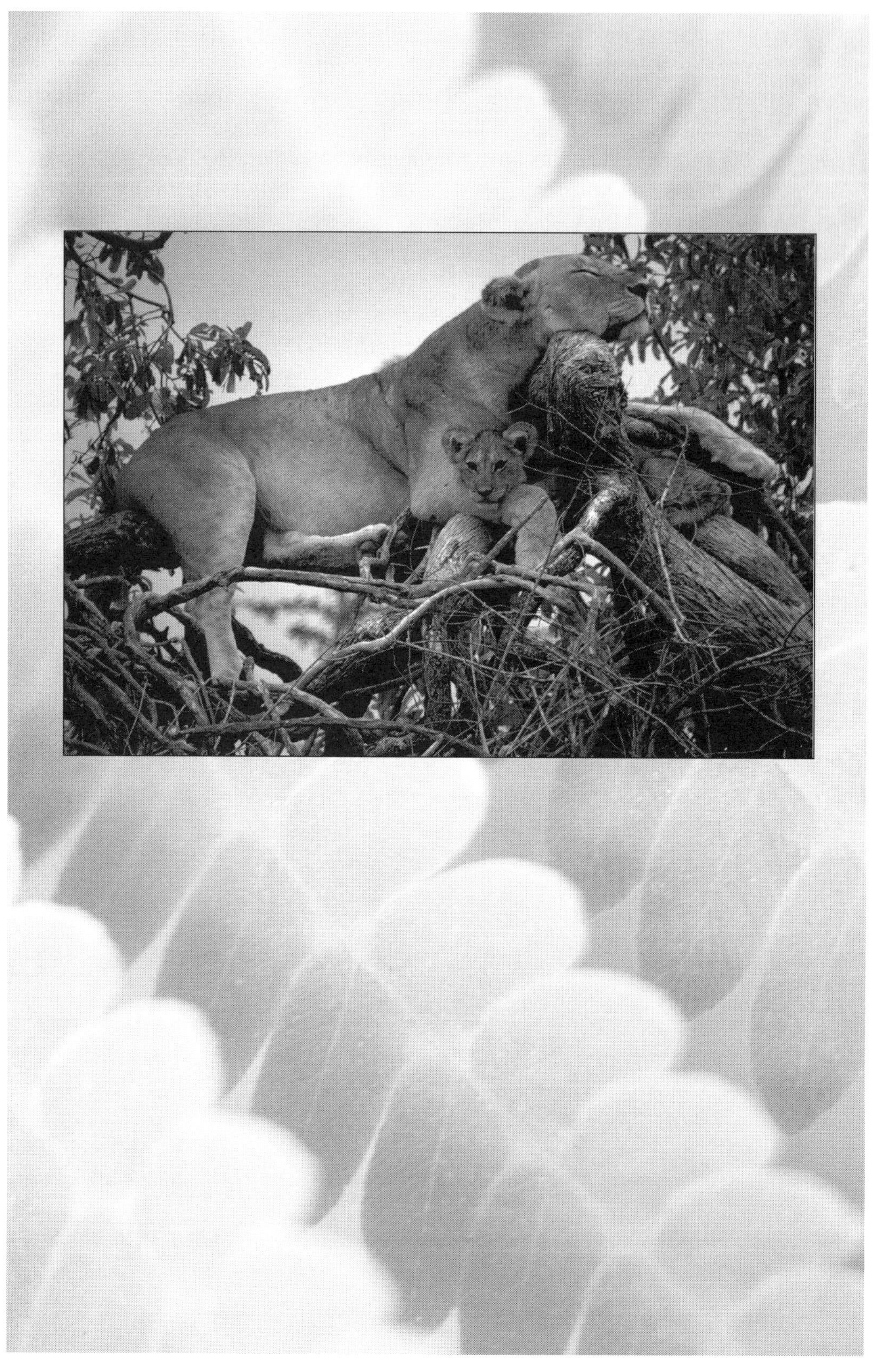

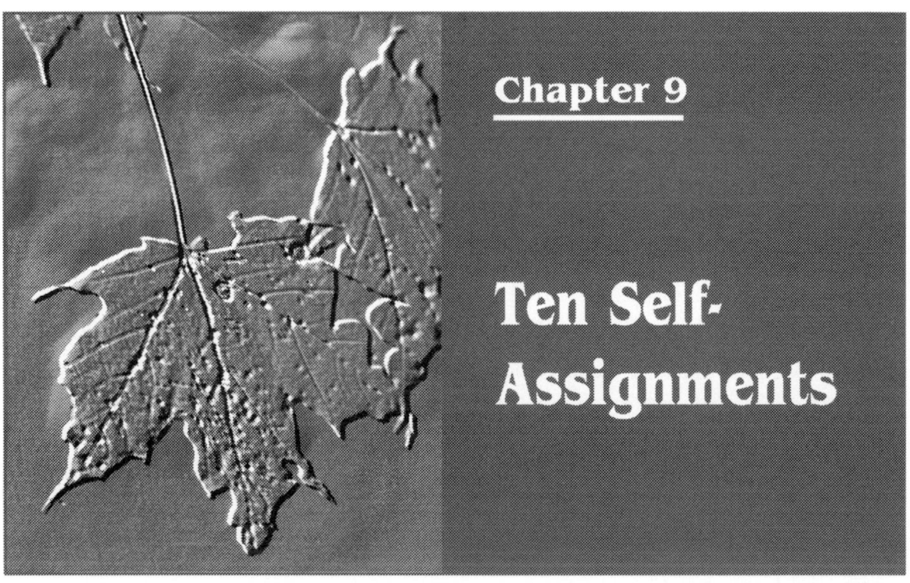

Chapter 9

Ten Self-Assignments

The projects suggested here cover many of the physical and technical skills needed for nature photography, which apply to a greater or lesser extent whether you are photographing large or small wild mammals, pets, birds, insects, or plants. If you do the assignments conscientiously, re-shooting when you are not satisfied, the pictures you make should have value as a portfolio, as stock, as illustrations or records of scientific or outdoor projects, and as possible picture stories or features.

For the most saleable nature pictures, try to show creatures in action, and especially show eyes and whiskers, fur and feather, tooth and claw, scale and fin, in super-sharp detail whenever possible. With plants, don't forget to shoot leaves, reproductive organs, roots, and surroundings, not just pretty blossoms or berries. This is because the fine details in nature are fascinating, frequently educational, and can be seen most clearly when a picture is tack-sharp.

Many top nature photographers love revealing these details to the uninitiated; it takes a great deal of skill to do this with fast-moving subjects.

But, a grainy, soft-focus, "fine-art" style is currently in vogue with the trendiest magazines, so that if that "look" is your preferred style, persist. It will probably become acceptable to most nature clients sooner or later, and today some of the worlds' greatest nature and wildlife photographers are making impressionistic pictures of various kinds.

Whatever your own personal style, work hard to perfect it. Nothing will make you successful faster than having good, honest pictures done with an original approach.

Most nature-picture users prefer that you shoot the finest-grain color transparency film possible. Many landscape photographers use medium- and large-format cameras, and panoramic cameras, for maximum detail; but the great majority of nature subjects that move are still photographed with 35mm equipment.

Color is the norm today for landscape and wildlife pictures; but black-and-white is being used again by a few of the most sophisticated magazines and corporate clients, by many fine-art photographers, and still of course by many newspapers.

Self-Assigned Fine-Art and Personal
Nature and Wildlife Pictures

Of course, choose the subject matter that interests you most, and keep working on it until you feel you have exhausted the possibilities. You wouldn't be reading this book if you did not want to make excellent pictures. These, as you probably already know, take patience, practice, and passion. Only you can supply the patience and passion. These assignments are designed to help you sharpen you physical skills and your eye with practice.

Shoot as often as you can, especially in early and late light. Don't overload yourself with equipment. Use a tripod almost always! Edit slides on a light box or with a projector, pin work prints to the wall for a few days and study them carefully before making (or having made) the best possible final prints for exhibition, an album, or wall art.

Self-Assignment # 1
An Animal "Portrait"

Photograph a frontal or right-facing vertical close-up of the head of a wild animal, bird or even a pet; large creatures are the easiest subjects for the inexperienced); shoot outdoors in wildlife reserves, game parks, nature reserves, city park or other natural surroundings if possible.

Shoot indoors in a zoo as a last resort, because the lighting usually requires heavy filtration for acceptable color.

The object of this assignment is to make a good portrait, and to get familiar with the use of long telephoto lenses. Choose a "model" that is attractive and in top physical condition; not scarred, molting, or with missing horns, teeth, or claws, and not wearing a radio collar, ear tag, or other identifying mark. The "look" should be editorial and have a soft background (with no bars or other evidence of captivity in sight), and the animal (or large bird) should not appear too passive or posed. Try for overall sharp focus, plus an interesting angle or movement of the head. A sparkle in the eye (which should always be in sharp focus), a quick flick of the tongue, a snarl or growl with bared teeth, or an open beak, adds life to any nature portrait.

Imagined Uses: The close-up could be for a magazine cover, or a poster, or for full-page use inside a magazine. (Compose some shots to allow plain light or dark space at top or bottom for type.) Pictures of animals with expressions that somehow illustrate human characteristics are big stock sellers.

Possible Markets: Sale to a magazine or newspaper; sale to the park or refuge or zoo where the picture was taken; portfolio material; stock. (Professionals shooting stock aimed at the high-paying advertising market should get an animal-model release signed by a qualified person before shooting in any privately owned animal-model facility.)

Equipment: You will need a 35mm single-lens reflex (SLR) camera with a 200, 300, or 400mm lens (or equivalent lens for medium-format cameras) and a sturdy tripod. The type of head used on the tripod is to some degree personal preference, but most people who shoot nature/wildlife, including myself, prefer ball heads, with pressure that can be adjusted to permit following animal movement. A cable release is helpful, and a small flash may be useful to give sparkle to eyes in shadow.

Film: Professionals shooting for stock should use slow or medium-speed slide film outdoors. Stock agencies like pictures shot on Fuji Velvia Professional (50 ISO) and Kodachrome 64 Professional (KPR). Many professionals also shoot Fujichrome 100 (RDP) and Ektachrome Plus 100 (EPP). If you must shoot indoors in a zoo, use faster film (and appropriate filters) for indoor fluorescent, tungsten, or mixed lighting conditions.

Additional equipment: Use of a motor drive (integral or added) at several frames per second is sometimes helpful to catch fast movement, but gobbles up a lot of film. Autofocus is sometimes very helpful too (indispensable if your eyesight is not perfect) but, also try focussing manually. Manual focus is often more precise in experienced hands. Compare to see which gives you better results, you may be surprised. Getting animals' eyes sharp is always critical!

Carry a second camera (identical to the first to prevent finger-fumbling and lost shots) as insurance against equipment failure, as a way of changing film quickly (exchange bodies), and because you can use a wide-angle lens (20 or 28 or 35mm), or short zoom lens (in about the 28-80mm range) on the second camera to get pictures of the animal in its habitat.

Filters: Professionals will need color compensating (CC) filters (or gels) and/or light balancing (LB) filters, for indoor zoo lighting. Make advance color tests.

Research: Try to find out as much as you can about the animal and its natural environment and normal behavior. If your subject is in a zoo, avoid inappropriate vegetation in the shot.

Suggested Subjects: In a national or state park or refuge: stag with short velvet-covered horns in spring or big antlers in fall. Whatever other large animals/birds inhabit the park. Any animals or birds with young. Smaller "cute" or cuddly animals like cottontail rabbits, prairie dogs, chipmunks, marmots, raccoons, and hedgehogs are popular stock staples. In some places, these little creatures are fairly easily found and approached; but with most animals, locating them may be the hardest part of the assignment!

Best Times of Day: Almost all wild animals feed early and late.

In City and Suburban Parks: Photograph plump squirrels or any species resident or transient in your park. Stock agents say there is an unmet demand for urban wildlife pictures.

Use Fast Shutter Speeds: 1/250 of a second or higher to stop motion and show detail is good. Almost all animals and birds are fast moving, and will require quick reflexes. Patient waiting is needed, and in parks (not in the wild!) the judicious use of a bag of nuts or sunflower seeds, some corn or even bread pellets, is often helpful too!

In Zoos: Photograph a tiger, lion, grizzly or polar bear, eagle, great ape, any animal mother with young, owl, bright parrot or macaw. Do not show bars, stone walls, or evidence of captivity in zoo shots.

Permissions: From superintendents of refuges or parks, or landowners, may be needed to shoot "off-road," on private property or outside normal opening hours.

Transportation: For dirt roads/wilderness areas, a vehicle with a sunroof than can be opened and four-wheel drive is top choice. In national parks and refuges, shoot from roadside or from an open vehicle window. You can't use a tripod inside a vehicle, use a window clamp, or a beanbag instead. Cars make fine "blinds" for shooting many types of shy animals or birds from the roadside. The dedicated will hike into backcountry or wilderness areas, and should own a good camera backpack. In the city, take the bus and help cut down pollution!

On the Shoot: Keep the camera on the tripod, fully loaded with film, and ready to shoot at all times. Set manual exposures, if used, to the prevailing light conditions. I usually use automatic/autofocus cameras on S (shutter priority) setting, and choose the highest possible shutter speed. I favor manual over autofocus.

On a very sunny or very dull day, try using a flash for fill to supplement the available light (up to a distance of about ten feet, maximum for a tiny flash; thirty feet for a Vivitar 283 or similar unit). Flash used in sunshine will lighten harsh shadows; expose normally; add flash. On a dull day aim for slight underexposure and add flash. This will give highlight to the eyes, and perhaps a gleam to dark hairs or feathers (important for creatures with deep-set eyes and dark coats/feathers).

Variables: Time of year (for best light, breeding and courtship habits, color of vegetation, migration habits, young, and so on.) Time of day. Weather. Avoid rain almost always. (Animals in snow, however, often look wonderful.)

Results: An interesting, saleable portrait.

Look at: Picture books suggested in the bibliography, nature magazines. See also chapters 2, 4, 5, and 10.

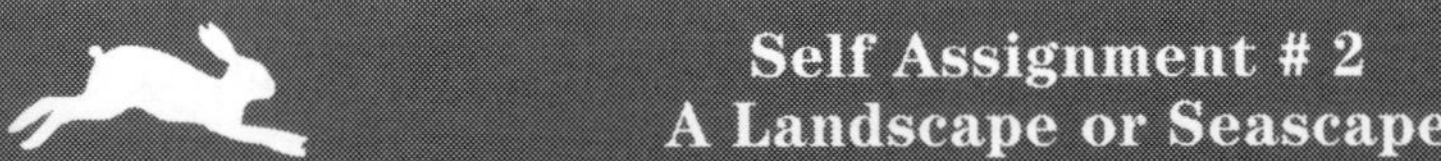

Choose an unspoiled landscape (with no telltale signs of man in evidence). The place can be mountains, plains, lake or river view, rolling hills, or a seascape. Photograph at different times on a sunny day.

Start shooting before sunrise until an hour or so after sunrise, take comparison shots at midday, and then photograph again in the late afternoon until sunset and through dusk (which I call "blue-time").

The object is to show how changing angles of the sun, different cloud effects and the color temperature of the light at different times, affect a scene (even if the sky is not used in your composition); and, to make the best landscapes possible.

Possible Uses: Part of a nature/environmental or travel story; a local, regional, or national tourism promotion; stock pictures; postcards; calendars; portfolio pieces; fine-art/wall decoration.

35mm Equipment: You will need as a minimum one (or better two) cameras to shoot fast in changing light; wide-angle and zoom telephoto lenses. I like a 20mm or 28mm lens on a 35mm SLR for most landscapes, but sometimes use moderate zooms — 35-70mm or 80-200mm — for precise framing and to bring say, distant mountains closer.

Medium- or Large-Format Equipment: Use your favorite camera, and two different focal length lenses.

A sturdy tripod for long early and late exposures is a must (use one that extends at least to your eye level for comfort). A cable release is handy. Carry plenty of spare camera batteries to remote places; a backup meter is good.

Film: Use slow- to medium-speed film (shoot at least two rolls, or equivalent amount if you use medium- or large-format cameras). I use Kodachrome 25 Professional or Fuji Velvia Professional (50 ISO; I rate it at 40) for most landscapes.

Research: Do some driving/traveling around and choose the most beautiful place you can find, or the best overall view you know. For true nature photography do not include any man-made objects whatever! (The less pure can show a distant farm, bridge, or road if they wish.)

Variables: Weather and time of year. Check forecasts and wait if necessary; a very clear day with sunshine and nice white clouds in a deep blue sky would often be ideal. Before or after storms you often get dramatic cloud effects. Winter views with snow can be stunning. In winter too, animals and birds often migrate to one place, and can be included in the landscape. Autumn colors are favored above all for stock landscapes; I also love early spring with acid-greed trees and new grass, and late fall/early winter landscapes are often subtly beautiful, with a few brown leaves clinging to trees, fog, and mist.

Curiously, high summer is often the least interesting season for landscape photography. Many beautiful places are hot and crowded then; in northern latitudes, the overhead sun is harsh and the color temperature of the light very high (blue) for much of the day; mountains often appear a distant, misty blue in photographs; bland blue skies can be boring. In late summer in the U.S. plains and West though, you quite often get thunderstorms and great cloud effects. (Before and after storms and awful weather in all seasons, anywhere, clouds and light can be spectacular.)

Alternate approaches: The stock specialist or nonpurist photographer (like me) may take some shots that include roads, railroads, small farms, distant hikers/climbers/skiers, a boat, or a lighthouse; all these should very small in the overall scene.

Look for vantage points, often high ones looking down are good. Bridges, fire towers, scenic highway overlooks, observation towers, piers, river and lake fronts all make potential "picture points", as well as do hill, mountain, and cliff tops.

Permissions: Arrange in advance to arrive very early, return and then stay late, at an observation tower, state or local park, and private property.

Transportation: A car is normally a must to "scout" locations and to move heavy equipment, but big-city dwellers manage to get out using public transport! Hikers should own a good backpack to carry equipment.

On the shoot: Arrive at you chosen spot a good half-hour before sunrise, and well before sunset; set the camera on the tripod and be ready to shoot fast in rapidly changing early and late light.

Compositional tips: Don't cut the picture in half with the horizon

124

line, unless of course that's just what you want. Take time to make sure the horizon line is level, wherever you choose to place it in your composition. If you have difficulty with horizons because you wear glasses, consider getting a grid-style view finder for your camera. A small spirit level is helpful with panoramic and view cameras (if not already built in) and can often be useful when using wide-angle lenses in any camera format.

Take all the landscape pictures from the same spot for maximum comparison of changes in light effects. Mark you tripod position with tape, stones, whatever, so you can find it again. Do variations on the composition also.

Meter off the nearby sky, not the sun itself, during sunrises and sunsets or you will get underexposure. (Use a 135mm lens or longer on the camera as a substitute for a spotmeter.) Shoot from about half an hour before until about fifteen minutes after sunrise; half an hour before sunset through the pink afterglow and then the darkening blue sky of dusk.

Bracket (vary) your exposures. If fast-moving clouds are present, photograph different sky effects.

Stock: Photographers who plan to sell for advertising or promotion should get a property release from the owner of private property. I am told that even shots of hills, or trees, or lakes, that can be identified, need releases for commercial (not for editorial) use.

Results: A landscape with a variety of moods. The color range should be from reds, warm oranges and pinks at sunrise and sunset, neutral to blueish at midday, and light, royal and midnight blue effects before sunrise and after sunset, without the use of filters.

Note: The midday pictures are normally for purposes of comparison only; very rarely are they better than the early or late ones. However, there are exceptions to every rule, so don't omit them.

Look At: Landscape photography books listed in the bibliography, and nature and travel magazines.

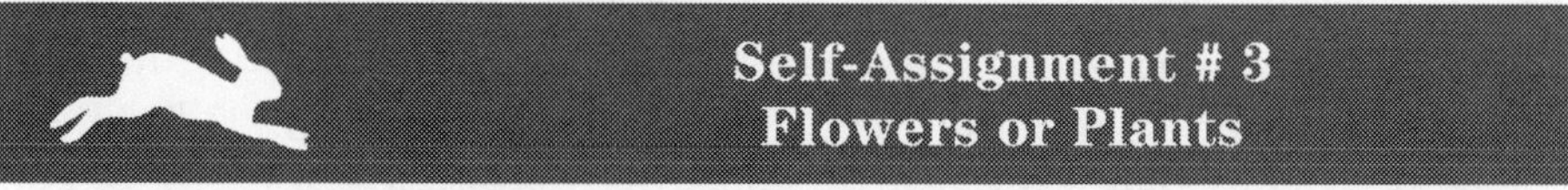

Make a series of five to ten carefully composed pictures of flowers/plants at the peak of their beauty. Work in a national, state, or city park, a field, private garden, botanic garden, or arboretum.

Include horizontal and vertical "portraits" of single blooms; if you have the equipment make extreme close-ups, as well as showing masses of blooms in fields or flower-beds. Put the camera on a tripod and take some super-sharp, small f/stop, wide-angle-lens shots of the whole landscape or garden, keeping the foreground flowers as large as possible, and the background in as sharp focus as possible.

The object of this assignment is to show off the bloom or blossom, its habitat in the wild, or its place in a garden.

Possible uses: Stock; sales to calendar, greeting card, or poster companies; landscape architects/contractors; gardeners and home owners; municipal park and other authorities; wall decoration, personal/fine-art.

Equipment: 35mm, medium-format, or field camera. Extension tubes for 35mm/medium-format lenses for close-ups. A sturdy tripod that can be used close to the ground and a cable release. Macro, wide-angle, normal and moderate zoom or telephoto lenses are all useful here. A folding white reflector may be helpful on sunny days.

Professional Equipment: 105mm macro lens; longer lenses and 8mm, 15mm and 27mm automatic extension tubes for 35mm SLR cameras; equivalent for medium-format equipment. (Some specialists will use field cameras with shifts, tilts, and swings for increasing depth of field (the zone of sharp focus).

Film: Slow- or medium-speed daylight transparency film.

Research: Finding the flowers or garden, and best time of year/day to photograph them. Getting permission from property owners, or from botanic/public garden authorities to shoot early or late for best light.

Transportation: The usual car or taxi, or public transport and feet.

Variables: Weather, time flowers are just approaching their peak, time of day; times place is too crowded to photograph. Times when there is no wind. Cloudy day pictures of flowers are often excellent.

Depth of field and movement from wind are the critical items here. Use the stop down preview button on you camera to see depth of field. (Stop-down may be electronic on some new program cameras; read the manual carefully.) Working with lens stopped down takes some getting used to; not too much light comes to the viewing screen when the aperture is f/11 or f/16 needed for maximum zone of sharp focus. Use the A (Aperture Priority) setting on an automatic camera.

Select only perfect blooms to photograph. Watch the direction of the light, and shoot back-, side-, and front-lit versions of your composition. Use an 18 percent gray card (or the palm of your hand) to meter exposures. Don't meter directly off white or light-colored blooms, or you will get underexposed flowers.

Note: Low backlighting (light from behind the subject) is especially beautiful for flowers, revealing their translucency. Care in exposure is necessary for this. Select good viewpoints for massed wildflower displays.

Bracket exposures (use half-stop increments). You don't know exactly which effect may be best with a delicate blossom or flower. Probably all of three or four half-stop exposure variants will be fine, but one will certainly be better than the others, even if only you can tell the difference.

Caution: Certain flower colors, especially intense blues, are difficult to reproduce precisely on film (they come out purplish). Color-compensating (CC) filters may be needed for professional work. (See interview with Heather Angel, in Chapter 13, for more.)

Alternate Approaches: Photograph wildflowers with insects or butterflies feeding; arrange picked garden flowers in beautiful bunches. If photographing uncommon wildflowers, show surroundings, leaves, and if possible, roots; they help identify plants. Never pick those! The garden specialist should include the house in the background, and even the gardener or garden designer, in a few shots. And, think about morning dew, color combinations, and the overall design of a formal garden. (Also see the interview with Curtice Taylor in Chapter 13.)

Results: Pictures for magazines, sales of prints to garden designers/owners, brochures, advertising, or wall decoration/fine art. Other possible uses of flower pictures are as greeting cards, covers of religious bulletins, calendars and note/postcards, as well as portfolio pictures.

Flower pictures are relatively easy to do well, and I am told they are over-photographed as stock subjects. Don't let this discourage you if flowers are what you love most to shoot. Great pictures of anything will always find a market!

See the interviews with Heather Angel, Dwight Kuhn and Curtice Taylor in chapter 13 for more on photographing plants and flowers.

Look At: "Shelter" (house and home) and garden and "country" magazines for examples of top professional work. Also see relevant picture books listed in the bibliography.

The aim in a bird portrait is usually to show as much detail as possible; of the hard rings around the bird's eyes, the texture of feathers, beak, feet; and to stop, or nearly stop, the motion of wings in flight. If you can photograph small birds well, you can do almost any nature subject well, in my opinion!

Photograph in a garden, park, zoo aviary, or anywhere birds are fed on a regular basis. You could even take tiny bread pellets, corn, or sunflower seeds and photograph city-park dwelling sparrows, pigeons or ducks if you don't have easy access to uncommon birds. Common perching (passerine) birds are tricky to shoot; but, if birds are what you love most to photograph, make these pictures as exercises in technique and composition and as excellent practice for more unusual bird shots that you will make eventually.

Equipment: The longest and fastest lenses made are needed for serious bird photography. If a feeder is reasonably near your house, a 200mm lens on a 35mm camera, not slower than f/4, can be used to start with. If you get serious about bird photography, you will soon get a longer lens and/or a tele-extender. (See chapters 2 and 5.)

Subject for the Inexperienced: A feeder with perches that's close (but not too close) to a house; ideally it should be no more than about ten feet from the house, and clearly visible from inside. Stock the feeder with commercial birdseed mix available from supermarkets to get common birds of your area; suet hung in a mesh bag will get you woodpeckers if any are around. Try to anticipate and catch birds alighting, not with their heads obscured inside the feeder.

Subjects for Advanced Bird Photographers: Take pictures with a fast flash setup (see chapters 3, 5 and 8). Unusual, colorful (and more saleable) birds can be attracted to feeders with thistle seed. (This costs about the same per pound as sirloin steak!) Humming bird feeders, that take syrup made from glycerine and water, and with red flowerlike tops, attract those colorful birds in season. Attractive feeders of different types, at reasonable prices, are sold at Nature Company stores and through specialized catalogues such as that of Connecticut Valley Biological Supply Company (See Resources); or, make your own.

Alternately, find birds in zoos, commercial aviaries, and the like.

Film and Specialist Equipment: Use slow film if you have a fast lens; medium-speed otherwise. Bird photographers always use the fastest, longest lenses possible; high shutter speeds are important to stop wing motion in daylight. All super-long, fast lenses are their manufacturers' top-of the-line; all are very expensive, and all are heavy. Some are very heavy. (For 35mm, I am talking about 300mm f/2.8, 400mm, 500mm or 600mm f/4 or f/5.6 and even 800mm f/8 lenses here!)

Patience, anticipation, and fast reflexes are the keys to good bird photography!

Possible Uses: Feature on local bird life for newspaper or regional magazine. Stock. Greeting cards. Possible promotional/advertising use. If you live in the Florida Everglades, the Texas Panhandle, along the Mississippi flyway, or close to the Brigantine National Wildlife Refuge in New Jersey in the U.S.; near Canadian nesting grounds in late spring/summer; or near say, Slimbridge, Gloucestershire in England, your local birds will be of more than local interest!

Birds that are golden, red, blue, green, or with at least with dashes of these colors, not surprisingly sell better as stock than plain brown or gray birds!

Also see interview with Roger Tory Peterson in chapter 13, just about any issue of *Wild Bird* or *Audubon* magazines (or the many other specialist bird magazines), and bird books listed in the Bibliography. These will help you judge your technical and artistic progress.

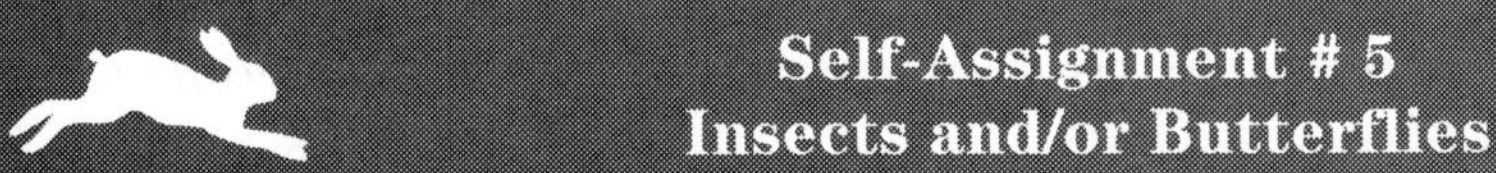

The object of this assignment is more practice in shooting very sharp, detailed close-ups, this time of things that move! Also, to produce material for professional research and record purposes, stock, material to illustrate scientific articles and books, and childrens' books.

Equipment: For minimum equipment, see self-assignment # 3. In addition to the camera, lenses in the 100-300mm range (for a 35mm SLR) plus extension tubes and/or macro lenses, and, sometimes a folding silver or white reflector are useful here. A small flash is often used for fill (and occasionally as the only light source) for insect pictures. (Tripods are not much used for insect or butterfly pictures, as they move fast; they are sometimes used for slow moving creatures like spiders and moths.)

Film: Use the slowest possible daylight film to reveal maximum fine detail of small/tiny subjects; this film is also best when using flash.

Research: Selecting the spot where your subjects gather; try if possible to locate some wild flowers where butterflies or bees feed. A summer meadow with flowers in early morning, when insects are slow moving after the cool night, is a good bet. Or, try attracting moths with a light, and photographing them with a flash at night. Alternately find spiderwebs (good stock sellers) in shady corners (best photographed backlit with low sun), or turn over some rocks or stones in damp/swampy areas to find who knows what! The seashore will provide tiny marine organisms in tidal pools.

Project for Professionals: Photograph a story of the life of a small creature.

Variables: Season, time of day, tides, climate, terrain, and such.

Permissions: As always, from property owners if needed for access.

Possible Uses: Insects in general are not over-photographed. There is a demand for stock shots and picture stories of all types of insect. Childrens' books and high school textbooks in particular use a lot of color pictures of unusual insects, spiders, and other tiny creatures. Pictures of butterflies and pretty insects will possibly sell as greeting cards.

Look At: Many issues of *Audubon, Natural History, Geo* (in German or French), *Airone* (in Italian), and *BBC Wildlife* magazines carry insect stories (these publications almost all available at good magazine stores in the U.S., Canada, and Britain) and of course the *National Geographic* (available by subscription only). Also see biology textbooks and the relevant books listed in the Bibliography.

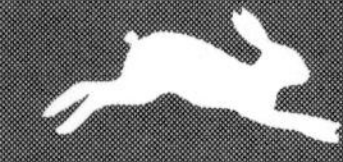

Self Assignment # 6
Basic Underwater

The object of this assignment is practice in getting sharp, correctly exposed pictures, and accurately framed subjects underwater.

I strongly suggest you practice in a swimming pool close to home and master these basic skills before going on any expensive trip to a far away place!

You Will Need: A well-fitting mask, plus snorkel and fins, or, scuba equipment (if qualified to use it).

Photo Equipment: An underwater camera equipped with an underwater sports finder. (If you do not have this accessory, it is extremely difficult to frame accurately underwater because the mask you must wear makes it almost impossible to see through a standard-size 35mm view finder. I speak from experience!

A small underwater flash is essential if going down below about twenty feet. An underwater meter is needed unless the camera and flash are TTL/dedicated.

Caution: "Disposable" and "point-and-shoot" underwater cameras can make fun vacation pictures on the beach, or from rafts or small boats, but in my opinion are of limited use underwater, except perhaps when shooting a fellow swimmer/diver close to you. If you get truly sharp pictures of fish or tiny marine life underwater in the ocean with these cameras, even at very shallow depths, it may be more by luck than skill. (Again I speak from experience!)

Film: I use 200- or 400-speed daylight film for underwater photography, because I don't use a flash. The new Kodak Ektachrome Underwater (UW) film that minimizes blue is designed to be excellent for this, but I haven't had a chance to try it yet.

Use fairly high shutter speeds and apertures around f/8 even close to the surface to get sharp underwater pictures underwater, because refraction makes everything underwater appear about 25 percent larger.

Note: Most top specialists prefer to use wide-angle, 15mm or 20mm lenses underwater, unless shooting extreme close-ups. (For much more, see the interview with Robert Rattner, in chapter 13.)

Research: Locating a scenic underwater spot if one is close by and you can already swim, photograph, and dive well (close to the surface of a very clear lake or river will do). If a total neophyte, find a fair-sized outdoor swimming pool with a deep end, where you can practice both basic snorkeling/scuba skills and underwater photography without having to worry about currents, sharp coral, sand, mud, or strange creatures. (Some underwater life can look quite scary, 25 percent bigger than life, peering out of grottoes, this is experience talking again!)

Important: Scuba divers must obtain certification, carry proof, and are tested before being allowed to dive in most places (learn theory at dive shops and practice basic skills in pools almost anywhere).

Variables: Location, time of day, season, weather. (Plan to shoot between about 10: A.M. and 2: P.M. on sunny days for best results at shallow depths without flash. Skilled divers can take flash pictures earlier or later, but many underwater shots look best with some daylight visible.

On the Shoot: Wait for calm weather! The main thing to practice is getting sharp, in-focus pictures of fairly small objects, especially fast moving objects. (Use something heavy like a paperweight on a pool bottom to start, then progress to a friend swimming underwater.)

The more advanced underwater photographer, at a tropical ocean location, should try to show schools of fish, close-ups of coral, and colorful underwater scenes with a diver included in the background. If you plan to market stock, you should know that close-up shots of very pretty individual fish, large schools of fish, and marine organisms with bright colors sell best.

Professional Tips: It will take you a lot of practice (and film) to become very good. Get model releases from recognizable divers photographed underwater.

Results: When you are skilled, you will produce photographs that are marketable for research/record purposes, tourism advertising and brochures, as public relations/magazine/newspaper features, and stock. You will also have portfolio material, wall art and mementoes of vacations. I am told there is not a great demand for pictures of average "wrecks"—boats that were sunk in the last twenty-five years—because there are too many of them, and they are not very hard to photograph.

Look At: *Dive* and similar magazines, some issues of the nature magazines previously mentioned, and relevant books listed in the bibliography. Also see Caribbean or Pacific island airline, resort, and hotel advertising and brochures.

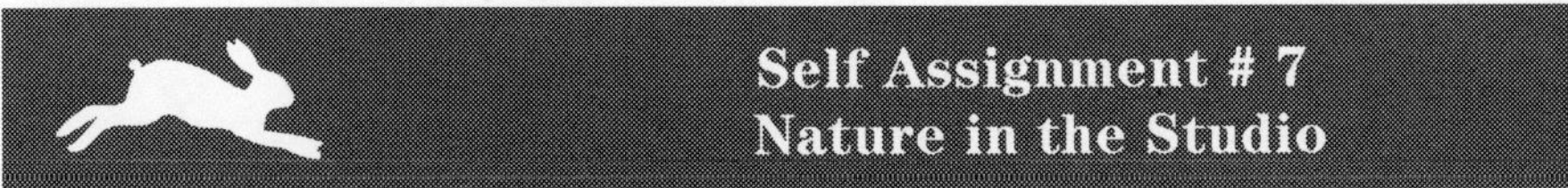

Animals, Reptiles, Insects, or Fish Photographed with Flash/Strobe in a Studio Environment

The object is practice, because the skills of a studio photographer are needed by most professional nature/wildlife photographers at times.

Equipment: Any type of camera. A tripod is usually used. Flash or small strobe is used, as preferred. If you are photographing fast moving subjects, use portable flash, for the following reason: Portable studio flash/strobes run from continuous AC power, and are mostly used for portraiture, fashion, still-life, travel, location, and similar work. They do not have flash durations as short as small portable battery-powered flash units (like Vivitar 283s or Nikon SB 24s) turned down to 1/16 power or lower, and therefore standard studio strobe/flash units do not stop fast motion. (If you want to test the practical flash duration of a studio strobe, you can do so following my method of photographing a revolving wheel, outlined in chapter 3.) For more on portable flash in practical use, see chapters 5 and 8. For information on custom made high-voltage ultra-high-speed flash units, that will stop the motion of the fastest mammals, birds and insects, see chapter 3. Also see the interview with Merlin Tuttle, in chapter 13.

Creating a Studio Habitat: A fair-sized aquarium is often used to create a natural-looking background for very small animals, insects, and reptiles, as well as for fish. Use dirt, rocks, and sand as appropriate, and correct, very fresh-looking vegetation. Keep the habitat you make damp, use a mister (unless creating a minidesert!) but don't make it too wet. Do study what your subject creature needs to have available to stay comfortable and healthy, before transferring it to the environment.

Be careful setting up lighting, and angle lights to avoid reflections on glass. Diffuse or bounce the lights to avoid double shadows. Flash or strobe in a soft light bank often works best. (For more on studio-type lighting with flash and small strobe, see chapter 8.)

Professional Tip: Many of the close-up pictures of rare animals, birds, reptiles, and so forth that you see in stock catalogs and on greeting cards are taken under controlled conditions, not in the wild. Game ranches that have beautiful animal models (often used in movies and TV commercials) and trainers to direct them, exist (mostly in the northwest); still photographers can use them too. Prices to shoot in these places is high, and worth it if you get excellent stock. (See chapter 10; also see interviews with Leonard Lee Rue III and Len Rue, Jr., and Art Wolfe.) Other places to shoot close-ups under controlled conditions are "rehab" centers for injured wildlife (ask your state/province/county wildlife or fish and game department for locations); animal hospitals and some entertainment complexes and zoos.

Film: Use fine-grain color transparency film for stock sales.

Permissions: Get a release signed if shooting an animal "model" at any commercial facility.

On the Shoot: Get as many poses/positions from your "model" as you can, some with eye contact if possible, some facing right and left. Don't forget to shoot verticals, and pictures that have sky, out-of-focus green, or other bland space around the subject (for type placement) as well as frame-fillers.

Results: Good stock shots, practice, portfolio pieces.

Pictures for greeting cards, calendars, childrens' books.

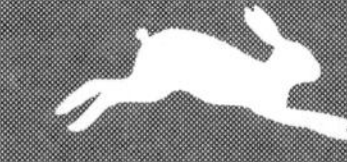

Self Assignment # 8
Safari at the Zoo

The object of this assignment is preparation for foreign travel to photograph exotic animals/birds.

Equipment: Ideally, use at least two cameras, possibly three (to have different lenses quickly available at all times), and fast telephoto, wide-angle, and/or zoom-telephoto lenses. Use a tripod when shooting any lens over 200mm. Carry all this in a sturdy backpack, or use an inconspicuous waterproof case wheeled on a sturdy luggage cart.

Film: Depending on weather, I use slow- or medium-speed daylight transparency film. Fujichrome 100 Professional is my current medium-speed favorite. (If you want prints for a personal album, or fine-art pictures, and don't care about stock usage, use any film you like.)

Permissions: In major zoos, try to get special access. Apply well in advance. Otherwise, arrive early or late, try to avoid holiday weekends.

On the Shoot: Check schedules for feeding times. Be early for them to set up your tripod in a good position. The giant panda at the National Zoo in Washington is fed daily at 11:00 A.M., and big crowds often surround his enclosure by 10:45 A.M., for instance. He takes an hour or more to chomp down bamboo (and an occasional carrot) and you can get great shots.

Use your own style; try photographing fast moving animals in large enclosures, expressing movement by using slow shutter speeds and "panning" with the animals. Try to show behavior: individuals and groups feeding, drinking, playing; creatures interacting with mates, young, and rivals. Good animal behavior pictures are not easy to get, even in zoos and are top stock sellers.

Professional Tips: A small, light, aluminium stepladder is sometimes helpful to get up high (where permitted). It is not normally easy to get animal model releases from zoos, but carry a few forms with you just in case you photograph a famous, recognizable animal. (My zoo pictures have sold as editorial stock without releases.)

Alternate Approach: Photograph in a nearby national park or wildlife reserve that you know has plenty of animals.

Results: Stock pictures, possible editorial feature, portfolio shots, fine-art personal pictures, pleasure.

Look At: Publications aimed a zoo-going public and zoo professionals, childrens' nature magazines and books, and guide books about the animals and places you plan to visit. To study animal behavior, see *Serengeti*, by Mitsuako Iwago, a great book.

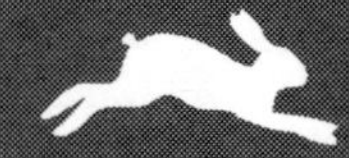 ## Self-Assignment # 9
A Nature Pictures Story

The object of this long-term self-assignment about a region, eco-system, or animal or bird habitat is practice in working for top editorial markets, a possible book, stock, fine-art, portfolio material.

Equipment: Two or three professional cameras, with wide-angle, normal, telephoto/zoom, and macro lenses. A sturdy tripod with a good ball head. A backpack or waterproof case. A reflector and/or small flash for fill light. You will need camping equipment if you choose to work in a backcountry or wilderness area. A luggage cart to help carry all this is almost a must!

Film: Carry plenty of your favorite slow- or medium-speed film, plus some fast film just in case.

Variables: Seasons, weather, habits of migratory species.

Transportation: You will probably need a car, or best, a truck or sport utility vehicle with a high cab. Hikers can arrive by public transport. Big city parks are worth showing in this way too.

On the Shoot: Aim to show the whole ecosystem. Photograph landscape, types of water, trees, other vegetation, geology, and as many as possible of the large and small creatures that inhabit the area, over the course of one year.

Try for variety in your shots; think of the needs of the art director or editor; previsualize situations laid out as an interesting magazine story or varied book. You will need close-ups, medium, and wide-angle pictures. Think of color, too many blue, green, and brown shots are boring together. Vary colors by shooting at different times of day, especially at dawn and dusk, for best animal, bird and insect activity, colorful skies, fewer crowds. Different seasons will give maximum color contrasts too. Don't be afraid to work in the cold. (See the Interviews with Jim Brandenburg, Nathan Farb, and Frans Lanting, in chapter 13, for more.)

Professional Tips: Try using flash fill of nearby creatures against sunrises or sunsets (see chapter 3.) Keep notes of places and times that interesting things happen. Write the story too, if you can. A picture story is the best possible portfolio for a photographer who wants to crack the top magazine market; a story with words and good pictures is even more saleable that pictures alone.

It's worth spending considerable time on this project if you have professional ambitions. Try to get any good story published as a whole before letting the best shots be used singly as stock.

Look At: *The National Geographic, Airone, Audubon, BBC Wildlife, Geo,* and other top nature magazines, also many of the picture books listed in the bibliography.

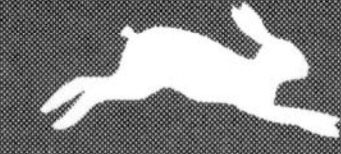

Self-Assignment # 10
An Environmental Project

Support any cause you believe in with your photography.

Equipment: Use any equipment and film that you like. The organization that uses the pictures will be grateful.

Film: If for publication, use color transparency film for stock, black-and-white film for small newspapers, and newsletters. Color negative (print) film for is often useful for public-relations albums or exhibit prints. Or, you can check ahead of time with possible users as to their specific needs.

You can photograph pollution and disaster of course, and use the powerful pictures to gain political support for improvements. Remember also that there are areas where progress is being made, or even triumphs recorded— a stream restored to health, a small or large park created — and these things need photographing too. My friend Patricia Fisher, a Washington, D.C.-based photographer, recently gave her services to documenting the annual beach clean-up at Assateague Island National Seashore. She photographed about 200 volunteers from all along the eastern seaboard (including me) picking up about eight tons of garbage from the beautiful place, on a late September day.

Approach: Use any style you wish.

Results: Satisfaction gained from doing something for a good cause, possible feature story, portfolio material, stock, personal/fine-art images.

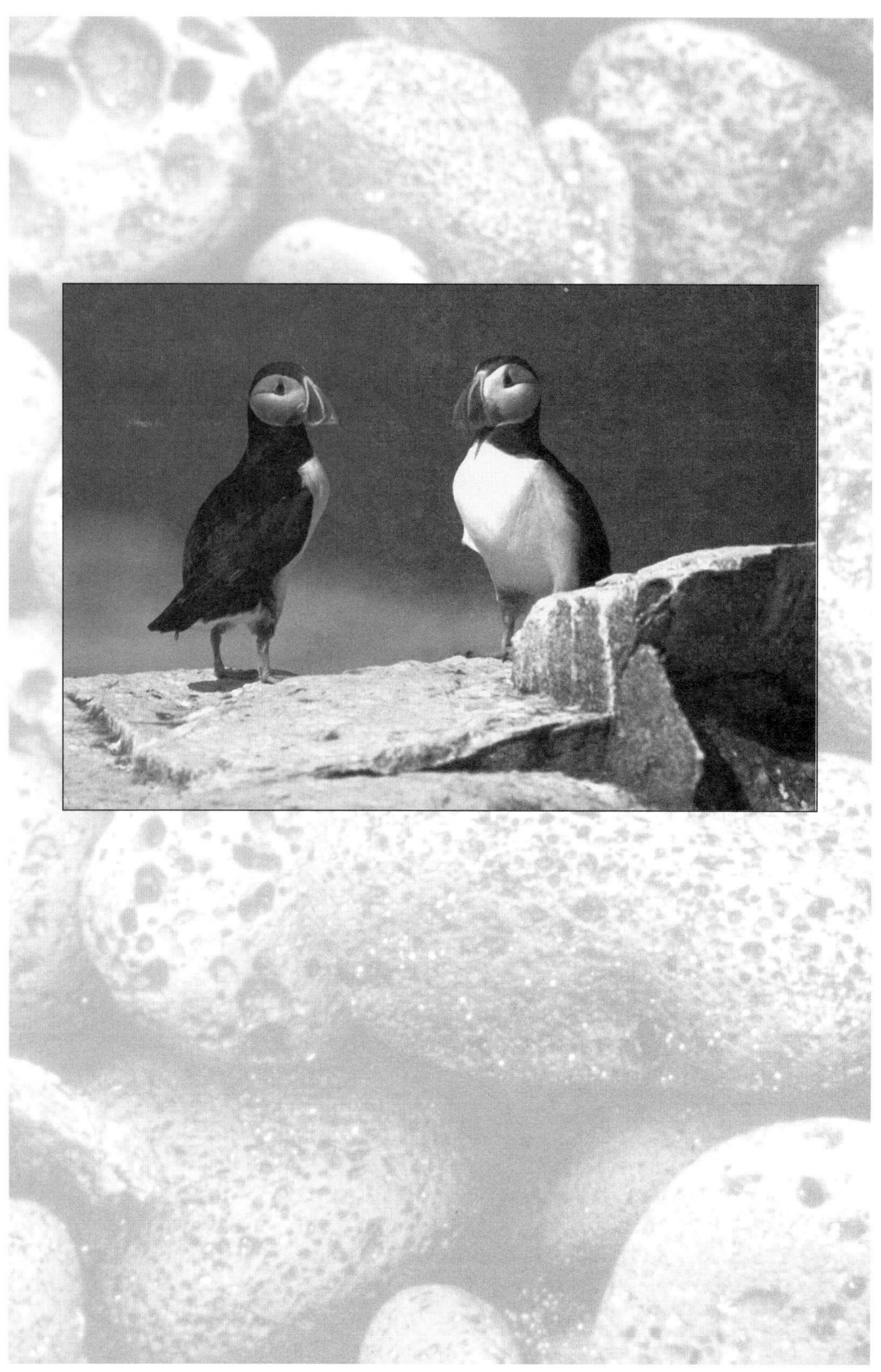

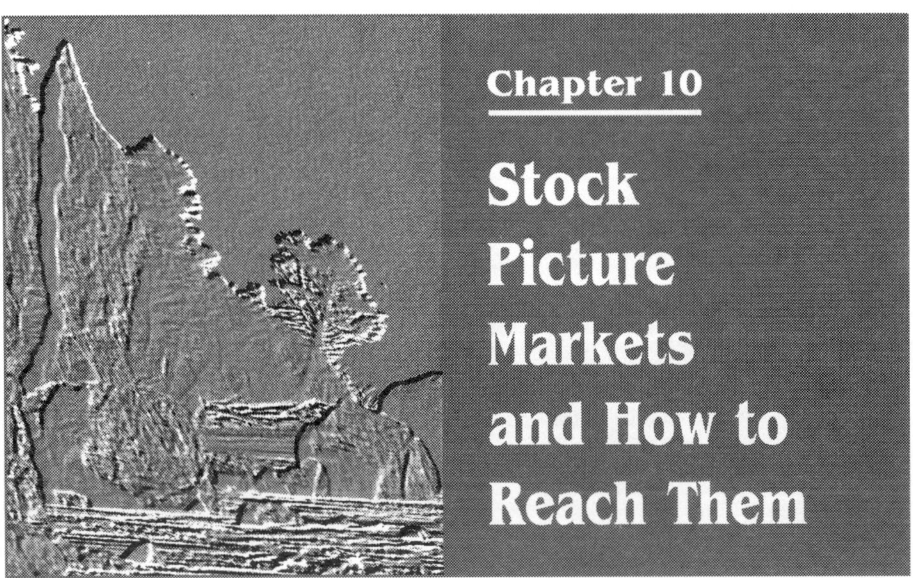

You perhaps have amassed a fair quantity of very good or excellent nature and wildlife images if you are a professional photographer who gets outdoors as often as possible, or if you are a professional natural scientist or outdoorperson. Or you may be a skilled, dedicated but as yet strictly amateur nature photographer, animal handler, birdwatcher, conservation professional, pro or good diver, forest or parks ranger, gardener or horticulturalist, mountain guide, outdoor-program leader, teacher, travel photographer or perhaps a writer/photographer, or anyone who frequently takes pictures of large or small animals, or birds, plants, marine life, or landscapes as part of your work or for personal pleasure.

Stock is such a currently hot topic that you have almost certainly heard something about it. Perhaps you are interested in a professional career in nature photography and know this is a way that some photographers make big money, or you like the idea of getting some pictures published, marketing your images to make money. Maybe, you have seen nature pictures used in advertising, or want to get nature stories printed in newspapers, magazines, or books, or you think your pictures would be excellent for calendars or greeting cards. This chapter is about markets for all types of nature, wildlife, landscape, plant, flower, marine, underwater, close-up, and related photographs and specifics for teaching them.

A Quick Guide to Stock as a Business

The practical way to learn about the stock business is first to ask questions:
What exactly is a stock picture anyway?
Who sells stock?
Who buys stock?
How is stock sold?
How are stock prices determined?
How do photographers get paid?
How can photographers locate good stock agencies?
Can stock be sold without an agency?
How does one begin to sell stock?

Here are some answers (for more details see the rest of this chapter):
A stock picture can be any existing picture.
Stock is sold by stock agents, photographers, scientists, zoos, more.
Stock is used by ad agencies, magazines; text, trade, and childrens' book
publishers; graphic designers, corporations, calendars, more.
Stock is normally licensed for a specific use, not sold outright.
Stock prices are determined by negotiation, based on extent of usage.
Contact PACA for a list of about 100 member stock agencies (see text).
Agency photographers get paid after agency is paid, less commission.
Photographers who market direct get paid by client.
Yes, but setting up your own stock operation requires time, work.
Edit, caption, organize work; mail subject list to known stock users.

The Big Business of Stock Today

A stock picture can theoretically be any existing picture, available for viewing before purchase (as opposed to pictures taken on assignment or commission, which cannot be seen before a user invests money).

Today, stock is a multimillion-dollar business. (It is also a pounds, yen, francs, marks, pesos, kronor, and many other currency business, because stock is marketed all over the world.) The biggest stock agencies are international, well organized and highly competitive, and now quite hard to affiliate with unless the work is exceptional.

There are also some midsized and smaller stock agencies, which are somewhat easier to crack.

Most of the stock pictures that are sold (more accurately, licensed for use) are marketed by stock picture agencies (sometimes called picture libraries). Some stock is marketed by the owners or copyright holders of specialized, often historic, picture collections. A small number of photographers function seriously as their own stock agents, employ a staff, perhaps marketing the work of a few other photographers in addition to shooting themselves. There are a few stock cooperatives of photographers who get together to share office space, and the cost of staff. Finally, a few organizations, like certain publishing companies, zoos, and museums, market their own specialized picture collections. Most individual photographers sell only their own work, and usually operate the stock business with the help of a spouse or family member.

All serious stock photographers and agencies, have carefully edited collections of filed, indexed, easy-to-access, captioned pictures. Many do careful research to find out what subjects are in current demand. Some photographers, and a few stock agencies, function rather like TV or movie production houses, setting up shoots, traveling to prime locations at the best times of year on a regular basis, and even paying for wildlife models.

Promoting Stock Pictures

In today's competitive business climate, even top photographers who are widely published in magazines and books (which is wonderful advertising) also send out stock lists, promotional mailers, and buy space in sourcebooks (distributed free to major stock users). Advertisers get reprints for promotion pieces.

Most important picture collections are known about by picture researchers (who can be staff or freelance) and big stock users. Individuals who meet criteria (a certain number of published credits, and quantity of pictures available as stock) can pay for an (all-type) listing in *The Green Book*, which is considered the standard reference source for nature stock users. The cost is quite moderate (currently around $500). A rather newer venture, *Stock Direct*, is a catalog where individual photographers can buy space to showcase pictures that they feel will sell well as stock; again there are specific criteria for inclusion. This book showcases many general stock pictures of the most popular categories (people, travel, industry, and the like) besides nature and wildlife images, and currently costs about $2,000 per page. Also see interview with directory publisher Ann Guilfoyle in this chapter, and chapter 14.

Iit is rapidly becoming standard practice for the largest agents, and stock photographers, to market collections of pictures on CD-ROM discs. These are in effect catalogs and are distributed to major stock users.

Marketing Your Own Stock

Individual nature/wildlife photographers who want to start marketing stock without an agent must work hard so that potential buyers become aware of the pictures they have. If you want to try to market stock, first edit and accurately caption your best pictures. Then, make a detailed listing of the subject matter. Next search in libraries to see who uses

---

Animal Model or Talent Agencies, and Game Ranches

There are now several game ranches where photographers can spend a day or a month photographing rare and popular wild species under controlled conditions in natural surroundings. Pioneered by the movies, then by TV production companies, the use of animal models by professional wildlife photographers was a fairly well-kept secret for years. Rates are quite high, in the region of $500 per day, for one prime species, such as a cougar, and one smaller animal, like a raccoon. Some stock specialists find the investment profitable. Today, several photo tour companies catering primarily to affluent amateurs organize groups that spend a few days getting up close and personal with bobcats and mountain lions and more, which reduces the per-person cost. Two of the best-known game ranches, Triple-D and Wild Eyes, are in Montana. They, and others, and group organizers often advertise in *Outdoor Photography* magazine. Professional film and photo sourcebooks list other sources of animal talent. Some commercial wildlife parks permit individual photographers to work (supervised) close to animals and big birds, for a fee; usually the cost is much lower than the top game ranches, which have superb beasts.

---

those types of picture. Browse among nature magazines, science textbooks, and childrens' magazines and books to begin with. All of them use a lot of nature and wildlife pictures. Then, send out your stock list, perhaps with a photo card or inexpensive print, follow up with phone calls to show a portfolio.

Locating Stock Agents

PACA —The Picture Agency Council of America— is an organization of about 100 member stock agencies of various sizes, most are in the U.S., but many also have international affiliations. All members have agreed to adopt a code of ethics for dealings with photographers and clients. They publish a directory of their members, with phone numbers, contact names along with agency specialties. Obtain a copy of this directory by writing to the president of PACA, c/o a member agency (which changes each year). The directory currently costs $10. It can also usually be obtained from any PACA member agency, and also is given away at major photo shows where PACA exhibits.

The British agency organization is BAPLA, the British Association of Stock Picture Libraries and Agencies. Their directory costs £10 by mail. (For current addresses of both, see resources, chapter 14.)

```
┌─────── (SAMPLE) STOCK PICTURE DELIVERY MEMO ───────┐
```

(SAMPLE) STOCK PICTURE DELIVERY MEMO

Photographer or agency letterhead
(List both phone and fax numbers)

Attn: Mr. Charles Client
Eco-Equipment Manufacturing Company
25 Greanleaf Avenue
Nicetown, MN 12345   Date:

Notice: The pictures listed below are submitted, at your request, for examination only. They may not be reproduced, duplicated, photocopied, electronically scanned or stored, or used as artist or photographer reference without a signed licensing agreement from photographer or his (her) agent. The client agrees not to project these valuable images, or expose them to sunlight, heat, or dust, or to subject them to damp or humid conditions. Client (named above) is responsible for loss or damage from moment of receipt until returned to the photographer.

The pictures may be examined free for two weeks *(or period of your choice)*. After two weeks a holding fee of $1 *(or other fee)* per picture per day will be charged, unless noted to the contrary below.

Please check count and acknowledge receipt of images by signing below. After five days, count will be assumed correct and pictures acceptable for reproduction.

QNTY	SUBJECT	FORMAT	COLOR/ B&W	AGREED VALUE
1	Mt. Robson, BC, pink dawn	35mm vert	color	$2,500*
2	Mt. Rainier, WA	"	"	$1,500 each
1	View of Green Mts, VT, snow	"	"	$1,500
1	Butte, Monument Valley, AZ, sunset	"	"	$1,500
1	Yellowstone peaks, MT	"	"	$1,500
2	Mt. Evans, CO	"	"	$1,500 each

As per our agreement, a research fee of $60 (or other amount) will be charged if no images are used. This fee is deductible from license fees of over $500.

*Denotes especially valuable image, as per our telephone agreement.

Return: This submission is conditioned on the return of all items, undamaged, unaltered, and unretouched.

Client (named above) **assumes all risks** for the items listed from the time of receipt by client to the time of receipt by photographer or his (her) agent.

Your carrier loss or damage: Reimbursement for loss/damage shall be amount(s) indicated indicated above. Do demand a receipt from your carrier, and insure shipment.

Receipt acknowledged for client:

(Signed)____Date:____________

Selling Stock Overseas

Britain, France, Germany, and some other European countries are excellent, quite high-paying markets for stock. There either is, or soon will be an EAPLA—European Association of Stock Picture Libraries and Agents. Inquire further if interested c/o BAPLA (see above).

I do not know of any organization of Japanese or Asian stock agents, but there are a number of good agencies in that fast-developing part of the world. Japan of course is the top (and very high-paying) market; Singapore, Hong Kong, Taiwan, and Korea have good agents too. Argentina and Brazil are the top-paying markets for stock in Latin America.

Note: Despite the fact that many agencies today require exclusive representation, this is open to negotiation *if you have images agencies particularly want.* The very successful wildlife photographers Leonard Lee Rue III and Len Rue, Jr., have dealt on an individual basis with a number of agencies in the U.S. and overseas for many years. So has top stock specialist Jim Pickerell (but he is not a nature photographer). To learn much more about stock business, read the *ASMP Stock Picture Handbook.*

Presenting Your Work to A Stock Agent

Check out the PACA Directory (see above), stock sourcebooks, and books listed in the bibliography. Ask photographers about the stock agency(ies) they are affiliated with. Then edit the original pictures you are prepared to part with, very carefully. (Do not show dupes or any technically poor work.) Sort these pictures into groups, stamp them with your copyright notice, and put them into twenty-slide plastic sheets. Write a short letter or list summarizing what you have. Call, write, or fax an agency that interests you and ask if they are interested. If they say yes, ask how many pictures they want to see (average is 200-500). Arrange an appointment with a picture editor, or drop off work, or send the pictures by certified or registered mail.

Physically Caring for Your Pictures

Excellent nature pictures are highly prized by all kinds of publications, are widely in demand, and, over a period of years, may be worth considerable money, and sell over and over again as stock.

If you are talented, and persistent enough to make fine images, value them highly, protect them, and have reproduction-quality dupes (duplicates) made of the very best ones. Do not send out or project precious originals. (Increasingly, photographers are having their best images scanned onto computer disc [photo CD's] to preserve them safely.)

Store all slides, but especially treasured originals, carefully. If you market, or plan to market images, arrange them so you can locate pictures quickly. To minimize the risk of scratches, dust, or fingerprints, put your choicest 35mm slides (or "selects") into individual Kimac slide covers, made of stiff, nonharmful plastic, and then then in twenty-slide plastic sheets, grouped by subject.

Current Best-Selling Nature Stock Subjects For Advertising:

- Animals/birds large in foreground of beautiful/magnificent landscape possibly with water, flowers, mountains (symbolic of healthy ecosystem)
- Drops of clean water, clear blue water, flowing waterfalls (symbolic of purity; industries' concern for the environment)
- Eagles (all species, but especially bald eagle, symbolic of U.S.)
- Green pristine landscapes in general (symbolic of the environment)
- Large flights of birds (symbolic of migration; nature's bounty)
- Large herds of moving animals (symbolic of fears about extinction of wildlife; nature's bounty; also herd instinct)
- Large schools of fish (symbolic of clean, healthy ocean)
- Magnificent old trees (symbolic of maturity, continuity)
- Mountains (symbolic of permanence, strength; pure clean air)
- Owls (all species, symbolic of wisdom; burning midnight oil; also northern spotted owl, current symbol of conservation causes)
- Pandas (cute, cuddly; almost extinct, currently in the news)
- Penguins (amusing metaphors for humans; symbol of Antarctica)
- Primates in general (amusing symbols of human traits and emotions)
- Rain forests, pine forests, mixed hardwood forests (symbolic of concerns about logging, global warming, and the future of the planet)
- Salmon (currently in news because concern about decline in numbers)
- Sharks (symbolic of business climate; ruthless power; in the news currently because of overhunting, declining numbers)
- Wolves (symbolic of freedom in nature; current subject of intense debate between conservationists and those wishing exterminate wolves)

The following Nature/Wildlife Subjects are Perennial Bestsellers:

- Animal families
- Baby and young animals
- Bears (all species, especially in the wild; can be shown as cute or magnificent; currently much-photographed so competition is intense)
- Beautiful or hardworking insects (butterflies, bees, spiders, ants)
- Big cats, all species (symbols of beauty, grace, speed, power)
- Birds leading V-shaped flights (symbolic of change of seasons; also purpose, business leadership)
- Close-ups of leaves showing veins (symbolic of human vascular system)
- Coral reefs with colorful fish (symbol of tropical vacations)

Best-Selling Nature Stock Subjects— Continued

- Colorful small birds, especially bluebirds; and cardinals or robins in snow (used on greeting cards)
- Elephants (but today should be taken in the wild to sell as stock; symbolic of wisdom, longevity, long memory; endangered)
- Females of all species with young (symbolic of caring, compassion)
- Fighting animals; not too bloody (symbolic of business competition)
- Fluffy, furry, pretty small animals (used a lot on greeting cards)
- Frogs, green tree frogs (these are now the symbol of the rain forest)
- Lions (the king of beasts; even good close-ups taken in zoos sell)
- Male animals of any species with magnificent horns or antlers (symbolic of power, pride, assurance, virility)
- Parrots, macaws (very colorful; symbolic of rainforests; endangered)
- Primates; all kinds, especially with expressive faces, humorous shots, or actions mimicing human behaviour
- Romantic flowers, bouquets; roses and violets, white flowers, and lately, lush fields of wildflowers, and seasonal images of fall leaves and snow scenes sell for greeting cards and some calendars.

Archival storage sheets for all formats are sold in professional photo stores and through catalogs. Store the sheets in a file box or good binder to begin with. When you get enough sheets, hang them in file cabinets or even store them in a fire-resistant safe as I do. (I store nonselected slides in the original boxes from the processing lab, in metal file cabinets.)

Digital Images, CD-ROM and the Stock-Picture Business

The use of digital cameras in professional news and sports photography is increasing quite rapidly. Time is more important than picture quality in these areas; the images can be transmitted over phone lines. But digital images are still of very low resolution (translate: less clear, sharp) compared to those made on conventional film. The same thing is true of video images; the resolving power of even professional videotape is not as good as that of 35mm film. It seems likely that most still nature pictures will be shot on conventional film for many years to come. However, the scanning and digitalizing of both professional and amateur photographs shot on conventional film onto computers, either as discs for viewing only, or discs for viewing and downloading to other computers for publication, is now a fact. Photographs are enjoyed, marketed, retouched, and printed via computer.

For amateur photographers this is all good news. They can purchase

Kodak's CD-ROM (Compact Disc-Read Only Memory) player and view pictures on the TV screen. Negatives (reversed to positive) slides (even older favorites) and prints can be scanned onto disc by labs equipped to do this.

Images can be scanned at varying resolutions. Scans can be transferred to computers and manipulated and undetectably retouched , and amazing results are possible. If you see an ad showing an apparent photograph of the Statue of Liberty looking bewildered in an Iowa cornfield, with the Rocky Mountains close behind her, you should know that today three, four, or more photographs are scanned onto a computer, parts of each image are silhouetted, then assembled, and blended seamlessly to get the desired effect.

Scans can now be made by relatively small, inexpensive machines, and quickly transferred onto today's sophisticated home computers. Quite a few photographers, and many graphic designers, now manipulate images. Scans to disc are now the method of choice for preserving valuable fine-art, historic, and stock images. Imported onto a computer,

---

Protect Your Copyright

If you want to market stock, or authorize an agency to market it for you, you must own the copyright of the photograph.

Stock photographers and agencies almost never sell the copyright in a work outright, but license limited usage.

Note: Copyright laws vary in different countries.

(For more on copyright law, see the *ASMP Stock Picture Handbook*. In Britain, see the *Artists' and Writers' Yearbook*.)

Always mark each picture (original or duplicate) with rubber stamp or computer type small enough to fit on the mount,with your name, the international copyright symbol (©), and the year the picture was taken, thus:

**Photograph copyright©
Fabulous Photographer 199?
(or use Roman numerals, MCXM?)**

Never, never send any pictures anywhere unsolicited, or send any requested pictures anywhere without a stock delivery memo listing subjects, stating the value of each image, and setting out client's responsibility in case a picture is lost or damaged. In the case of valuable images, reduce risk by sending out duplicates (dupes). These can be made by professional labs, or make them yourself.

When the client wants to use any image, send a stock licensing agreement, stating the licensing fee, and and the terms and conditions for reproduction.

---

they can be digitally retouched, repaired, or otherwise manipulated, before they are either "outputted" onto film again, or separated directly for reproduction (which lowers the cost of color printing considerably).

Collections of pictures scanned onto CD-ROM discs are now being used to market stock by some agencies and by some pioneering photographers. (It is cheaper to show work on disc than to print it in a catalog.) All of the advances are good for most professional photographers.

Not so good are the possibilities that exist for the less-than-honest user to transfer pictures from discs onto computers for use without payment to a photographer or agency.

Professional organizations and individual stock photographers (most notably Jim Pickerell) are working very hard to raise consciousness and to have copyright laws strengthened to make it easier for photographers to collect damages for willful copyright infringement, and to perfect "watermarks" on scanned images intended for viewing only, so they would be very difficult and expensive to retouch for reproduction.

Copyright-free Photo CD disks are not good news for most professional photographers.

The Money Side of Stock

I meet quite a few would-be stock photographers who are a bit hazy about the money side of the business. Here is my summary:

Stock at one time was mostly a by-product of assignment photography. Income from any subsequent use of the pictures, perhaps including syndication of stories overseas, belonged to the photographer. If the stock was put with an agency (there were not too many agencies until the 1970s), of course a commission was deducted from stock sales, but stock income was considered to be more or less "found money" until as recently as about ten or fifteen years ago, when stock specialists became prominent.

Today, there are comparatively few big magazines that give assignments, fewer still that give lavish ones, and the great majority of stock is produced by photographers who must bear the expenses involved up front. Quite a few photographers today specialize in shooting only for stock. The sucessful ones spend much effort researching what sells best, and must have some money to invest, because it takes time for stock to circulate, be selected, published, and paid for.

If a photographer uses a stock agent, or agents, the agency edits new work submitted, keeps the images they think will sell on file to show to interested buyers; most today advertise.

Stock agencies make their profit margin, and pay expenses, by a taking a commission from the licensing fees received. (Agency commission is often, not always 50 percent.) Agencies get paid when the pictures are leased, not before. Photographers receive their fees with commission deducted. Normally the photographer does not receive any money up front. I know of one agency that pays small amounts to encourage photographers when a large body of new work is accepted. A few agencies give their top-producing and top-grossing photographers a minimum annual guarantee. (But both these arrangements are exceptional.)

Almost all stock photographers are paid after pictures are licensed, used, and the agency has been paid. Photographers are then paid on a time schedule negotiated with the agency. Payment policies vary and are negotiable to some extent. Some agencies pay monthly, some quarterly; photographers with few sales may get checks every six months, or even annually.

Marketing Your Own Stock

Photographers who market their own stock of course get paid directly by the client at the time of use. They can then keep all of the fee, but for this they have to negotiate fees, "pull" (edit) pictures for clients, log them in, send them out, negotiate prices, log returned used or unused pictures back in again, check them for damage, bill clients, collect fees due, keep track of slow or nonpayers, and more. It is, as Len Rue, Jr., says, a labor intensive business.

I for one think that stock agents earn their money!

Making a profit from stock may not be as important to you as getting published. But you should charge a fair price so as not to undercut the market. Donate fees to a conservation organization if you don't need the money! Professionals of course must make a profit!

To deduct photography expenses from taxes, the IRS person (or their equivalents in other countries), will want to see evidence of substantial business activity (i.e. income!) from stock. Watch expenses carefully. Keep records. For a definitive guide to the business side of stock, see Michal Heron's *How to Shoot Stock Pictures that Sell* even though it's not about nature photography. Also see the *Guilfoyle Report,* the well-respected newsletter of nature and wildlife photography. (See the interview with publisher Ann Guilfoyle later in the chapter). Also see: *Pricing Photography,* by Michal Heron and David MacTavish. and/or *Negotiating Stock Picture Prices*, by Jim Pickerell.

Taking Stock is a bimonthly newsletter edited by stock photographer Jim Pickerell. It is devoted to business and to industry trends. Subscribe especially if you are interested in keeping up with the latest about digital imagery. Jim is an acknowledged expert and a passionate crusader for photographers' rights, in this area.

The Stock Photo Report is another extremely detailed well-regarded newsletter. It is edited by Brian Seed, a British photojournalist, stock agency founder, and stock expert.

The Photo District News (PDN) has an annual stock-picture issue. This trade magazine is indispensable to professional photographers.

The Photographers' Market is an annual which includes many nature stock buyers in its listings, good especially for calendars, paper goods, greeting cards, and poster companies. Not all top-paying magazine markets are included. Also see resources, and the bibliography, at the end of the book.

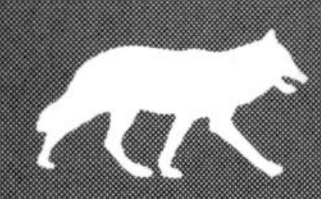

John Kapriellian *is director of the Nature Source division of Photo Researchers Inc., a New York stock agency:*

JK: We represent the National Audubon Society collection, the Jacana nature agency in Paris, and Okapia, in Germany. In addition to many of the finest U.S. nature photographers, we represent quite a few of the best British ones too, including Stephen Dalton and David Hosking, and the pictures by his father, the late, great bird photographer Eric Hosking.

I edit all new nature material from our photographers. When I review portfolios by people who want to be associated with Photo Researchers, I need first to see technical quality that is competitive—pictures must be sharp, correctly exposed, and on the film stocks we prefer (of course exceptions may be made for special images or unusual subjects).

I usually speak to new photographers by telephone first, asking what kind of film and equipment they use, how long have they been shooting, how many transparencies they have, to try to get a feel for their work. When I agree to review, I want to see a tight edit of 200-400 slides. I must be impressed with style, technique, and subject matter, and I shouldn't have to look at soft or poorly exposed images in a portfolio.

Nature photography has exploded in the last few years, with many improvements in equipment, especially in very fast telephoto lenses, which though very expensive most of my photographers are now using.

Kodachrome remains my film choice for finest image sharpness, grain, and longevity, but newer E-6 films, especially the slower professional Fujichromes, are excellent and have advantages in many situations.

In order for a portfolio to truly stand out, it must have either very broad coverage of many subjects, or great depth in a specialized area.

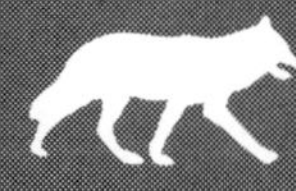

Excerpts from an interview with
Norman Owen Tomalin

Norman Owen Tomalin *is the owner of Bruce Coleman Inc., a New York stock agency specializing in nature.*

The Bruce Coleman Agency was established in 1970, by Bruce Coleman and myself. We had branches in London and New York. I liked New York, he liked London, so I bought out the New York branch a few years ago. I usually encourage my photographers to seek representation in the U.K. with Bruce Coleman Ltd., in London. He does the same for me in reverse!

The perennial nature best sellers for the last twenty-three years have been primates, big cats, and birds of prey. I don't think I ever have enough primate pictures. And right now, wolves are a very, very hot subject. Jim Brandenburg's work has certainly contributed to the excitement.

Textbooks often want the esoteric. I had a request for the Galapagos tool-using finch the other day. Not many people have it using the tool.

The advertising user has finally discovered nature photography. It can illustrate practically anything. And of course, "green" is in right now, that ties in wonderfully. Advertising is where the money is. Most nature stock for advertising is taken under controlled situations. There is so much money to be made that many people find it pays to go where they can get prime specimens in authentic surroundings. Belize zoo is for jaguar, Montana game ranches for American big cats, Ranthambore reserve in India for tigers. Phoenix zoo has a fine tiger compound. The Sonora Desert Museum in Tucson is particularly good. Research to locate rare species. Modern zoos can be very fine, pictures should look as if they were taken in the wild if possible; show the zoo in some shots too.

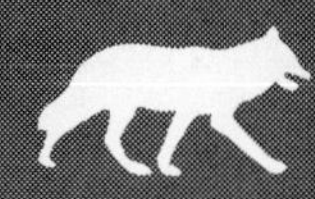

Excerpts from an interview with
Ann Guilfoyle

Ann Guilfoyle *is the publisher of The Guilfoyle Report and the Green Book Directory of Natural History and General Stock, in New York City.*

AG: I was photo editor of *Audubon* magazine from 1967-1976 and started *The Guilfoyle Report* as a forum for nature and wildlife photographers in 1982. There are now about 1600 subscribers. The GR is a quarterly magazine in newsletter format that offers in-depth descriptions of photo markets and "Happenings" listings of current photo needs from such buyers as *National Geographic* and *Natural History*. Our subscribers include many of the world's best nature photographers, some of whom work fulltime at their photography and others who have additional sources of income. This reflects the composition of the nature field in which the delineation between professional and avocational photographer is not always clear cut. Only a relatively small percent are able to make their livings from photo sales alone. One is Art Wolfe. Many pros, like John Shaw, write and do workshops as well. Some have other specialties besides nature. One is Richard Hamilton Smith whose nature work is widely known, plus he has a successful agricultural photography business. Many teachers also photograph; their knowledge of curriculums helps them produce saleable images for textbook markets. Dwight Kuhn worked that way for years, but now he does nothing but photography.

Our *Green Book* is a biannual, indexed directory of natural history and general stock that provides a place where people can advertise their work to editors and researchers. Anyone starting out could do worse than study it. It's in some libraries, and of course we sell copies. To advertise, we require a minimum number of published credits.

Editorial Markets for Nature Pictures

Magazine users of stock nature pictures include internationally known publications like *Audubon, BBC Wildlife, National Parks*, and *Natural History*, as well as smaller magazines like *Animals* and *Birding*. Gardening, travel, and outdoor magazines use nature pictures from time to time. Nature magazines for children, include *Ranger Rick*, and National Geographic's *World,* and also various *Scholastic* and other classroom publications. While magazines do buy individual pictures, what they most like to see are stories. Some stories may take months or years to shoot. Top New York stock agent Norman Owen Tomalin told me, "If I have a nature story, I can market it. If I have single pictures, they have to wait to be discovered."

Newspapers should be interested in goodpictures of local wildlife, and in local picture stories; query the picture editor.

Trade books (general interest), childrens' books, and textbooks of all levels are users of nature pictures too. Browse in a good magazine store or bookstore, or a general or school library. Then call and find out how to submit to a publisher whom you think your work will interest, or "fit."

Most picture and textbook publishers, and magazines, employ picture researchers, either on staff or freelance. Many of them belong to ASPP, the American Society of Picture Professionals. (See chapter 14.)

Most often today, even if you are within reach of a publisher, you will be asked to leave or "drop off" the portfolio, overnight or for a few days, because art directors' and picture editors' time is limited. Ask for a receipt if you "drop off" a portfolio. If the publication requests you to do so, you can send it by certified mail. Envelope, enclose a detailed list of the pictures, and keep a copy.

Many publications will send guidelines outlining wants, submission requirements, and rates paid. Send for this, enclosing a stamped, self-addressed envelope for the reply.

Other Markets for Stock

The last market for nature pictures of all kinds is loosely called "paper goods," this includes publishers of calendars, posters, and greeting cards. Check stores that sell these goods, look on the back of calendars and cards for publishers' names, and consult the annual *Photographer's Market* directory.

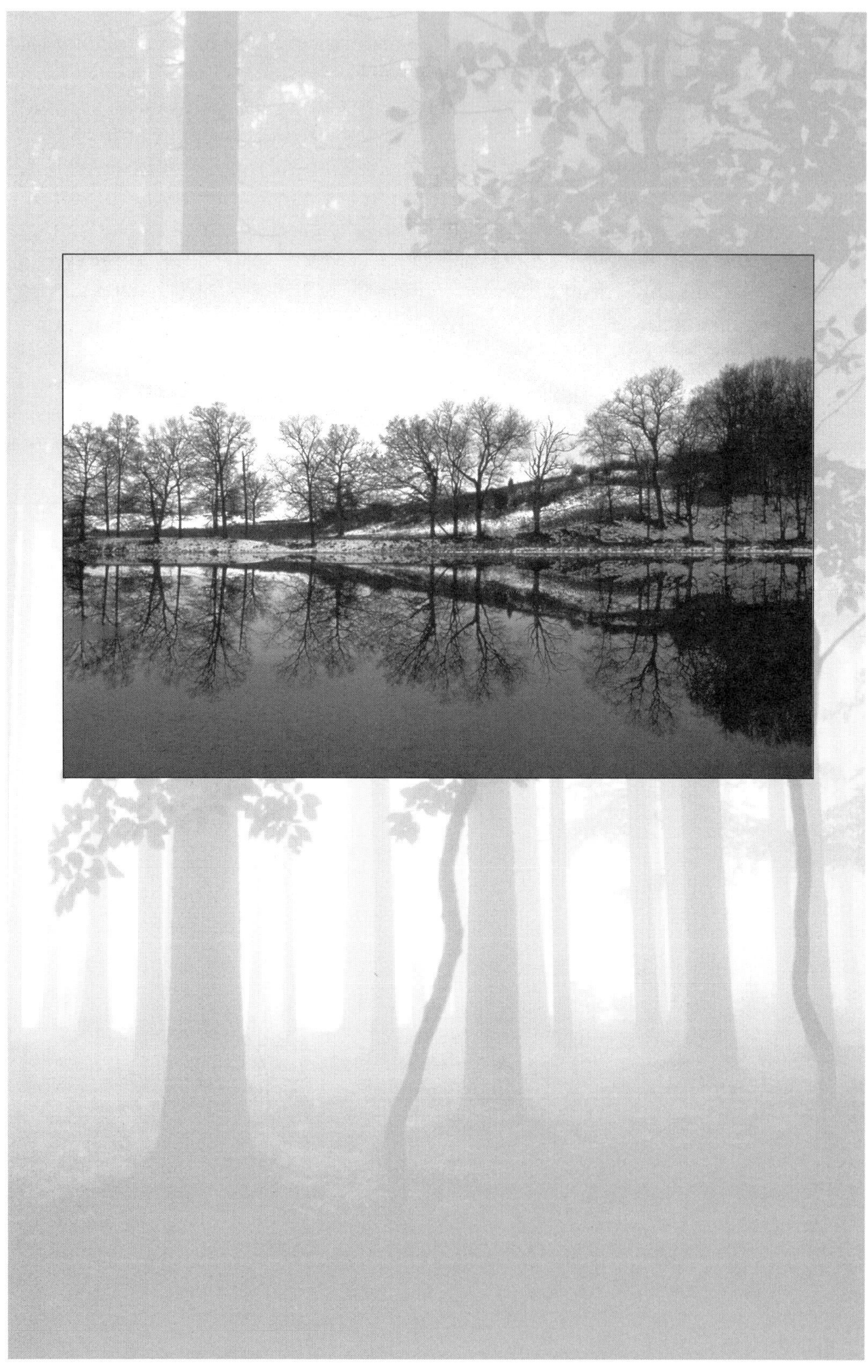

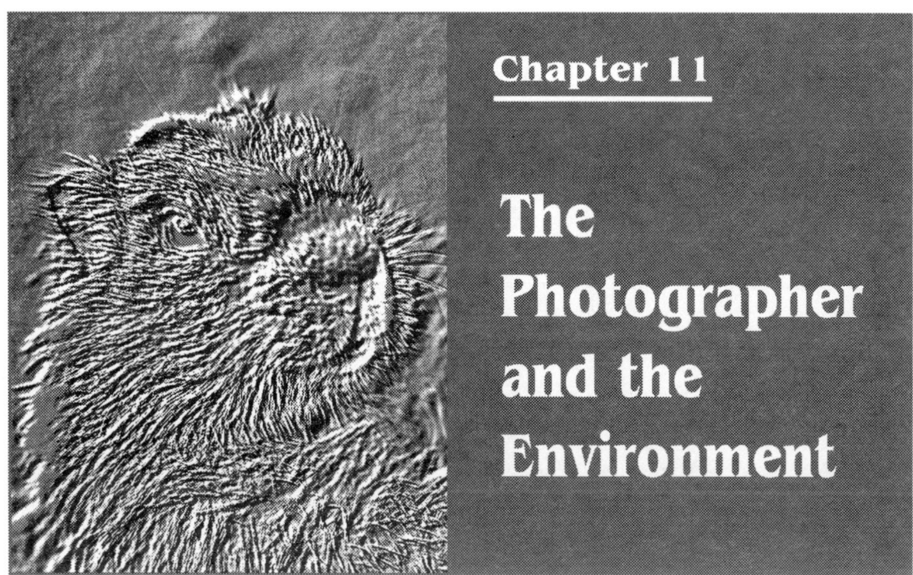

There can hardly be a nature, wildlife, or outdoor photographer today who would not like to aid the environment, reduce pollution, help to preserve endangered species, and make sure that we do not knowingly contribute to harming the world's fragile ecosystems. But the world's environmental problems are enormous, the scientists don't know everything, and individuals can feel extremely powerless.

The way to feel less powerless in any situation is to do something positive, however small. People cause pollution, so small actions taken by individuals can cumulatively have great effect. I have listed a few things that any photographer can do that will help our planet and our future, without a large financial investment.

Improving the Photographic Environment

Keep pressure on all photo manufacturers at home and overseas (and indirectly on their shareholders, employees, localities, and governments) by sending letters to management about their environmental policies. Press manufacturers to clean up messes made in earlier times, and give photographers and other consumers the latest accurate information.

Ask questions and make statements at photographers' meetings detailing your concerns. It is not enough today for any company to make pious statements in tasteful brochures printed on recycled paper.

Call on all manufacturers to continually research cleaner products, and on labs, even small ones, to use the best environmental processes.

By not patronizing polluters, whether large and international or small and local, you will be sending the most powerful message of all.

Practical Steps Any Photographer Can Take
to Help the Environment

The way to start solving environmental problems directly related to nature photography is first to define them:
- Many chemicals used in photographic processes can pollute water.
- Silver can cause water pollution that affects aquatic and wildlife.
- Even a home darkroom may pollute local water supplies.
- It is hard to learn which photo processes are "cleaner" than others.
- Laws governing disposal of chemicals vary; are hard to learn about.
- It takes effort to learn if a lab is obeying environmental laws.
- Photographic packaging uses plastics.
- Photographic packaging uses paper and cardboard
- It is hard to learn which manufacturers are reducing pollution.
- Whatever I can do will make so little difference it's not worthwhile.
- Photographers hurt wildlife by disturbing breeding/feeding grounds.
- Large numbers of tourists, even photographers, may spoil a habitat.
- Even one photographer may unintentionally harm/kill a living creature.
- Is so-called ecotourism just a hot commercial gimmick?
- Does ecotourism benefit indigenous peoples in any true sense?
- Some ecotourism companies contribute to environmental causes; which?
- It's hard to know which environmental group to support.
- Should photographers become environmental activists?
- Should one despair about the future of large wildlife?
- Can photographs themselves help wildlife and the environment?

Some answers, and some ways to start tackling problems:
- Ask for manufacturers' environmental policy statements.
- Ask manufacturers what they are doing to to correct past problems.
- Learn which chemicals and processes are least polluting, and use them.
- Read manufacturers' literature on their products and processes and comply with their recommendations for safe disposal of chemical waste.
- A high percentage of silver can be reclaimed/recycled at low/no cost.
- True, but following recommendations in this chapter will help, and there are now many waste disposal companies who will know local laws.
- People as well as commercial enterprises affect the environment, actions taken by individuals will collectively make a huge difference.
- Ask lab (or sewer authorities) if a lab has a sewer discharge permit.
- Patronize manufacturers and labs who recycle, and minimize packaging.
- Manufacturers and politicians are all extremely concerned about their image. Do not patronize/vote for the unenlightened!

Helping the Environment — continued

- Photographers must never intentionally harass or harm wildlife.
- Low-impact tourism will do less harm than logging, mining, ranching.
- Ask ecotourism companies how profits contribute to local economies
- Patronize ecotour companies that financially support causes and specific projects aiding local peoples, wildlife, and ecosystems.
- Support organizations that spend a high percentage of contributions on the cause, not on salaries, offices; ask to see financial statements.
- Become an activist if you wish. Contribute photographs to help causes.
- Photographs of unspoiled landscapes can help preserve wild areas.
- Pinpointing pollution with pictures can aid clean up campaigns.
- Photographs of threatened/endangered species can aid conservation.

Finding Out What You Want to Know from Manufacturers

The major photographic manufacturers listed will, if requested, send information on their record of compliance with local, state/provincial, and/or federal/national environmental regulations.

Ask smaller companies you patronize for similar information also.

For free or low-cost information on chemical processes and ingredients and for copies of MSHDS (Materials Safety Handling Data Sheets) plus literature on corporate environmental programs and policies, pamphlets on safe effluent/waste disposal procedures, recycling, and the like, contact:

3M Corp. Environmental: 612-733-1135. Ask for the program manager, environmental affairs. They will send a brochure on the 3M 3P program (Pollution Prevention Pays), a special report on the environment, and more.

3M markets Scotch films in the U.S. (which are manufactured by Ferrania in Italy and sold there as Ferraniacolor.) 3M also manufactures and markets photo chemicals in the U.S. and overseas.

Agfa. (Now, Agfa Division of Miles Laboratories.) 201-440-2500. Ask for Environmental Information. Agfa manufactures 85 percent of its film, photo chemicals, and paper in the U.S.; manufactures also in Germany, Belgium, and Argentina. (This company was formerly known as Agfa-Gevaert.) They will send a brochure on Agfa and the environment, and photography and the environment. (This last gives names, addresses and phone numbers of members of the Agfa Business Group in twenty-eight countries.)

Eastman Kodak: Environmental Support Program: 800-242-2424 (Kodak Information Center), 716-477-3194 (Environmental Hot Line.)

Kodak manufactures photographic products in the U.S. and Canada, Mexico, Australia, Brazil, France, Germany, India, and the U.K., and owns or has an interest in labs in the U.S. and most other countries.

Kodak has taken an industry lead in recycling film cassettes, spools, and paper cores; it now even accepts certain of other manufacturers' products for recycling. Kodak provides detailed advice to users of its products under an umbrella program called CIESS (Customer Imaging Environmental Support Services). To contact CIESS call 716-477-3194. To obtain a copy of the annual *Eastman Kodak Company Health, Safety and Environmental Report,* contact CIESS, or the Kodak Information Center.

Some free or low-cost publications from Kodak:

*Choices-Choosing the Right Silver-Recovery Method etc. J-21 $1.00
*Disposal and Treatment of Photographic Effluent (38p) J-55 $8.00.
Disposing of Minilab Effluent J-20 50¢
Effluent Sampling J-98P
Health, Safety and Environmental Expertise From Customer Imaging
 Environmental Support Services CIESS-01
*Kodak Index to Photographic Information L-1
*Kodak Professional Photographic Catalog L-9
*Safe Handling of Photographic Chemicals J-4 $1.00
(Especially useful.)*

Fuji. 800-473-3854 (ask for environmental specialist). To the best of my knowledge, all Fuji film is manufactured in Japan. Some chemicals and photographic papers are now manufactured in the U.S. Fuji will send free brochures on *Customer Assistance Programs, Green Care, Plant Operation* (in Japan), *Recycling Programs,* and more; they have videos on recycling, handling/disposal of hazardous waste, and more, available on free loan to labs. Videos may be purchased.

Ilford. 800-535-9205 (ask for environmental information). They will send a free technical brochure on the *Ilfochrome Classic Process* (formerly known as Cibachrome), respected for image permanence; plus literature on D*isposal of Photoprocessing Wastes and Disposal of Ilfochrome Process P30 and P30P Processing Effluent* (these are used with the Ilfochrome Classic print materials.) Ilford also prints position papers on *Photography and the Environment, Health, Safety and the Environment, and Environmental Aspects of Ilfochrome Processes.*

Ilford, originally a British company that still has extensive manufacturing facilities in the U.K. and Europe, is now a division of the multinational International Paper Company, an American corporation.

Polaroid. Customer service 800-353-5000. Polaroid manufactures its films, cameras, and chemicals in the U.S., Mexico, the Netherlands, and Scotland. A spokesperson told me that Polaroid has had an environmental policy since 1977, and since 1987 has published an annual report on the environment. The corporate communications office (617-577-3124) will send a copy, and marketing environmental programs, (617-577-3890 or 617-577-2007) will answer questions about post-consumer waste initiatives.

Safe Disposal of Photographic Chemical Wastes

The discharge of quantities of photographic (or other) chemicals into septic tanks can cause problems, because some inhibit bacterial activity, and the chemicals can reach the groundwater and even your neighbors' well. If your darkroom wastewater discharges into a septic tank, amateurs should collect, store, and evaporate used photo chemicals, and use the services of a low cost or free municipal hazardous-waste disposal program to dispose of the residue. (Professionals must use commercial services.)

It is illegal almost everywhere, as well as polluting, to discharge contaminated wastewater into streams, rivers, ponds, or lakes, or to dispose of hazardous waste anywhere other than to designated and regulated facilities.

Silver Recovery

At present, the most regulated water contaminant found in photographic processes used by the average amateur or small studio is silver. Silver is contained in used black-and-white fixer and color bleach fixers. Recycle silver inexpensively with a steel-wool cartridge filter device that exchanges silver in fixer with iron. Such "tailing" devices can be ordered through many professional photo dealers.

Kodak Chemical Recovery Cartridge, Junior Model II, 3-1/2 gallon size, is catalog # 166 9431; the Model II, 5 gallon size, is catalog # 173-4953. (For how these work see: Kodak publication J-9, *Silver Recovery with the Kodak Chemical Recovery Cartridge, Model II.*)

CPAC of Leicester, New York, make the IMG Trickle Tank device for photographers, doctors, dentists, and other small users of photographic chemicals. A unit currently costs about $90-100, depending on whether one or two steel-wool cartridges are required.

In the Kodak or CPAC system, cartridges last for months depending on volume passed through them. The residual silver sludge recovered should be rinsed and stored according to manufacturer's instructions. When four or five cartridges are full, they are sent to a refiner (get names from cartridge manufacturers); the price received for recovered silver may eventually offset the unit's cost. For the home or professional darkroom worker using tanks and/or trays for processing (not a processing machine), plumbing is not required.

Another option used by almost all commercial labs and large studios is to install an electrolytic silver-recovery device. These cost about $2,500 for small units. The silver recovered is very pure and can be sold; after silver recovery, some fixers can be reused. (Kodak offers an electrolytic Silver Recovery Unit, model ML, catalog number 142 0173.)

After silver removal from fixer or color bleach fix by either method (the acidity is also somewhat reduced), the discharge of small quantities of most black-and-white chemicals into sewers and eventually wastewater-treatment systems is currently considered not to be harmful, if the chemicals are flushed down the drain mixed with wash water (which should run moderately for several minutes after chemical disposal).

Dr. Bob Cappel, director of Kodak's Environmental, Health, and Safety Support Services, informed me that the company no longer recommends the use of limestone filters installed under home darkroom sinks. Twenty years ago, limestone helped to neutralize acidity of chemicals then in use. Today, after treatment through a silver-recovery device, Kodak says that spent chemicals mixed with wash water, give an effluent well within the recommended pH tolerances, and limestone filters will actually increase chemical traces in wastewater. The EPA recommendations for the acidity/alkalinity [pH] of chemicals discharged into wastewater treatment systems is currently a low of pH 5-1/2, a high of pH 10-1/2.

U.S. federal requirements for wastewater discharge into sewage treatment facilities are set out in the Federal Clean Water Act of 1977, and the Water Quality Act of 1987. Federal regulations do not cover discharges into groundwater. Local community standards are often stricter than federal EPA standards. Unfortunately it is often extremely difficult to find out what local standards or requirements are; you can try by calling the local sewage treatment or water authority.

A local permit may be required to discharge photo chemicals even from home darkrooms into wastewater treatment systems. Some communities now forbid this, requiring that chemicals should be first evaporated, then treated as hazardous waste. Information on waste disposal should be available at town, city, or county government offices. Hazardous-waste-disposal companies (see Yellow Pages) will have information.

Some potentially harmful chemicals must still be used in color printing and color-film developing (and are used in just about all industries, including papermaking and printing). Regulations (and common sense) may require that these chemicals be disposed of as hazardous waste. Many communities today (and the number of these is rising all the time) operate low-cost or free hazardous-waste-disposal services.

Keeping Water Clean

Never discharge harmful chemicals into a septic system, you could end up with a clogged septic tank (very nasty) contaminate groundwater, and even well-water supplies.

Of course, you should never discharge any chemicals into ponds, streams, rivers, estuaries, bays, or even the open ocean.

Individual photographers and labs in unregulated rural areas can call the Environmental Protection Agency at 800-424-9346 for information about federal standards for small/very small hazardous waste generators.

Copies of the Federal Clean Water Act of 1977, and the Water Quality Act of 1987 are available from U.S. Government Printing Office branches.

If you use color chemicals in your home or small professional darkroom, dispose of them safely. You will avoid harming your plumbing (acids eat copper pipes) and the local sewage-treatment systems or the water supply, and avoid a stiff fine if you are caught breaking the law.

Even if you live/work in a big city, you should still recover the silver in fixer before sending used chemicals down the drain.

Finally, it is no use making the U.S. photo industry a scapegoat. While it is a large user of chemicals, other industries consume more. The total runoff from pesticides and fertilizers used in agriculture, and golf course and garden maintenance today is probably much more dangerous to groundwater and surface water today than photographic processing effluents. We also have little knowledge of waste-management practices in Mexico, Japan, Europe, or other countries.

Finding Environmentally Friendly Commercial Labs

Most labs today are environmentally conscious (they have to be!), and almost all must follow strict laws regarding safety for employees and safe/legal disposal of hazardous/toxic chemical waste. Many labs now work with the largest photographic chemical manufacturers, and use the latest silver recovery systems, evaporate and dispose of hazardous chemical residue safely, use processes that eliminate or minimize pollution, and recycle plastic boxes and steel film cassettes.

It does seem as though a few photo processors are less strict in following the letter and spirit of the law than most. There is nothing to prevent you from asking labs, or any other entities, about methods and procedures they use. Ask a school or workshop about where they dispose of their chemical waste, and whether they practice recycling. You can withdraw your business from a lab that is not up to scratch. If you do so, tell them why. If enough clients respond that way, they will get the message. You can even report a lab polluting water supplies.

Free or Low-Cost Community Hazardous-Waste Disposal Programs

Low-cost or free disposal of harmful chemicals is available in many places to householders, including amateur photographers, who generate small amounts of chemical waste. These services are not available to commercial photography studios. (Kodak has an excellent program with Safety Kleen; contact Kodak CIESS if interested.)

Chemical Disposal By Commercial Hazardous Waste Services

If you use a commercial hazardous waste-collection/disposal service, follow their rules for evaporating or storing solutions separately before collection. (Chemicals can change composition and emit gasses when mixed together in unintended combinations.) Make sure that a disposal service is reputable; find out where they send the waste. It has been heard of for a few bad apples to dump it in the local landfill!

Recycling

The motto of the environmental movement is: Reduce,Reuse, Recycle. Sorting of household wastepaper, plastics, and metals is now required by most local governments, at least in theory, and many are now enforcing local ordnances strictly. Even if not yet required to do so, if you generate any quantity of photo waste (silver, chemicals, paper, film, or metal) use a recycling service. One I know of is Boston Recovery Company, which is licensed in the six New England states and New York State. They conform to the guidelines of the Commonwealth of Massachusetts, which are stricter than most federal standards. To contact them, see resources, at the end of the book. In other areas, check Yellow Pages, or ask local authorities for recommendations.

Read labels! Avoid using photo products or processes utilizing ingredients that are heavy pollutants. (Many classic processes used in fine-art photography fall into this category.) Chemicals are listed on packaging, (with cautions if they are known to be harmful). Ask manufacturers for MSDS (Materials Safety Data Sheets) on chemicals.

For Environmental and Your Own Health Reasons, Some Photo Ingredients to be Cautious about Are:

Formaldehyde (still used in some stabilizers, harmful vapors).

Silver (used in film and photographic paper, should be recycled).

Potassium ferrocyanide (used in some print bleachers, also reducers).

Metol (an ingredient in some older developers).

Hydroquinone (a solid used in many developers) can be harmful if inhaled, and can be a skin irritant. It is treatable in a sewage system, but can kill the bacteria in a septic tank if discharged in quantity.

Sodium and/or ammonium thiosulfate (hypo, a.k.a. fixer; used in color bleaches also).

Glacial acetic acid (concentrate, used in stop baths) Always dilute by adding acid to water, not vice versa.

Ammonium sulfite, potassium sulfite or sodium sulfite (used in some archival print washing processes).

Selenium toner (hazardous, not recommended for archival treatment of films and papers).

A Few Ways to Help the Domestic Environment

Use rechargeable batteries and battery packs wherever possible.

Avoid buying anything in spray cans using freon/butane propellants - these are harmful to the ozone layer. Pump bottles work quite well. (But freons are still used in some air conditioners and refrigerators.) Try to use air conditioning sparingly. Buy recycled paper and plastic products when possible.

For a contribution of $20, Greenpeace will send *Stepping Lightly on the Earth*, a guide that includes a list of biodegradable cleansers you can make at home, replacing chemical ones; some will save you money.

The Nature Photographer and the Larger Environment

All of us affect the global environment, so does travel, tourism, and even (we hope to a minimal extent) ecotourism. Nature and wildlife photographers should be in the lead in helping save our planet, including in my opinion, supporting political and social initiatives to stabilize population growth of our own species. We must also support enlarging existing national parks and wildlife preserves, and adding new ones worldwide. We must do whatever we can to preserve old-growth forests, rain forests, and wetlands, and save endangered species.

Many more people than ever before are traveling to natural and wilderness areas; huge numbers of people and too many large vehicles are

Two Important Books

The information about chemicals in this chapter was adapted from ***Over-exposure, Health Hazards in Photography*** by Susan D. Shaw and Monona Rossol, published by my publisher, Allworth Press, New York, in 1991.

Read this important book for much more information relating to chemical use, storage, handling, disposal, and related topics. For how to order a copy, see the last page of this book.

Coauthor Susan Shaw is a doctoral candidate in immunobiology at Columbia University. She is also a talented nature photographer who has exhibited her work, and the founder and president of MERI—the Marine Environmental Research Institute, of New York City and Brooklin, Maine (see resources, chapter 14.) She wrote the original version of *Overexposure* in 1983 at the request of The Friends of Photography, and Ansel Adams.

Coauthor of the revised, expanded edition, Monona Rossol is a chemist, artist, industrial hygienist, and lecturer, the founder and president of ACTS (Arts, Crafts and Theater Safety) of New York City.

This Land is Your Land, A Guide to America's Endangered Ecosystems, by Jon Naar and his son Alex J. Naar, is an important new book.

It has maps and charts, identifies environmental problems, and suggests solutions. It also lists just about every conservation and environmental group you can think of, plus U.S. government agencies, and some resources that you would never think of on your own. Read it.

Jon, who is a friend of mine, was for many years a New York professional photographer. He is now an international authority on solar energy, and spends much of his time lecturing and writing books on environmental concerns. Son Alex is a former professional fire fighter, an environmental activist, and amateur nature photographer, who is currently completing a JD in environmental law while working summers as a National Forest fire control specialist.

now by far the biggest problems in the most popular U.S. national parks.

More and more people want to go to the places where wildlife can still be seen in concentration. There are now crowds of nature-loving tourists in some remote places where a few years ago only the dedicated scientist or professional wildlife photographers would venture.

Are even serious nature or wildlife photographers, or people on well-organized study tours (along with "ecotourists" from all over the world), who travel to get close to, say, monkeys in Costa Rica or penguins in Antarctica, contributing to the destruction of habitats? Or does ecotourism preserve wildlife because tourists bring more money to local economies than hunting or poaching?

Should national parks and wildlife refuges limit the numbers admitted by requiring advance reservations at peak seasons? Should mobile homes equipped with air conditioners be allowed in national parks?

These are of course, all matters of personal conscience. I believe we should live life to the fullest and travel anywhere we can, but favor low-impact travel, camping especially, and don't think we need deluxe facilities or anything but a few basic food shops and information kiosks in wild places, including I may say, the U.S. national parks. Make your own decisions, and let politicians and others aware of them!

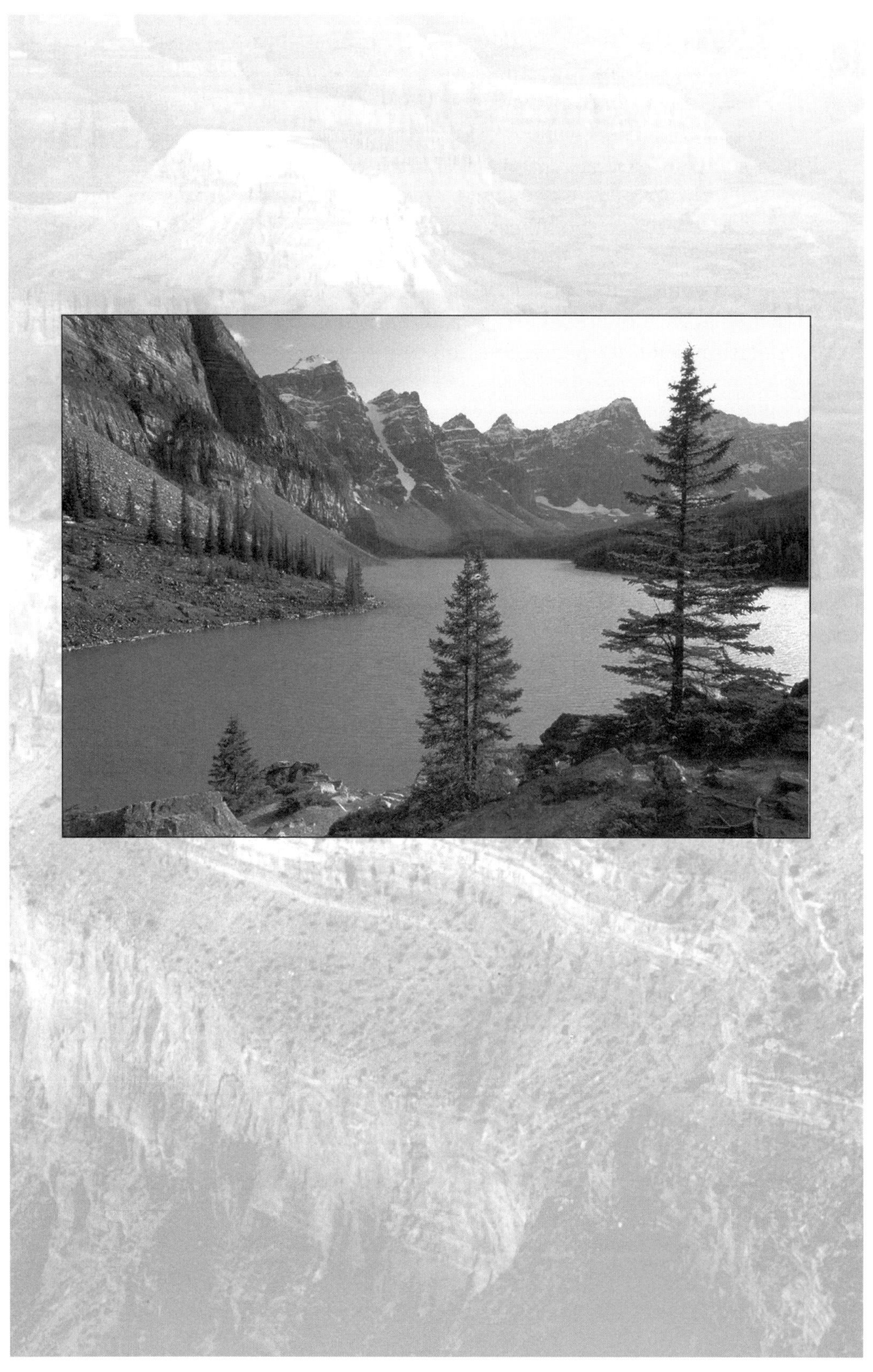

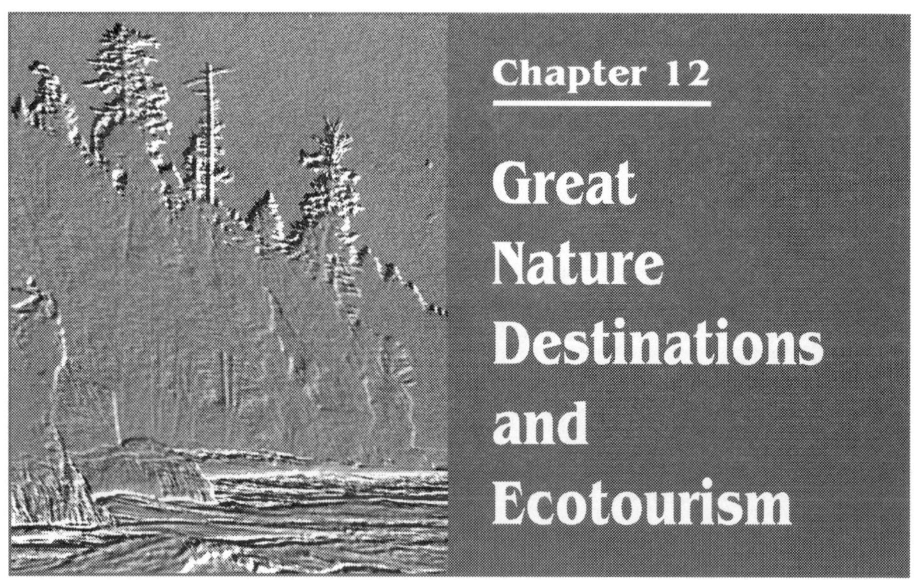

Great Nature Destinations and Ecotourism

There are now more and more affluent people willing to pay several thousand dollars (or pounds, francs, marks, or yen) for an escorted odyssey to the rain forest, the Antarctic, the wild rivers of Alaska and the Yukon, or the remote vastnesses of Tibet, Mongolia, or Siberia. Sometimes ecotourists travel to photograph specific species in their habitat —gorillas, tigers, grizzlies, and more. They have spawned a new industry (sometimes called green tourism). Where once only anthropologists, botanists, zoologists and the most professional nature photographers ventured, and where travel often involved torturous journeys, there are now comfortable hotels and lodges that cater to anyone who can pay the fare.

Whether ecotourism is helpful to the less wealthy of the local people, or to so-called "primitive" tribespeople, or harmful to fragile ecosystems and endangered wildlife is a hotly debated topic in some circles. Pro or con, ecotourism seems unstoppable and harmless compared to the poaching of big game, indiscriminate logging, or strip-mining and oil drilling in wilderness areas.

Of course the idea of killing animals to promote tourism, as in the postponed idea of shooting several thousand Alaskan wolves from the air, theoretically enlarging reindeer herds, is truly disgusting.

I asked Dr. Thomas E. Lovejoy, an internationally known expert on the Amazon rainforest, what he thought about the ecotours where visitors are hauled up on ropes to walk at the top of the forest canopy. He said that it was better for a tree to have a few tourists crawling around on it than for it to be cut down by logging companies!

I hope that you will want to travel, take tours, stay in hotels and lodges, or participate in photo workshops that are run by organizations that have at least some community participation. Before you sign up, ask for specifics on just what an ecotour company is giving back. This could be in the form of contributions to conservation causes, or by providing jobs that are not just menial to locals, or by training locals as nature guides, park rangers and the like.

Quite a few respected museums and conservation organizations now operate ecotrips: the Sierra Club has been doing this for 100 years!

The Ecotourism Society is an international nonprofit organization of ecotour companies (this has come to mean commercial operators of tours to underdeveloped countries and/or wilderness areas), conservation professionals, ecotourists, government officials, guides, lodge owners, park managers, students, and more. Members are pledged to adhere to practices that promote "responsible travel that conserves natural environments and sustains the well-being of local people." They publish a quarterly newsletter, and publish and market some interesting books, including, *Ecotourism, A Guide for Planners and Managers,* and *Ecotourism, the Uneasy Alliance.* For information on membership, and whether a tour company or traveling workshop you are interested in is a member, you can contact them. (See resources, at the end of the book.)

Buzzworm, the environmental magazine, has recently published an interesting book (on recycled paper) — *The Buzzworm Magazine Guide to Ecotravel.* I recommend this book, which describes 100 different wilderness trips and experiences, with prices, maps, and details about the operating companies. Some of the programs are expensive, but the book can also serve as inspiration for planning your own itinerary.

I have recently been on an ecotour of Ecuador, a country I had never previously visited. I went down there as a guest of SAETA airlines and the Metropolitan Touring Company of Quito. I photographed that city, as well as volcanoes, fine Indian markets, and the gateway route to the rain forest, and want to go back to the Ecuadorian mainland. The final, portion of the trip was to the Galapagos Islands. I took a week-long cruise on a very comfortable thirty-passenger cruise ship, the *Isabela II,* with an alumni group from an Ivy League college. Though it was not a photographic tour there was plenty of time to take pictures at the right times of day, early and late. The management, air and ship's crews, and excellent guides and naturalists were almost all Ecuadorian. (I do not know who the shareholders in these companies are.) I highly recommend Ecuador to any nature-lover. The Galapagos wildlife is still extraordinarily tame, and anyone who is sincerely interested in nature will enjoy the islands, with the caution that they are hot and humid. They are one of the world's great nature-photography destinations.

Independent Travel

For maximum photographic opportunities and flexibility, there is no question that it is best to travel independently to many places. F.I.T. (foreign independent travel) to East Africa for instance, means that you don't have to share a minibus with several others, nor will you be dependent on their schedules. But F.I.T. (for photography, with serious equipment, not at the student backpack level) is usually not cheap, and in remote places it is still neither especially comfortable, easy, or risk-free. But, as Frans Lanting quotes to the dedicated, "Where there's a will there's a way!"

To research independent travel, first read some of the guidebooks listed in the bibliography, and ask questions of anyone who knows anything about the place you want to go. Travel agents, I regret to say, are often not too well informed about off-the-beaten-track places.

The Photo Traveler Newsletter, a bimonthly published in Los Angeles, features wildlife, scenic, nature and travel destinations (mostly in the U.S. and Canada) and publishes periodic *Photo Opportunity Reports.* (See resources.)

Travel Advisories

Call the US State Department Citizens' Advisory Center at 202-647-5225 for information and warnings if planning travel to troubled areas. (Many other countries' governments have similar information.)

Some Great Nature Photography Destinations

Adirondack State Park, New York—For stunning landscapes, at all times of year. Winters extremely cold (Nathan Farb).

Baja California—For whale watching, seabirds. Independent travel to see whales is not easy to arrange (Heather Angel).

Baxter State Park, Maine—Go in Spring, summer, and fall. Moose, black bears, deer, much more (Dwight Kuhn).

Belize—Noted for national parks, fine zoo (Norman Owen Tomalin).

Blue Mounds State Park, Luverne, Minnesota — Classic prairie ecosystem; pronghorn, bison, uncrowded (Jim Brandenburg).

Bombay Hook, Delaware—Go in May, to see millions of migrating sanderlings, plovers, sandpipers, and more (Jake Rajs).

Bonaire—Excellent snorkelling in relatively shallow water, large flamingo reserve (Bob Krist, Phil and Edith Leonian).

Boundary Waters National Park (Minnesota and Ontario)—Moose, wolves, and much other wildlife lives in this famous, rather remote canoeing area, where George Shiras III made his pioneer wildlife studies. (Recommended by Jim Brandenburg who has a camp there, and by travel photographer Bob Krist.)

Canada—Most of the country is close to wildlife, there are thirty-nine national parks and reserves. Some have large populations of polar and grizzly bears, caribou, elk, moose, wolves. Top western parks are Banff, Jasper; Kootenay, and Waterton Lakes (by me.)

Cape May, New Jersey—One of the world's birding hot spots. In spring and fall, hundreds of thousands of migrants pass by. Brigantine National Wildlife Refuge is somewhat restrictive to photographers (Gerry Bailey, me).

Cayman Islands—Superb diving, many different sites (Robert Rattner).

Camargue, France—Great marshy delta of the Rhone River, a large national park with wild horses, important shorebird colonies (me).

Chincoteaugue National Wildlife Refuge, Virginia—Wild ponies, seabirds, shorebirds and ducks. Huge populations of migrants in April/May, September, October and November. Crowded in August for annual wild pony roundup. Thanksgiving week peak of bird migration. Assateague National Seashore is connected to it. (Pat Fisher, me.)

Costa Rica—Has excellent national parks, many diverse species, one of the first countries to recognise importance of ecotourism industry (Robert Rattner).

Custer State Park, South Dakota—Uncrowded, beautiful, large and small mammals, close to Badlands and Black Hills (me).

Denali National Park, Alaska — See Denali, but go to wilderness areas in midsummer if possible, the park road is crowded in July and August (Art Wolfe, Leonard Lee Rue III and Len Rue, Jr.).

Devil's Tower National Monument, Wyoming—Rather tame black-tailed prairie dogs in a huge colony at roadside (me).

Ding Darling Wildlife Refuge, Sanibel Island, Florida—Wonderful "hot spot" in January-February for wading birds like roseate spoonbills, herons, egrets. Avoid weekends (Pat Caulfield, Roger Tory Peterson).

Domenica — Lush rainforest in the Caribbean, phenomenal tropical vegetation a flowers, parrots and other birds, waterfalls (Robert Rattner).

Everglades National Park, Florida—Still beautiful December to May, though drainage has depleted amphibian population. Some damage from recent hurricanes still visible (Pat Caulfield).

Farne Islands, Northumberland, England—Great in June/July. Get up close to nesting kittiwakes, Atlantic puffins, cormorants, more (me).

Fort Niobara National Wildlife Refuge, Nebraska — Bison, prairie dogs, more (Jim Brandenburg, Pat Caulfield).

Hawk Mountain, Pennsylvania—On the predators' migration route, many species can be seen in April/May September/October, but they often soar very high. A 500mm lens is suggested as a minimum (Robert Rattner).

Galapagos Islands, Ecuador—Photograph seabirds, seals and sealions, giant tortoises and iguana up close. Visits to the Galapagos National Park are strictly controlled; groups must be accompanied by a parks naturalist. The majority of visitors take tours. Superb. (Nathan Farb, me).

Ile d'Ouessant, Brittany, France—Part of the Armorique National Park, rugged rocky shore, beautiful island of fisherfolk, many migrant seabirds in spring and fall; hostel for ornithologists (me).

Katmai Peninsula, Alaska—July-August. Large numbers of bears fishing for migrating salmon, to store up fat for their winter hibernation —one of the great sights in nature (Heather Angel, Art Wolfe, more).

Machias Seal Island (Maine/New Brunswick—both claim the spot) —Atlantic puffins, razorbills, murres, Artic terns and eiders breed here (May-September). Permanent blinds for photography are in place. Boat trips from Jonesport, Maine (me).

Madagascar—Many unique species (Heather Angel, Frans Lanting).

Monument Valley (Arizona-Utah)—Extraordinary landscapes. Avoid summer crowds (me).

Ngorongoro Crater, Tanzania — Go anytime, for lions, zebra, and more (Leonard Lee Rue III).

Olympic National Park, Washington State — Spring through fall, hike into wilderness beach areas especially (Art Wolfe).

Okavango Delta, Botswana—Superb (Frans Lanting).

Ouse Washes, Norfolk, England—About 6,000 Berwick's swans from Siberia stay in this great bird refuge from December - February (Heather Angel).

The Pantanal, Mateo Grosso Province, Brazil—June-November. Copybaras, alligators, exotic birds, butterflies, a great and seldom-photographed wildlife destination (Robert Rattner).

Ramble, Central Park, New York City—In winter, red tailed hawks are among birds you can get close to (NYC Audubon Society member Deborah Allen).

Red Sea near Eilat, Israel—Go spring, summer, fall to dive, also see migrating hawks in fall, and the Sinai desert, and any of the 48 nature reserves in Israel anytime (underwater photographer Zvi Livnat).

The Serengeti, Tanzania—The migration of zebra and wildebeeste is one of the great nature sights in the world (Leonard Lee Rue III, me, and a great many other photographers).

Trinidad—The Caroni Nature Reserve, plus flora and extensive bird life that reflects the fact that it is off the coast of Venezuela (Art Wolfe).

Yellowstone National Park, Wyoming and Montana — Fall is best time for elk rut, spring second best, for babies (Leonard Lee Rue III and Len Rue, Jr.).

Check state, provincial and national tourist offices, eco and photo-tour operators, for details on getting to these places.

My first book, *Travel Photography: A Complete Guide to How to Shoot and Sell,* contains a lot of information about the mechanics of travel. You don't have to take organized tours to most places.

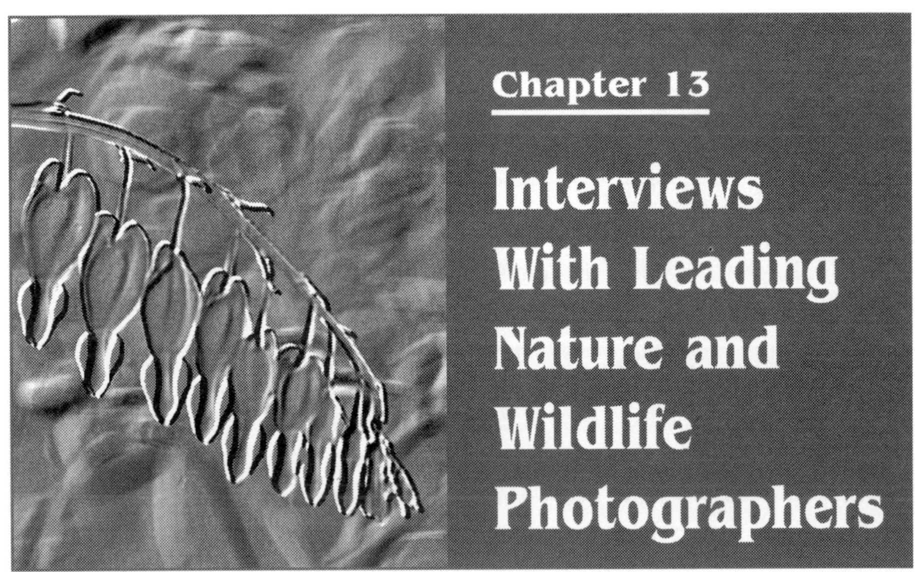

This is, if you like, the graduate school chapter of the book. A person can know all there is to know about the technical aspects of photography, be in excellent practice, own the finest cameras and longest and fastest lenses, and even know a great deal about the habits and habitats of their chosen subjects. These things alone, while they all contribute to making a good photographer, do not make a great one.

The photographers I have interviewed here are very different in style, but all alike in their love for their work. What makes the difference between good and great is not so much technique or even talent, but passion and commitment. Great photographers have a love for what they do, and a drive that overcomes the difficulties that arise during a career in any of the arts. The photographers I interviewed gloss over the labor they have expended, but all have worked until technique became second nature, leaving them free to think about what they want to express in their photographs, about nature, the wild things of the world, and even the future of our planet.

Just as watching great athletes is deceptive, because they make the hard look easy, these photographers make what they do seem rather simple. It is not. But if you read between the lines, think about what they say, and especially if you study and think about their pictures, your own work cannot help but benefit. I know mine has.

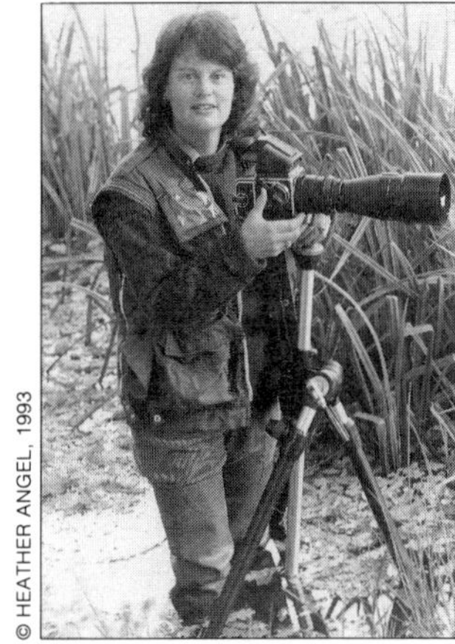

An Interview with

Heather Angel

Heather Angel, DSc., MSc., FBIPP, FRPS, is one of Britain's most admired and successful nature photographers and writers. Her pictures are published in magazines around the world. She has produced forty-one books to date, the latest to be published in the US is *A World of Plants, Treasures of the Royal Botanic Gardens at Kew.* She operates her own stock agency, Heather Angel/Biofotos, writes a weekly column for the *Amateur Photographer* magazine, and has served as president of the Royal Photographic Society. She lives with her husband and son in Surrey, where I interviewed her.

SM: Would you tell me what you do, exactly what you consider you are?

HA: Some people call me a nature photographer, but I suppose I prefer to be called a wildlife photographer, because I do much more mammals in the wild than plants — although I like photographing plants. I trained as a marine biologist. I photographed marine life exclusively for a while, but then got a label as a marine life photographer that persisted for years, although I was doing a lot of other things. But by writing books and covering anything from a blue whale down to a flea, I find I don't restrict myself.

SM: Did you have photographic as well as scientific training?

HA: I'm 100 percent self-taught. By trial and error. I didn't even own a camera until I was twenty-one. But when I was going to Norway on a scuba-diving expedition from Bristol University, I knew I needed to record the things we would come across. I got a perfect twenty-first birthday present from my father, an Exacta Varex IIA. It was a pretty good camera in the 1960s. I couldn't even load a roll of film at first. In Norway I shot lobsters and crabs and whatever else we found. Not, I'm sure, very well. I then got very keen and learned how to develop film and print. I did a lot of adult-education lecturing, and used my shots of marine life to illustrate my lectures.

In the late 1970s, early 1980s, I used to photograph a specific area, such as the Galapagos or the Seychelles or Mauritius or Madagascar. I set out to photograph life on isolated oceanic islands because they have a high proportion of endemic species found nowhere else. I came back with landscapes, habitat pictures, plants, animals, and birds that are special to those areas, which continue to sell, even though many people have been since. For the past few years I have enjoyed concentrating on a prime species, for instance going and sitting at Churchill on Hudson Bay, spending three weeks doing nothing but polar bears. That way you can get some lovely behavioral and action pictures. It's putting all your eggs into one basket, because if the weather's bad, or winter comes early and all the bears move out on the ice, you've lost the chance of bears for another year.

Taking photographs is the most relaxing part of my job, but it is hard work. It's exhilarating, sometimes totally draining of every ounce of energy in your body. When the excitement is there and the adrenaline is flowing, it's tremendous. When action starts, you don't have the luxury of time or thinking. Technique has to be totally instinctive, you can't fiddle around deciding what lens to use, what filter to put in. You simply have to get going and do it. Afterwards you think "Gosh, could I have done it better?" Sometimes it's all over in only a matter of seconds, there isn't time to think. A lot of what I photograph is planned minutely. But sometimes it's just seeing a lovely pattern or design that catches my eye. No amount of planning can cater for that.

SM: When did you start doing color?

HA: From the beginning. Color in nature is there for a purpose. It's not just to make a pretty picture. It's there because the animal needs it to survive, to lure a mate or deter a predator. Color is important for the editorial-type pictures that I do. If one is treating nature photography in a pictorial, fine-art way, color is not so important.

I'm trying to produce photographs that are striking and interesting to look at, but also tell a story that is saleable. I think authentic color is important. One could argue for hours about what is authentic color? Because no two people see it the same way. About 10 percent of the male population cannot distinguish red from green, for instance.

Inaccurate reproduction of color in nature occurs with films where the color is exaggerated and the greens are not true greens. Greens come in a very subtle range. They're not always bright, bright green. They can be yellow-green or something that doesn't quite leap out at you but is there. In the natural world, the greens have to be right.

I think the average person is perhaps not so perceptive about what true, natural color is. The brighter the better is their sort of attitude. Sadly. In many homes the color on the television set hasn't even been properly tuned. I've been a user of Kodachrome forever. To me, that's always been the wildlife- and nature-photographer's film. And so it has in America, until Velvia came along. My friends in the States now seem to have switched to Velvia. I think Velvia is brilliant for autumn colors. I've done a lot of fall colors in the States, and over here in Britain this year. I did some comparative shots with Kodachrome 25, my normal landscape film. I must say, the Velvia leaps off the light box.

SM: But if you're doing polar bears you still prefer the Kodachrome?

HA: Yes, I do. I definitely do. Kodachrome 200. The greens of Velvia I do not like. And I did a big test last May of bluebells; there is this enormous problem of trying to reproduce their authentic blue color, I don't know if you know why?

SM: No. But I've photographed gentians in the Alps; getting their blue color right is very difficult too.

HA: Bluebells and morning glories are even worse than gentians. Bluebells reflect some far resonant infrared wave lengths that we don't see, but which some color films are very sensitive to. If you plot the film sensitivity to the visual spectrum, then Kodacolor Gold negative film drops very markedly at the end of the visual spectrum. I don't use color negative film. But I did this bluebell experiment with everything I could lay my hands on, and I have to say that Kodak Gold is a 100 percent success with bluebells! I tried the various Kodachromes, but they are all a bit on the magenta side. I didn't like the result with Velvia. The best slide film for blue is Ektachrome 100 professional (EPN), but you can improve the color of other films by shooting on an overcast day with a 20CC blue filter, and avoid showing the leaves!

SM: Ektachrome Plus 100 (EPP), is very good for blue.

HA: I like EPP. I use it with my Hasselblad quite a lot.

(NOTE: The new Kodak Ektachrome Lumiere [Panther in the UK] professional slide films were not available when I did this interview.)

SM: I'd like to ask about close-ups, because you're a great expert.

HA: Certainly use a macro lens. If someone asks me, "I can afford only one macro lens, what should it be?" I answer, "Get the 105mm." I have three macros, 55mm, 105mm and 200mm. The one I use 99% of the time is the 105mm. It's a lovely, lovely lens. The reason the 105mm macro is better than the 55mm, although much more expensive, is that you've got a greater working distance. Particularly with dragonflies and butterflies, you don't have to approach the insect as close as with a 55mm macro to get the same size image. It's a very good lens for flowers also.

Some people say you mustn't use slow shutter speeds for insects. But even when something is moving, there's sometimes a lull. I'm one of those people who is prepared to take a risk and will use quite long exposures repeatedly. Not all the time, obviously.

I use, it's no secret, Nikon F4s. (I also use the Hasselblad system and have done for a long time.) I have various macro lenses for the Nikon. They only make autofocus ones now. I think autofocus is mostly extremely bad news. I want to demonstrate a problem to you about autofocus for close-ups (well, we need a little flower)...

SM: The autofocus lens may not focus where you want it to.

HA: Exactly. It's going to focus on the front edge of this dahlia here. You don't want to focus on the front. To get the maximum depth of field, you want to focus part of the way back and stop the lens down. But, from my experience of judging a lot of photographs for various societies, one is seeing - I'm sure this is because of autofocus - an increasing number of pictures that are not focused in the best possible position, not maximizing depth of field. And so many of close-up images now have the main point of interest placed bang in the center of the frame. Only the most expensive autofocus models have multiple sensors, most autofocus cameras have only one, in the center of the frame.

SM: Many autofocus cameras have a "focus lock" (or something like that) and then you can reframe.

HA: Yes, but very often people don't bother to learn how to do that. I don't think autofocus helps real creativity at all.

I think the other bad news about auto-everything is that people put a camera on auto mode and don't fully appreciate why their white flower, or white bird, or white polar bear on snow, came out gray, because the automatic camera isn't a miracle.

This is something I went through at my last class at Kew [The Royal Botanic Gardens, in London]. They were horticultural photographers mostly. I said, "Look, here's a magnificent peony. It's just off-white. Pinkish, almost powder-puff pink." Floppy, huge thing. Very special. I said, "You are going to have to be careful about how you meter that, because it's going to reflect bags [a lot] of light, it's going to give a false high reading, and you're going to have an underexposed picture. What I suggest you do is meter off the lawn beside it." A green lawn is not a bad average reading if you don't have an incident light meter.

SM: Or a gray card to meter off.

HA: That's fine for plants, but not for polar bears! But my student metered her way. What did I see a few hours later? A pinkish gray, underexposed flower. "How did you meter?", I asked her. "Oh well, off the flower." She just didn't have the courage to meter off the grass. She got it right the second try.

A technique that I've used a lot with extreme close-ups in the last two years is fill flash. Until recently I've been quite against using flash for plants because one sees so many horribly lit pictures where the exposure isn't balanced and the background dark. But with dedicated flashes that meter off the film plane, it couldn't be easier. I use a weak fill. It just lifts the flower out a bit, brings out a little more contrast and makes the picture more interesting. I've used the Nikon SB 24 flash so much in the last two years and I'm delighted with it. I underexpose the fill by a stop, or even more sometimes.

I also have a double flash bracket that I call a boomerang, which I used for doing insects years ago. I don't use it so much now. It was made by a friend from Australia. I use it with two little manual flashes, one as a main light, the second little flash covered with a layer of opaque white plastic sheet, for the fill in light.

SM: That outlines the insect's wings on both sides? Wouldn't you use a reflector?

HA: With insects there's often there's no time to set up a reflector. As well as the SB 24, I always carry a cheap tiny flash. Not to light up an animal in any way, but to get a catch-light [highlight] in the animal's eye. Nothing looks deader that a black bird with a black eye, or brown-eyed mammal with brown fur and no light in the eye. If it's a dull day, or the creature faces away from the sun, the flash highlights the eye, making it look alive, and that's good news.

SM: If you had to go away and there was only one treasured gadget or special lens you could take, what would it be?"

HA: My 200-400mm f/4 Nikon zoom lens! I wouldn't hesitate! It's the most amazing lens. I'm terrified of losing it, because Nikon don't make it now. In Africa, I hardly use anything else. I even use it for landscapes and plants sometimes.

SM: I have a 400mm lens, and an 80-200mm lens for mammals. I use them with

1.4X or 2X tele-extenders. Cheaper and lighter!

HA: The 80-200mm is a nice lens, but not long enough for birds. I would use that more on boats, for whales and so on. They come up fairly close. The 200-400mm zoom is ideal for precisely cropping groups of animals, or for portraits of individual animals.

Besides photographing, I write an enormous amount; a regular column for *Amateur Photographer* magazine here in Britain, and I've just finished my forty-first book. Normally I resist being commissioned (assigned) to do specific pictures because animals rarely behave to order. I prefer to select my own subjects, then I can write about pictures I want to be used. I find that by writing and researching, it gives me ideas for photography. Obviously, I write about my photographic experiences, things I've seen and done. But also, through writing, I'm suddenly thinking, "Ah, I haven't actually seen that or done that—I really ought to do that." Many nature photographers would argue writing is a waste of time. But I often write when I couldn't possibly photograph, when I'm sitting on location and nothing turns up. Also, I'm one of these dreadful people who writes on planes. And I write at the airport—I realized I was wasting time at airports that I could be using so much more productively. I write an enormous amount. When I come back I dictate what I have written, embellish it, probably add. Then it gets input, and printed out. Then I edit that version. I carry so much camera equipment, a laptop could be the straw that broke the camel's back.

SM: How much time a year do you actually spend behind the camera?

HA: Quite a lot. If you look at last year's schedule you will see I traveled about five months during the year in two- and three-week periods. That's the time I'm abroad (overseas). But, of course, I work in Britain, too. Then I have to come back and caption the pictures!

I don't want to photograph constantly. I prefer shorter trips, going, let's say, to East Africa for two weeks, which I do nearly every year. It isn't difficult to shoot material there. That's the easy part! The hard part is editing and captioning. That has to be done well in order to sell pictures. There's no point in shooting if when I'm away my staff can't find pictures and send them out to clients.

I'm doing a lot in the Arctic now. Working in very cold conditions is an enormous problem photographically. Batteries fail, film breaks, hands become so numb that you can't take a picture. This has happened to me on pack ice with harp seals. Your mind is telling you to take the picture, but your finger just doesn't move because it's so cold.

SM: When you go to Churchill for the polar bears, what equipment do you take?

HA: Okay, I take my British-made Benbo tripod. I've been using it for over twenty years, so it's second nature. I helped promote it. It is a unique and amazing tripod. I sometimes use the smaller Trekker model as a second tripod, or for supporting a flash. When I work in the cold, I use Tripads, the tripod leg protective covers, which are produced in America.

I've found that the F4 body doesn't conduct the cold as efficiently as the F3 did, so it works better in the cold. I've made a sort of a woolly coat for my F4s.

SM: Like a dog coat?

HA: Not knitted! Made of thermal fabric actually. When I first produced this there were hoots of derision from my professional colleagues. But as everybody else's cameras were going down like nine-pins, mine actually survived. Handwarmers are another thing for when it's very cold. I went to Japan in January this year, to Hokkaido, and never experienced such conditions. It was minus 25°C at dawn. We were doing cranes in the river. As I was breathing, frost was forming instantly on the outside of my camera. One camera body packed up; then the other. I had some of those chemical handwarmers. Do you know them?

SM: For hunters? I know a guy who gaffer-tapes them onto his cameras.

HA: I don't want to cook the film. So I put one under the camera battery area, inside my homemade thermal jacket. That does the trick.

What else do I use? I have a brolly, a very cheap, clear plastic umbrella, which I bought in a market in Japan years ago. It doesn't cut out the light even if you are doing close-ups. To protect the camera from snow and rain, you put the brolly up. Then I have a very natty thing that I'll show you - it's British made - called the Camera Mac. It covers the body of the camera and the lens.

SM: That's very British — a brolly and a Camera Mac!

HA: When I'm going to a tropical rain forest or a desert or whatever, I have a checklist for each habitat. It is important not to leave something that may be inexpensive but will make a world of difference. Bad news with electronic cameras is that if you get any water inside, they start shorting. So I take little towels in case my hands get wet.

I always take lots of spare batteries, of course. Very important.

SM: You don't use Nicads?

HA: I can't always guarantee if I'm changing countries that the charger will fit, so I use disposable batteries. In Britain, I use Nicads all the time. They're cheaper and you're not adding to the landfill dump. I totally approve of them. But, I have had problems with them in some places, and not been able to recharge.

SM: Do you advise people going to a tropical rain forest or somewhere very wet or humid, not to rely on electronic cameras?

HA: Coming back to what I said at the beginning, about working instinctively with animals, and not thinking about the camera. If you go back to a camera you're not familiar with, you're going to be slower and fumbling around a bit. But, for plants, I think it would be a very sensible insurance to have a mechanical camera in the rain forest.

SM: Do you work with camera trips, radio beams, setups like that?

HA: I have done. I've had cross light beams and done studio pictures of frogs leaping and field mice, and so on. Having done studio nature photography, I'm not bursting to do a lot more. What I like first and foremost is to be out in the field stalking wildlife.

SM: Can you define "stalking?"

HA: First, you don't stalk a polar bear on foot, you do that from a vehicle. Stalking is literally going out and walking when you're sure that you've got a good likelihood of finding deer or whatever else you're after. You must know which way the wind is blowing, because most animals' sense of smell is acute. You want their scent to be blowing towards you, rather than your scent to them.

I've stalked musk-ox in Greenland, for instance. Stalking is gradually weaving your way forward, normally zig-zagging from tree to tree. In Greenland, where there are no trees, it's from rock to rock or hollows in the ground. Sometimes you have to crawl on your belly. With practice, you'll soon know how to move very slowly so as not to disturb the animals. Inch your way forward.

Noisy, rustling clothing is very bad news. Unfortunately quite a lot of photographic waistcoats [vests] have Velcro fasteners on the pockets, and you can be spending ages creeping up to something, or even be in a jeep in Africa, and you hear the RIP of Velcro. Sometimes, an animal will just stop feeding, but at worst it will scarper (run off). So I don't use anything with Velcro fasteners at all. Anyone that does needs to make sure the fasteners are open, secured back, before they stalk.

Obviously, clothing color should be sensible to blend in when stalking, but I think that people who put "camo" tape on tripods and lenses etc., are going a bit overboard. Camouflage isn't quite that essential. Though camouflaging old nonblack camera bodies and tripods, silver and shining, reflecting light, is a good idea.

When waiting for action, always, always make sure that you have enough film in the camera. I know that sounds elementary. But when you are doing something like whales from a boat, you never know when the whale is going to come up, you only have a few seconds to photograph, then it's down again. I work like a photojournalist when I'm doing whales. That's one time I have to abandon my tripod. I use 100-300mm, and 80-200mm lenses for whales mostly. I always make sure both cameras are loaded with a fresh roll of film. When you are working flat out, you can easily go through a whole film [roll] of a whale just coming up and down, if you are lucky and focussed early on. So even if I have a half a dozen, or even eight or ten frames left, I will wind off (rewind) and put a in new roll of film. You can't afford to miss the next action.

I try and get animals doing things, showing action, because however beautiful a portrait may be, pictures of animals doing things are very much more interesting, more salable, than portraits. A lion roaring is good news. A cheetah running is good news. Those action pictures have been done lots of times before, but they still sell. The grizzlies standing at the top of the falls at Katmai, with their mouths open, waiting, and the salmon just about to leap in, you know. Any of those things, rather than animals just standing there, is an extra bonus.

With still photography you have to try to encapsulate an action within a single frame. But, and perhaps this is another important point, many people today rush out, finger on the motor drive, bang bang, bang all the film gone. I've been with people on either side of me, with bears, grizzlies and polar bears, and they just run through roll after roll. They hardly take their eye off the view finder. That to me isn't the way to use the motor drive. I think you need to be constantly looking up, because with a long lens, you're only looking at a very small portion of the scene. You need to be anticipating. If you look up, you can actually see a second bear coming into the picture area. I need to constantly take my eye away from the view finder because I might miss a potential confrontation of a bear coming in from one side if I hadn't anticipated it. I don't always have the motor on continuous drive. I very often have it on single frame mode.

If you think about it, if you are shooting at 1/500th of a second, at say, five frames a second, you've got 5/500ths only of the action. You are missing 495/500ths! Some people think a motor drive is the answer to everything. But, if there's interaction, heads are moving, and one head blocks another head, that's a wasted shot. I've very often decided, "Right. I'm just going to wait for that peak moment," and get that one shot. You can always dupe up a really good shot. With fairly slow action, a continuous motor drive is great, because you can actually see the progression of something moving. So there we are!

SM: Thank you so much.

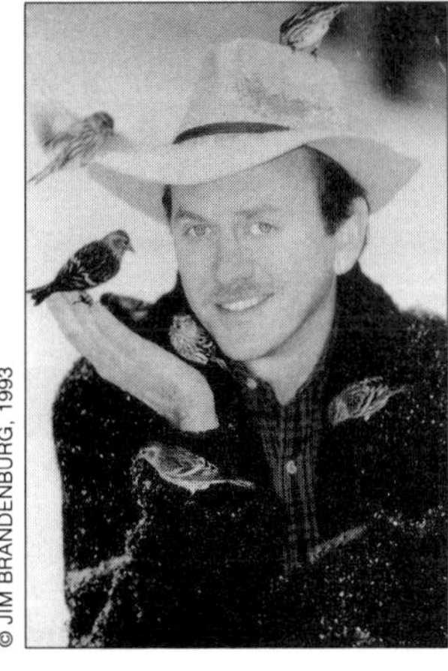

An Interview with

Jim Brandenburg

Jim Brandenburg, one of the world's foremost nature photographers, studied art, worked for a local newspaper, and was a contract photographer for the *National Geographic* for about twelve years. He has worked in Namibia, Nepal, and the North Pole among other remote places; his picture stories have appeared around the world. His acclaimed book, *White Wolf, Living With an Arctic Legend,* photographed over two long summers in remote Ellesemere Island, in Canada's Northwest Territories, has been an international bestseller. His awards include: National Press Photographers' Association Magazine Photographer of the Year (twice), BBC International Wildlife Photographer of the Year (1988) and United Nations Environmental Programme World Achievement Award (1991). Jim donates his time and work to numerous environmental organizations. His latest book, *Brother Wolf,* is about the gray wolves of Minnesota. I interviewed him in his studio outside Minneapolis.

SM: Thank you for letting me come. Can you tell me about your beginnings?

JB: I grew up in the prairies in the southern half of Minnesota, they are quite flat, quite featureless. There used of course to be great herds of bison, now it's cornfields.

SM: This was the land where the deer and the buffalo roamed.

JB: This is the classic prairie, one of the greatest ecosystems ever destroyed. It was the largest ecosystem in North America, and now it's virtually all gone. It's all plowed up. It grows wonderful cornfields, but that just creates more food to encourage more people to have babies... The population situation is a very delicate subject. I think there are feelings now, by far-forward-thinking scientists, that it might have been better if we had left the prairie be and harvested the bison.

SM: Is it possible the prairies could ever come back?

JB: The natural evolution of things is something you can't fake, or encourage, or accelerate. Nature's always going to be okay in my mind. We've been here for a very short time, us people. The dinosaurs came and went without us, not because of us; and we'll probably come and go, for other reasons. We're just another form of nature. I guess if there ever really was a sin, it's man causing extinctions with no remorse, or no ability to correct it. But you can bring some of these ecosystems back a little bit, correct some things. There are some people in the Nature Conservancy, here in Minnesota, who have done some remarkable acquisitions. Through burning and long-term thinking, in a hundred years, some of these prairies could approach what they once were. I think one of my fantasies is that 200 years from now, this land will all be back the way the way it was; there'll be some foundations, some stone work that people will dig through, if there are any people...

SM: I've read about places in the Dakotas that have been virtually abandoned because life is too harsh, and small farms don't make it...

JB: Yes. But, unfortunately, once you disturb this very delicate ecosystem of the prairie—it's taken 10,000 years to evolve since the glaciers scraped it clean—to start over again isn't easy.

SM: Only 10,000 years? That's not very long at all.

JB: The glaciers were here 10,000 years ago. We're so impatient, we think in terms of one lifetime, we think of what is possible, what did we destroy in terms of our short-term memory and experience? In the big, big, geologic picture, I'm not so worried. When you believe in nature as much as I do, you know that man is a flyspeck in the universe.

But nature is going to rule all. I think in the next ten, fifteen, twenty years, there'll be a major catastrophe, and all of a sudden, this mockery of environmentalism, "It's the economy that matters stupid," is going to be insignificant, because if we don't have a home to live on, whether it's the earth, or the air, or the water, what does the economy matter. We are losing the natural connection. I'm waiting for the day when man will be taught the lesson. It's almost a Biblical thing.

SM: Are you religious?

JB: No. I think I'm very spiritual, it all revolves around nature...

SM: Like the Native Americans?

JB: More like my ancestors, the Vikings. They had belief systems in their own deities and nature.

SM: You had this spiritual connection with nature, and you grew up in this vast, empty, rather austere part of the country, with a very severe climate. What did you study? How did you start in photography? You told me you worked in newspapers. Can you give me the five-minute bio?...

JB: I was interested in nature first, and that's the driving force. I wasn't interested in photography—just like I'm not interested in computers now though I work with them—but in odd ways both now bring me closer to nature. Starts out, I was a hunter; all young boys down in southern Minnesota grow up playing basketball and shooting pheasants, and fox, and rabbits. My dad was a hunter, all my uncles, all my friends. I hunted and thought that was natural, till I got to the age of sixteen or seventeen, and thought, killing animals is kind of a strange thing. So I got a camera and took pictures. Needed an excuse. Back then, you just couldn't go birdwatching, couldn't just go out and enjoy nature with binoculars, or go hiking, where I came from. One reason I like to go back to England is, you have a long tradition there of just enjoying nature for the joy of it. We are just starting to dwell on that now in America. The bird thing. Roger Tory Peterson had a big effect on that. I started using a camera as an excuse to be close to nature, because somewhere inside of me, maybe it's an old northern European work ethic, something said you couldn't waste the day looking at nature, you had to do something with it, shoot it with a gun, or take a picture of it! So the camera was used as a device to just be out there...

I started with amateur cameras, and then moved to my first interchangeable-lens body, it was an old J3 Yashica. I bought a 300mm lens for it. I kind of threw the normal lens away, didn't ever use it. So I always had the 300mm lens on the camera, it was my normal lens. So I started thinking in long-lens terms. To this day, when I look across the scenery, I think in telephoto terms. My next lens was a wide-angle; a 24mm I think, or maybe a 28mm, so I had the extreme wide, and the extreme long. I worked with those two lenses for years as an amateur.

I was very reclusive, a very shy boy, didn't talk to many people, didn't get involved, wasn't interested in education, or higher education. Finally the Vietnam war came, it was quite controversial to some, and I decided I'd better get into college, or I'd be drafted. I went to junior college, studied fine art, then got a job on a newspaper called the *Worthington Daily Globe* in southern Minnesota. Lucky for me. It was one of the most remarkable work experiences I've ever had. I had a publisher that believed in quality, was very supportive, let me shoot nature stories and articles for the newspaper, let me separate the color, lay out the pictures, write the story, even deliver the papers! I went straight from the *Worthington Daily Globe* to the *National Geographic,* without missing a beat! It's still published, but it's changed somewhat. The original publishers aren't there now. Mr. Jim Vance was crucial in my career, insisting upon the finest quality in everything. As I said, I did a stint of school, at the University of Minnesota. I've never taken a photography course.

SM: You studied fine art?

JB: Yes, art history also. The rest of it, to me, was being around good people, seeking out people that I really respected. If I have any advice for young people, any age people that want to get started, seek out the very best photographers you can find, and spend as much time as you can with them. Unfortunately, things have changed. Today that's not very easy. I get many requests from people, so many requests, that I just cannot physically find the time to do it. One of the first people that I sought out in my career was Ernst Haas, who was to me a god.

SM: Frans Lanting said the same thing to me. One of my favorite books is *The Creation.*

JB: So is mine.

SM: So is Frans Lanting's.

JB: Haas was a pioneer. Pioneer isn't the right word. He was a visionary. I called him up. You know how hard it is for me to be in New York City. Twenty years ago it was even more difficult! I found out where he lived from friends, went to his neighborhood, found a pay phone, called him. Instantly: "Come on up. No problem." I'll never forget it. And his eloquence, his vision, his intellect, his sensitivity. It's easy to look at his work now, the young people might see it and say, well, you know, I could do that. But would they have done it back then? When color photography was just beginning and a literal translation was always the norm, and so tempting. Get it as literal as possible was the standard. Haas was a translator, he was just great. Other people that have influenced me? Andrew Wyeth had an incredible influence on my life.

SM: I notice you have one of his prints hanging up. *Christina's World.*

JB: Something about his point of view of color, and his point of view of starkness, reminds me of how I grew up on the prairie. You'll see Andrew Wyeth in my work more than you'll see Ernst Haas. If you'll look through this—my book *Minnesota*—I've never said this before, you'll see a brooding Andrew Wyeth quality, kind of a heavy mood. I'm not talking directly about Ernst Haas or Andrew Wyeth, but my work has kind of a slightly detached, once removed, cool look. Not a real up-front quality. Painterly maybe. You don't think of my work in this way perhaps.

SM: This book is called...

JB: *Minnesota, Images of Home.* For obvious reasons it's kind of a limited edition book...It isn't found on the open market.

SM: It's a lovely book. I've never seen your black and white before.

JB: I'm proud of this, very proud of it. A little bit of that shows up in this other book, which I'm also extremely proud of.

SM: This is *White Wolf.* It's one of the most beautiful books ever done, I think. Haunting. It makes me want to cry sometimes.

JB: That's a nice compliment. There's something about photography, that we often lose track of, it's the very elusive ability that photography has, to be like painting, or poetry, or sculpture. People abuse photography terribly, it's hard to articulate. I don't often talk about it. People try to utilize photography's obvious... Make the literal translation, they turn off some of their emotional buttons... Get the exposure right, get the composition right, and frame it.

I don't know what I do, but I like to think that I get lost, in the emotion of it. Experience kind of allows technique to be used without thinking about it, and to use the lens more like a brush, and take some chances, make some mistakes, and go back on the editing table, and be surprised. Photography is the easiest medium to take chances with, yet it's oftentimes the one that's done (chanced) the least. Painters will take chances with painting, weeks they'll experiment. Photographers don't. I'm mostly speaking of not total professionals — someone like Jay Maisel probably takes a lot of chances — I'm trying to think of people in our profession that you would know, that go out and stretch it. Jay's a remarkable guy. Incredible. But photography is so often abused. It's so easy to be lazy with a camera. Many photographers that I see today that are quite successful, oftentimes are lazy creators, and obsessed workaholics. They know how to get their files in order and how to talk to the right people... Make the sale, go to the editors, make the deal, finesse everything, and there's something missing. You look at the work, and it's the soul that's missing. I think it's because it is deceptively, tantalizingly easy to make sellable photography, and forget about the essence. Of the pain...

SM: I was going to say, the correct word for the feeling in some of your pictures is, pain. Some of the pictures have real pain in them.

JB: Well, they do have pain, and that pain was real. It's twenty years of beckoning up a wolf situation. I was trying to tell a wolf story for twenty years before I came onto this scene. Planning in my head, almost a spiritual prayer, a wish. Someday it's going to happen. I lucked upon the scene. I was up doing a *National Geographic* story on a North Pole expedition. I heard someone on television yesterday—I do watch a little television—talk about what luck is. It's preparation meeting opportunity. Some people have accused me of being so incredibly lucky, stumbling upon this pack of wolves. But I had some major preparation for that. Not just biology, but the vision. Paint a picture, and some day you'll find a canvas to walk into.

People call me a dreamer, my boyhood teachers would give reports to my parents: "He's always daydreaming, he's always looking out the window, he's not going to amount to anything, he's not focused." I've got a son Anthony, he's just like me. I'm so hard on him. I say "Tony, you've got to get focused." Then I remind myself. Today, all the advice I would like to give, I'm afraid to give, because I'm afraid it would create a failure. This culture doesn't have enough patience to allow a personality to develop like I did. Today you've almost got to come out of school running, and be successful, otherwise the economy and expectations will beat you down. Today there are so many people out there trying to be photographers. The *National Geographic* for one place, can't cope with the deluge.

SM: Where do people get the idea that photography is an easy profession?

JB: It's something that's locked in our cultural psyche. I continually make apologies for being a photographer. The books that I do, the writing part is what I'm most proud of. My next one, *Brother Wolf* especially; I'm incredibly proud of the writing. More than the photography.

SM: *White Wolf* has been an enormous success. The book has not only sold a lot of copies, it's made people aware of wolves as they never have been before, as beautiful and lovely, not scary and terrifying. But, you were talking earlier about Vikings and our brief history on the earth. We are still animals underneath; think of us living in a little circle, in a large wilderness. It's very dark at night, and these howling animals are not too far away... Fear of wolves is embedded very deep in the human psyche... How did you get to be not "feared" of wolves?

JB: That's what my next book is about. That fear is imaginary. I've been around wolves for twenty years. They are not at all what most of us think of them as.

SM: They postponed shooting all those wolves in Alaska...

JB: That may still happen.

SM: People fear wolves. I grew up with the European legends, the Big Bad Wolf and so on.

JB: So did we. The European wolf has been a little different, the European wolf was more aggressive. Our culture has all the European legends.

Sometimes I try to reflect on what creates a certain ability. I came from a farming family, not a poor family, but with no advantages. I look at people I know in photography today, and that's not true of many of them. They've come from wealthy families where they have traveled as young kids with cameras. They take this portfolio at age eighteen, or twenty, or twenty-four. Back twenty years ago, they went to the *Geographic,* with an impressive array of places. From the Great Wall to the Kremlin. They were kind of dazzled, some of these editors. Often times these young privileged kids were very talented and very bright. There was no place like that for me. I had to do it the hard way. That's why I think that pain shows, the emotion shows, in my work.

SM: Nobody told me, when I started, that many photographers are quite well-to-do.

JB: They are!

SM: Not Leonard Lee Rue. He was a farmer boy from Blairstown, New Jersey. He earned his living as a wilderness guide, for seventeen years.

JB: It shows. Lenny Rue's a real, roll-up your sleeves, go to work photographer.

SM: My parents didn't have money. When I was starting out, photography, commercial photography, was a good way for an artist-type-person to make a living. But when I was talking about pain, I didn't mean the pain of not much money, or background, I wasn't even thinking of waiting around in the cold. I was thinking of the pain in the soul.

JB: It's the Joseph Campbell kind of pain. You have to look at his work. He was a great philosopher, that died a couple of years ago. PBS did a series of six shows on him. Myths, culture, things like that. But, physical pain can't help but dent the soul a little bit too. It's a lonely life I often had. But I loved the pain. The pain brings soul.

White Wolf, the book and the film, was a life-changing experience. It's almost as if it was a spiritually guided thing. I can't believe the journey that I was prepared to do; how I seized upon it somehow, it was almost as though there was someone watching me, on my shoulder. The *White Wolf* did have an effect I guess, and maybe that's really the message. Having a strong point of view as a photographer, and the rest will come easy. Follow your bliss—that's the old Joseph Campbell saying—follow your bliss, and the rest will come right along.

SM: Thank you. I feel as though I've reached the summit of a mountain.

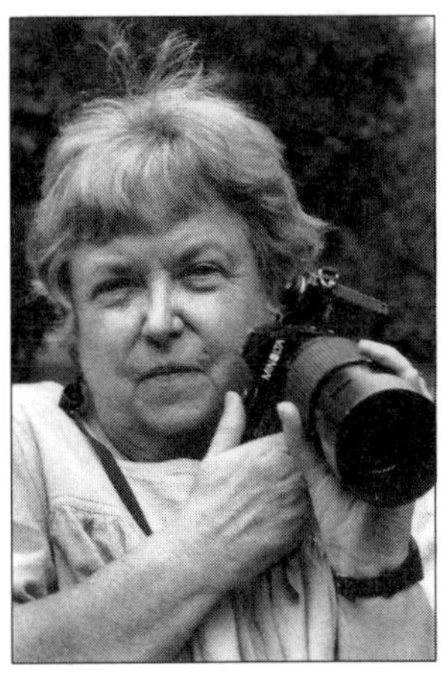

An Interview with

Patricia Caulfield

Patricia Caulfield is a native of Iowa and studied history in college. She has been photographing nature since the 1960s, and is especially known for her work in Florida. The Sierra Club published her book *Everglades*, and she has two beautifully illustrated how-to books: *Photographing Wildlife,* and *Landscape Photography,* currently in print.

Pat is a friend; I interviewed her in New York.

SM: I know that you learned photography on television. That is rare!

PC: Beaumont Newhall, the photographic historian, was doing a series about photography on TV in Rochester, New York. He needed a college-age person to teach, and there I was. I went into nature photography because I have been concerned about the future of the planet for ever. I was an environmentalist before there was a movement!

SM: You are so well known for your Everglades work. Can you talk about frogs, snakes, and alligators?

PC: There certainly are people who are better animal handlers than I. I have tended to work with another person. Most of my pictures of "herps" [reptiles and amphibians] are of animals that have been captured for study or photography, by someone who knows what they are doing. Sometimes you work with scientists, sometimes you pay a local person to catch snakes for you, for pictures. But you can't order a species, they catch what they catch. The handler puts the animal down in a good spot, where you are all ready and foussed, and you photograph it. He can also discourage it from slithering or jumping away before you are done. Snakes are later released unharmed back where they came from. This is true of most snake pictures you see anywhere. It's much safer to use someone who knows which snake is which. Some are poisonous. Frog pictures are done that way sometimes too, but obviously not alligators. Alligators you take where you find them. There are plenty of alligators within the Everglades National Park.

With the Everglades, it is a seasonal thing. You can't go down there in midsummer and expect to find a lot of wildlife. Summer is the wet season, the water covers everything, and all the animals are dispersed.

What you should do is go down in the winter, when the water has fallen, usually leaving standing water in alligator holes.

SM: The season for the Everglades is roughly when?

PC: I would say January to May. It starts to rain in June, then it goes into the hurricane season, and rains maybe into November.

SM: So you go down and stay somewhere in the park, or somewhere near the park for months, in a little motel room?

PC: Yes. Sometimes I camp. I have a van that I can sleep in. Now I also know people I can stay with.

SM: I suppose they help you find animals?

PC: Some of the people I knew who helped when I first went down there, in 1964 believe it or not, have gone on into the great swamp! But you meet new people.

SM: So you can't just go to Florida on your own, and expect to get great pictures?

PC: I think you can. You can go to Florida for a weekend with a car, at the right season, in the right place, and get great pictures. The two places to go for nature pictures are Everglades National Park and Sanibel Island.

SM: I've heard that the Ding Darling Refuge on Sanibel is a great place to photograph, but also that sometimes there's a solid wall of fifty people, lined up with the longest telephoto lenses, all taking pictures!

PC: It's not a wilderness experience. You are lined up elbow to elbow with a lot of photographers, at both the the Ding Darling, where you can get roseate spoonbills, American egrets, and coots, and in Everglades National Park, on the best trails like the Anhinga Trail.

SM: What about small animals? You are very good at small animals.

PC: One thing I want to say about photographing small animals. I don't set up every picture; I do often find animals in the wild. But, if you do find an animal, and are working alone and you approach it, the animal will probably just turn around and go in the other direction. It's very useful to have someone else with you to sort of direct, herd, shoo the animal in your direction, get it to face the camera somehow. Otherwise you will get a bunch of pictures of tails!

SM: Tails are not the best views of anything! Can you talk about handling snakes? I would be scared because I don't know which snake is which.

PC: Every snake that you meet is not going to bite you. But I think you have to be very careful with all snakes, not only because of protecting yourself, but because of protecting the snake, they are somewhat fragile. I do not handle poisonous snakes. I let someone else do that, I am afraid of being bitten. Everyone I know who has been bitten by a poisonous snake has been handling it.

SM: What about predatory birds? There's this wonderful flash picture in your book, of a barred owl flying towards you at night, with huge red eyes, in the Everglades. You say in the book that you lured him.

PC: He thought someone was entering his territory. There are ways to lure birds and mammals to be photographed. Most of the lures for mammals are scent lures. Most of the lures for birds are auditory lures. There are two ways to lure predatory birds. You can frequently lure them with a call of their own species, which is what I was playing when attracting that owl. Sometimes you can attract them with calls of small song birds.

SM: Dinner! I have heard that for predatory birds, you can also find a dead creature in the road, road kill, and put that somewhere as a bait.

PC: That's a scent lure. You can also buy scent lures in hunting stores.

SM: You have pictures of possums, and fox squirrels, and other little cuties. Until comparatively recently, I thought that photographers just went into the woods and found those things by waiting patiently, but it isn't so. Those cute animals on the calendars and greeting cards are often photographed in rehab [rehabilitation] centers, or are models bred specially for still or film or TV work.

PC: I have found a lot of little creatures in the woods, and it's rare. I think that like you, I was somewhat naive. When I started doing this, I found those species because I didn't know any better. I didn't realize that so many of those pictures are set up, that people work with captive animals. I have done relatively little of that. Some people have done enormous amounts of it. The pictures in my books are all of things that I found in the wild, except in a few cases like the endangered Florida panther, which as it says in the book was a captive in a place they are trying to breed them; it is almost impossible to find those in the wild.

SM: These pictures of a baby opossum, lit with flash, were they done in a studio, in an aquarium-type situation?

PC: No, they were done where I found them. I was walking around at night, with a flash on a bracket, seeing what I could find.

SM: In the backwoods of the Everglades, off the trails, did you use a guide to help you find things, find the trails, to track animals?

PC: I went with someone who knew their way around really well.

SM: On tracking. There are certain skills I don't have, never will have. Like most photographers, I hire people with skills if needed. I asked Leonard Lee Rue III if hiring a country person to help you track and find wildlife would be useful. He said, "Absolutely." Do you agree?

PC: Yes. I don't have tracking skills. Before I became a nature photographer, I was a magazine editor in New York City. Even as a child, when I was outdoor oriented, I didn't know how to track anything.

SM: When you're looking for cute critters at night, what do you carry?

PC: One thing I use is a headlamp like a miner's lamp, instead of a flashlight in my hand. It frees your hands, doesn't seem to get in the way of the camera. I wear it up high; they come with a strap. They are made for plumbers, electricians, people who have to hold tools and see into dark corners. You can get them in hardware stores. I also carry a flash on a bracket, as well as my camera of course.

When I first went to the Everglades there were a lot of snakes, you had to have light at night, and very carefully watch where you put your feet. Now there are far fewer snakes or amphibians, sadly. Drainage and water manipulation have greatly reduced the numbers.

SM: Do you wear snake boots?

PC: No, I never have. I wear sneakers. But I'm careful!

SM: Thank you for being so very specific. I expected no less!

An Interview with

Nathan Farb

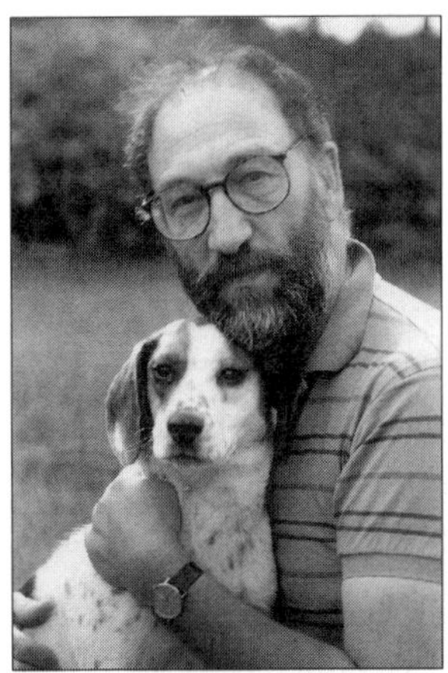

Nathan Farb was a psychology major in college, and has published nine books of photographs to date, including *The Russians*, *The Adirondacks*, and *Galapagos*. He specializes in large format landscape, and has shot assignments for the *New York Times Magazine*, *Life*, and *Condé Nast Traveler*, the National Audubon Society and New York State. His work is in the permanent collections of the Metropolitan Museum of Art, the Museum of Modern Art, and the International Center for Photography, New York; the Bibliotheque National, Paris; the Rheinisches Landesmuseum, Bonn, and numerous corporations including Polaroid. He has had nineteen one-man shows in the U.S. and abroad, is represented by four galleries, and maintains his own gallery at his studio in Jay, New York. He is a Trustees for the Lake Placid, New York, Center for the Arts. I interviewed Nathan at his temporary home in Washington, D.C.

SM: I wanted to talk to a fine-art oriented, large-format landscape photographer. I'll begin with asking the usual, how did you get started?

NF: I was born in Oklahoma. My mother's family was from Arkansas. That's not why I'm living in Washington at present. I'm here to be with my daughter, while she recovers from a bad auto accident. She goes to Gallaudet (university for deaf people). I studied psychology in college.

When I was twenty-five, my aunt, who was a professional, taught me photography. She had a little portrait studio, in Fair Lawn, New Jersey, and worked for a local newspaper. Her name was Rae Feldman. One day I expressed interest and she lent me a Rollieflex, told me the correlation between shutter speeds and f/stops, sent me out to take a roll of black-and-white in the park. Then she showed me to how to develop negatives and make prints. When she saw the first pictures she kidded me "Nathan, you're a regular Stieglitz." Positive reinforcement! She later gave me an old 4-by-5-inch camera. I didn't use it then, but my fantasy was that as I got older, more deliberate, I could do that kind of work.

When I first started photographing, I had a fairly good job on a newspaper. I tried my hand at writing, had also tried my hand at painting. I always thought that photography might be the thing, from early childhood, but never had the guts, or moxy, or whatever, to go ahead and jump into it. I feel like I found the right medium, when I was twenty-five. I think of photography as a wonderful cross between the painting aesthetic and the writing, with the ability to communicate. Within a year or so, I was making photographs that I liked a lot, and was occasionally able to sell. I had some feeling that I was doing the right thing for myself, and have certain respect for myself as an artist. It wasn't until I was about forty, forty-one, that I bought an 8-by-10-inch view camera.

SM: Did you do something else on the side, until you were forty?

NF: No, not at all. The first year or so that I photographed, I was on the newspaper, and all of my spare time I was going out and shooting. sometimes they used one of my pictures, but they would never have dreamed of hiring me as a photographer. I thought I was Cartier-Bresson. I was trying to capture the moment. I was living in the New York City on the Lower East Side, which became the East Village. There was still a strong feeling of the Eastern European emigrations, my work was journalistic, perhaps too a bit like the nineteenth-century people who documented the Lower East Side. Some of my pictures resembled Lewis Hine.

SM: So you did people?

NF: For the first fifteen years, my pictures were entirely on what I would call the human condition, including my own family. My daughter, who is twenty-one now, was born prematurely, and had some terrible problems. She has cerebral palsy, and is deaf. I was photographing that, the effect on the family, I was already in my thirties then. I became a great fan of Diane Arbus, I was very influenced by her. Also by August Sander.

I first went to the Soviet Union, to Novosibirsk, a city in Siberia, in 1977. I was looking for the mid-Soviet city, more for the average Russian than the Muscovite or Leningrad person. My own father was a Russian Jew, but I never knew him. He died before I was born. I only connected with his past in the most dim way. My book *The Russians* was much more about trying to find out who these people were, why we were at each others' throats so much. Really the Cain and Abel question, why do people have such strong aversion to each other? They often share some quite remarkable similarities. I had much more personal connection with Romania than Russia from my mother's side of the family. My maternal grandmother was from Romania.

I went to Romania after the Russian book was published, working for the USIA as part of a cultural exchange. I used August Sander as a sort of general construct, I tried to do types. When I was in Romania, I had never used strobes, never used the view camera. That's where I started using them. I worked in the countryside of Romania, in Moldavia. Very beautiful, very much like the Adirondacks. Lots of little rivers.

SM: When did you begin to concentrate on nature, the Adirondacks?

NF: I grew up in the Adirondacks. I was five years old when I went there. My father, as I said, died before I was born. My mother remarried, my stepfather was a rabbi in Lake Placid, New York.

SM: Did you run around in the wilderness as a kid?

NF: Sure. We all did that. We would fish, go out there to smoke cigarettes, escape from our parents, go in the woods, spend a couple of days drinking wine and getting sick, you know. As soon as I started working on my first Adirondack book, I knew it was the right thing. I had seen Eliott Porter's work of course. He was an influence, I love his work; went to see him talk and sat at his feet one evening.

SM: I haven't been to the high Adirondacks. How high is the tallest peak?

NF: Only one peak is above 5,000 feet. That is Mount Marcy, 5,344 feet high. (Showing SM Cibachromes) The Adirondacks look like the Alps, in places. Look at this river. Couldn't that be the Inn? And this summer one with its lush blues and greens. There are times, when I'm in the Adirondacks, when I feel as though I am in a tropical place, though it's extremely cold in winter. Every winter, you have days of minus 45° to minus 50°.

SM: Some of these icy pictures look as though they were taken in January or February. Absolute pain and agony to just stand there I should think.

NF: I've never felt agony. I dress appropriately for the weather.

Layers and layers. I have a jacket that looks like it's a moon-man jacket, and felt boots, and I wear layers of socks. My hands do get numb and raw. As a child I didn't have many clothes. We had very limited funds. I was poor really. I was cold all the time. I swore that when I grew up, I would be warm, and now I buy myself extremely good equipment!

SM: Triple-layer underwear and so on? Silk mittens?

NF: You don't have to have expensive stuff, it's just layers. I wear two pairs of socks, with felt boots, felt packs they're called. You can buy them anywhere where it gets cold, they're very available...

SM: What about your fingers?

NF: I seem to have the ability to have my fingers out in the cold for a long time. Some of my friends who are good outdoors people do marvel how long I can leave them uncovered. I work with bare hands when I'm setting up the camera. They do get raw. You can't get your hands wet, because then they'll stick to the metal. I stick my hands in my pockets constantly. I don't use handwarmers. I do use a kind of mitt that you can take off the top, made for film people. They cost maybe $35 or $40. I used not to have those. When you get successful, you get things that you don't really need. You could work perfectly well without them.

SM: This lovely deep-winter picture of a frozen pool, very snowy, with green ice. How long did it take you to get there, make the picture?

NF: That place is only a ten-minute walk from the road. That green ice is because there had been a thaw several days before. As the water runs it's just above freezing, colored plankton grow so all the river is green. Then the pools refreeze, and you get this beautiful-colored ice.

That's in *One Hundred Views of the Adirondacks*. That came out in '89, after *The Adirondacks*, which is still in print. It was first published in '85, I got a royalty check the other day! I think the count is about 46,000 now. I'm really quite pleased with myself!

This picture is of fallen logs in an old logging camp. People don't realize how huge the Adirondacks are, about one-fifth the area of New York State, bigger than the state of Vermont, bigger than Yellowstone National Park actually. It's not all state park. Doris Duke and the Rockefellers own thousands and thousands of acres.

SM: Do you always use 8-by-10-inch format nowadays?

NF: Almost entirely. I have a Deardorff, it folds up. I own several different lenses, but I did *The Adirondacks* with two lenses. A 210mm, which is a wideangle on an 8x10, equivalent to two-thirds normal focal length, and a 300mm, which is normal focal length for an 8-by-10-inch camera. It's easier to explain focal length in proportions of normal.

SM: Do you always use very small f/stops and long exposures?

NF: F/32 at between one-quarter and one second is fairly standard exposure for me. I use Ektachrome film.

SM: This slow-shutter-speed picture of the waterfall, it's the classic bridal-veil falls.

NF: Where I first saw that effect was in the work of a West Coast photographer I always loved, Wyn Bullock. He did a lot of bridal veil things, was a bit of a mystic. Of the West Coast people, he was ahead of his time I think. He did the first picture in the *Family of Man* book.

SM: That was a strange picture (of a naked child lying face-down on vines). I thought it looked as though the child had been strangled.

NF: I only saw that possibility after it was pointed out to me. I have always seen it more as how benevolent the wilderness is. I grew up in a a benevolent wilderness. No snakes. You can get lost in the Adirondacks, and freeze, but having grown up in it, it has always felt so gentle.

SM: Do you camp out when you are taking pictures?

NF: I like to move on. I generally will stay a day or two.

SM: When you know you have the picture.

NF: Sometimes you don't even feel that you have it; you just have to move on, you have a limited amount of time. There are places that I have gone back to many, many times. I have some views that elude me, I have gone back many times to two places I'm thinking of in particular, and never made a photograph of them that satisfies me. They are wonderful, powerful, historic sites, in the woods. They are very, very difficult places to get to. I've never got them right. They require a six or eight hour walk, with a lot of equipment.

SM: In winter it must often be very slippery, call for climbing skills.

NF: I use crampons sometimes.

SM: Do you have someone carry your equipment for you?

NF: Almost always now that I'm in my fifties. Even in earlier days, I often had someone help me.

SM: A trained assistant, or just a local lad?

NF: In the past six months, my whole life has changed, looking after my daughter. Under normal circumstances I have a full-time assistant, who hikes and carries equipment, and helps work on prints. The assistants have tended to be young women lately. Young women do everything today.

SM: You don't mind them lugging (carrying) huge cameras.

NF: When I interview them, I make sure they know it's a requirement. I have them pack up the camera gear, go on a trek. Including my own elder daughter, she's thirty. She has experience as a filmmaker. When I decided to take her to the Galapagos as my assistant, I first put a 45-pound pack on her back, and marched her until she fainted. That's the test.

SM: Nice Dad! Camera, two lenses, big tripod. How many film holders?

NF: Anywhere from four to ten. Sometimes I take a big changing bag and film on a longer hike.

As I said, I use Ektachrome film. For reproduction in books today, immediately you go to a digitized image, have them scanned. Once it's scanned, you have tremendous control of a picture. You can go into a dark area and pull it out, very easily. It's a matter of touching the computer a bit...

SM: The hiking preparations were for your Galapagos book, which to me captures the feeling of a very beautiful, strange place. How did that book come about?

NF: First, *The New York Times Magazine* sent me down there to do a piece, for ten days. I loved the place so much, I had to find a way of going back. When you do a successful book, the publisher gives you another chance. So I said I want to do the Galapagos. It took me a year to arrange it with the authorities in Ecuador. I sent letters of recommendation from about twenty people, including America's leading volcanologist from the Smithsonian. I had to deposit a $3,000 fee with the Galapagos National Park authorities. Finally, I got permission and went there for two months, the second time. I was frustrated at first with it being so difficult to make the arrangements, but finally I was glad they take good care to ensure everyone follows the rules. That was one place I used 35mm, for the birds, as well as 8x10 for the landscape.

SM: Were you afraid to shoot the place that the Ecuadorian photographer Tui De Roy, who has lived in the islands all her life, has made her own?

NF: I love Tui De Roy's work. But I thought I could bring something of mine to the place. Tui's brother Gil was my guide there. We went to some places he had never been before.

SM: You had special access?

NF: Finally, yes, we went to some sites not many people go.

SM: What is your next project?

NF: Getting my daughter on her feet again...

An Interview with

Dwight Kuhn

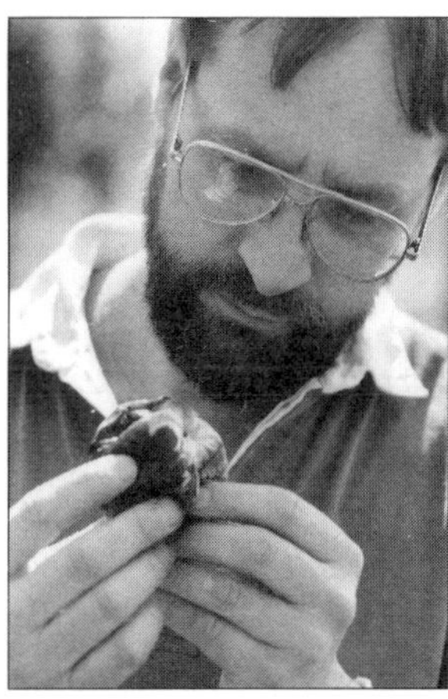

Dwight Kuhn has a B.S. in biology from Pennsylvania State University, and began his career as a high school chemistry and biology teacher. He started photographing for fun and to illustrate his lectures. He combined teaching with photography for eighteen years; about six years ago he became a full-time nature photographer, specializing in small creatures and extreme close-ups. His pictures have appeared in magazines and textbooks around the world, he has published eleven children's science picture books to date, and operates his own stock-photo business.

I interviewed Dwight at his office in Dexter, in central Maine.

SM: How exactly did you get started?

DK: I started photographing in summers in the late sixties. A friend in the school district got me interested. My first camera was a Pentax; I more or less played around. As I photographed, I realized I needed more equipment to do what I wanted, so I kept adding to it. Now I have three Nikons. One of my favorite lenses is an old Vivitar Series I 90mm macro; it was a very highly rated lens in its day—one of the sharpest ever made. It's still a workhorse lens for me, with a fast f/2.5 aperture that's good for viewing. I also use the 55mm Nikon macro lens quite a bit, sometimes reversed on a bellows. And I have a couple of special shorter macro lenses for the bellows for extreme magnifications. A 35mm and a 19mm macro lens, those do not need to be reversed. Mine are Nikon, but other companies make them. Olympus, and Zeiss, and Leica. You have to get the correct adaptor for attaching them to your bellows. A problem with most of those is they are not automatic, you have to stop them down manually. Also, they are expensive; now you pay more than $400 for one.

SM: This ladybug in your *My First Book of Nature* fills half the frame.

DK: Not such a big magnification, about two or three times life-size. You could photograph that with a 90mm macro lens and extension tubes. I can go up to ten, or even twenty times life-size with a special long bellows I made.

SM: Within about ten miles of Dexter you can take everything you need?

DK: There's a lot of things to photograph within ten miles of here. I center in on small things that aren't overly photographed. Smaller than robins let's say. Eighty percent of my files are probably of things that are smaller than a robin. Lots of insects, I like working with those, and spiders, and small plants. As I was teaching, I decided to build my files based on what was used in typical biology textbooks. I geared myself towards developing stock in those areas. In addition, I always like to have some major project underway, to work on a specific subject in depth. I did an entire study on aphids for instance. All aspects of the insects' life, the predators that feed on them, and so on. I tend to study and work with those subjects that haven't been overly done. I think that is part of my success. The stock sales started to take off, and looking after it took more and more time. About six years ago I found I got too busy with the two jobs, couldn't do full justice to either so I took up the photography full-time. I still shoot mostly in summer. Fortunately, most of the business work on the stock is called for in the winter.

SM: I notice you have great pictures of roots in this book.

DK: It's a subject I get asked for quite often. Fibrous roots, or tap roots. I have pictures of both, and sold quite a few images.

SM: So anyone who is talented and serious could make saleable nature pictures just about anywhere? Perhaps not in a big city too easily.

DK: You probably could come up with a lot of good nature subjects in a big city. But I have four kids, so I try to stay close to home. I can find enough subjects near here to keep me busy for the rest of my life.

I've had maybe eight different requests in the last few months for the water strider, the little insect that walks on the water using the surface tension. So I'm working on getting better pictures of it.

About 25 percent of my sales are to textbooks. About 25 percent are stock sales and assignments for magazines, especially nature and gardening magazines. More vegetables than flowers. Then there's about 25 percent to trade books and childrens' books, my own and illustrating other peoples' books. The other 25 percent is sales to calendars, greeting cards, and museums. Two stock agencies have some of my work. I mostly sell my own stock, and seem to do better at it than the agents. It's worth spending the time, though it takes away from photography, to do the business aspects. I do it to increase my profits. For promotion I send out a stock list and little photocards I have made up. I advertise in the *Green Book*, and subscribe to a couple of fax services that send out calls for pictures.

SM: Do you find those fax services worthwhile?

DK: They don't have a whole lot of nature-related requests. But I've gained some new clients, so it's worthwhile for me. That's mostly how I promote. I haven't got involved with any of the catalogs yet.

SM: Do you ever go to see clients, to show your work in person?

DK: I don't do a whole lot of that. I mostly promote by phone and mail.

SM: Do you think you are unique as a close-up specialist?

DK: There are a lot of good close-up people. John Shaw and Larry West to name two well-known ones today. When I was starting out, pictures by David Cavagnaro in *Life* magazine, award-winning pictures of dew, spiderwebs, ordinary things, in beautiful light, got me doing that also. Another person that stimulated my interest was Robert Sisson, formerly from the *National Geographic*. He did a lot of detailed natural history subjects, some of the oddballs. Those two photographers were my influences for the close-ups. I have a little different technique, I do different subjects than some of those other people.

Close-up is a difficult area to work with. Depth of field and lighting are two of the biggest problems. If you use natural light, you are usually talking about a quarter of a second exposure time or slower.

The basic is a single-lens reflex camera, a TTL-metering one is best. Then I would suggest people buy a good macro lens, a set of automatic extension tubes, and a good tripod and a cable release. Use those things as a starting point. If people find they aren't getting enough magnification, they can go to a bellows and special short macro lenses. Photographers should see if they like it, see what the problems are, before investing a lot of money. If they like close-up work, they can grow from there.

I suggest starting with a flower or plant, you can move around it to get the most interesting picture arrangements, and deal with where to focus for the best depth of field. Look at all the aspects of the plant, the spines on the stem, and the reproductive parts of the flower, finally focus in very, very close. First deal with the problems you have with a flower, like the least breeze blowing it out of focus, before trying insects that move. You can use automatic exposure settings first, but for best results, I bracket considerably on either side of normal exposure. You can use an 18 percent gray card, or even the green of the foliage, that's pretty close to a gray card. Usually, early mornings and late afternoons are good times to shoot, less breeze, and nice light. And early you have dew and water drops. A cloudy day can be good.

SM: If you had to name the one single quality that every good nature photographer should have, what would it be?

DK: Patience. No question. There's a lot of looking, a lot of searching for your subjects, a lot of waiting for the right time of day, waiting for the subject to do the right thing. I've sat for hours, waiting for something to hatch from an egg, you can't take your eye off it, or walk away for a minute, or you'd miss it. It only takes a few seconds for something to happen. There's a lot of sitting, in a blind if you're at a fox's den, or watching birds, or deer, or something else. You must have patience. With extreme close-up subjects, you need even more patience, for dealing with focussing.

I'm sure Leonard Lee Rue told you there's a lot of sitting and waiting. I have a portable blind bought from the Rue catalog, and it's a wonderful blind. Sometimes you have to sit inside a blind for hours. If you love nature, but aren't quite that patient, there are other areas of photography. Plants. Or landscape and scenics.

SM: How do you find your subjects?

DK: I've lived here for a long time, I know where many things are likely to be. Plus, a lot of people who know of my work call me if something interesting is around. Recently one of my neighbors called and told me about a fox den on his property. Park rangers are usually helpful. And I drive around a lot, and walk, just looking.

Last year I worked on a major project about kingfishers. First there was a lot of looking to find a place to get them diving into the water catching fish. I finally found a good fishing spot, then it was a matter of setting up a blind, and special lighting equipment, to catch them diving into the water, and waiting. Then there was nesting. Kingfisher nesting takes place in sandbanks. They dig a tunnel eight feet or so back into a bank, and have a large nest area at the back of the tunnel. It required finding an active nest first of all, then over periods of days and days and days, digging very slowly and very carefully down to expose the nest cavity, and then placing a piece of glass in there. It required a blind outside the cavity, so that the birds couldn't see me photographing as they flew into the nest. But, with the kingfishers, it just didn't work. They just couldn't accept that change, the glass there instead of the sand. So I had to back off so they would come back. After a while I could see that they weren't going to return to the nest with that glass there. They'd look in, then fly away. They were spooked even though it was done over a long period of time, and I've done that same type of thing before with woodpeckers and other birds and it's worked. So I had to take the glass out, and put the sand back, and give up on that aspect of the project. Those kingfishers came back and raised their young. At first I thought the problem was just the personality of that particular pair, but I tried with another pair, and the same thing happened. You have to know when to leave, when to give up. I don't recommend many people trying that technique. If you don't know what you're doing, you will spook birds off nests, and maybe destroy a lot of young.

SM: Supposing someone wanted information for a project, on, let's say, your aphids. Should you go to your local university biology department?

DK: I'd probably first see if there was anything on the subject in the well-known nature magazines. *Audubon, National Geographic, National Wildlife, Natural History. Ranger Rick* has a lot of good information even though it's a childrens' magazine. I might then go to the University of Maine library and search through their general files. Usually I can find enough in those places. If I still can't get the information I need, I might go to the biological abstracts file of research papers, at the university. From research papers you may find references, cited material, that might be useful. You can also get the names of experts to call. Some people are very busy, but most people are more than willing to help. For instance, I worked with a woman researcher at the University of Maine, on a mayfly that was recently re-discovered. They thought it was extinct. She was involved in the discovery. I did a major photographic study on it. I returned the help that I got from her with photographs that she can use for her lectures and papers. If someone helps me on a major book project, I send them a copy of the book, or try to be helpful in any way I can.

SM: How do you deal with the depth of field and sharp focus problems, with extreme close-ups of something that's on the move?

DK: You can work at certain times of day. On cold mornings, insects are sluggish, they are moving slower, and you can do daylight work. But for extreme magnifications, flash is useful. I often use flash to stop that motion. You can hand-hold the camera, and have the flash or two flashes, on a bracket. That's what I do, outdoors. You have to get fairly close, and work out your flash exposure for the distance with the guide number, or else use a TTL/automatic flash. I use f/16 or f/11, sometimes you must go to f/16 or f/22 because you need the greatest depth of field.

Your slower films are going to be better for the sharpest flash work.

SM: So you use flash for most tiny things?

DK: Yes. Unless I need natural-looking light, which sometimes you do, for instance if you're working with dew, or backlighting on flowers. I hardly ever use flash with flowers, just for the things that move.

SM: Do you tend to collect the ladybugs and bring them inside to photograph, or do you do them outside?

DK: Both. I prefer the natural light. But for very small things, like the aphid project you have to work indoors. Aphids are an eighth of an inch long, something like that. Almost impossible to keep in focus outdoors at the great magnification needed, let alone try to do behavioral things. In that situation, I brought entire plants, with the aphids on them, into the studio, kept the plants healthy, and the aphids just sat there, sucking their fluids, didn't change their behavior in the least. So I got the natural behavior, under controlled conditions, and I didn't have the motion problem from the wind. I would probably have missed 95 percent of the pictures if I had tried to shoot them outside. A lot of pictures shot at less than one-to-one ratio, life-size, are done outside. Extreme magnifications, and stopping fast motion, need controlled conditions.

Now I'm learning to use the electron microscope, to get even larger magnifications, up to 100,000X times lifesize. I haven't explored it all fully yet, but I'm starting to like what I'm doing. I'm getting a good reaction from the first pictures. The University of Maine is only an hour from here, so I'm alright working there for now.

SM: The enormous tiny world of Dwight Kuhn. Thank you very much for being so generous.

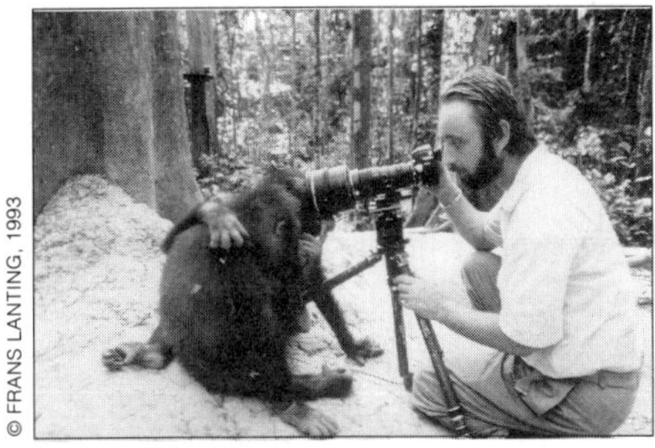

An interview with

Frans Lanting

Internationally famed wildlife photographer **Frans Lanting** was born in Holland, has an M.A. in economics from Erasmus University in Rotterdam, and came to the U.S. in 1978. He has spent much of the last ten years or so in the wilderness areas of the world, mostly photographing for the National Geographic Society. He was named International Wildlife Photographer of the Year by the BBC in 1991. His major photo essay about the Okavango was the longest wildlife conservation story in *National Geographics* 100-year history. This work, and stories on pygmy chimpanzees, and South Georgia Island, which have also appeared in *National Geographic,* and his books, such as *Madagascar, A World Out of Time*, have received worldwide acclaim. Frans is currently working in the Amazon Basin. He lives along the shores of Monterey Bay with writer Christine Eckstrom, with whom he collaborated on *Forgotten Edens,* just published by the National Geographic Society. I interviewed him by phone at his office in California.

SM: I'm very grateful for your time. I know you must be extremely busy. I love your work. I'm sitting with a copy of *Forgotten Edens* in my lap. To begin with, how did you get started? I know you're originally from Holland. I'm British, and I've been there many times. I don't think I've ever seen anything wilder than a rabbit in Holland!

FL: Well, there are a lot of birds.

SM: Oh, yes. Seabirds. So you started photographing seabirds?

FL: Shorebirds, things like that. That's what I grew up with; I always had a keen interest in nature. My interest in pictures came from that. But it took me a long time to realize, to acknowledge, that what I really wanted to be was a photographer. First I dabbled in economics.

SM: Is that what you studied at the university?

FL: Environmental economics, yes. I didn't really do that much with wildlife in Holland. As you say, there isn't so much of it to photograph. You can't approach anything very close...It wasn't until I moved to this country that (the U.S.) I got deeply immersed. The rest, as they say, is history.

SM: Did you take any photography classes?

FL: Not really.

SM: Who would you consider your great influences?

FL: Ernst Haas. A book he did many years ago, in the seventies, *(The) Creation...*

SM: I have it. It's probably my single favorite book...

FL: I think it still stands as unsurpassed...

SM: Any other influences?

FL: That book was my bible for many years... There was a man named David Cavagnaro, a front-runner in nature photography in the seventies. He cultivated a very poetic, impressionistic style, (his pictures were) suffused with an intimate knowledge of the subject. He published two books that were quite influential in the seventies. David and I got to know each other, when I came to California. He was very influential in shaping my attitudes towards nature and photography.

SM: How did you get associated with *National Geographic?*

FL: Like most photographers, I always wanted to be associated with the *Geographic.* It is very open to new photographers, they often give an assignment to try you out if they think you are promising, something not too critical. My first assignment was Madagascar. Madagascar turned into a Big Bang! That got me on a roll with the Society; for the last six years or so, they have kept me pretty busy.

SM: Do they more or less now let you do what you want to do?

FL: It's a synergistic relationship. We all come up with ideas and projects. Those are shaped by quite a few people. I think editorially and script, to some degree, my own stories. I work with the art people.

SM: You think about the layout (arrangement of pictures with type) and pacing the story.

FL: Yes, I very much operate like a movie director does.

SM: Do you make a list of things you have to cover and so on?

FL: Not just a list. Yes, there's the shopping list of pictures but it goes beyond that too. Every body of work, every collection of photographs needs to have a rhythm, needs to contain emotions, even though a lot of people say it's only pictures of nature and of animals.

SM: Oh no. This is what attracted me when I saw this book. It's a very poetic book actually.

FL: The flow of things is very important. In *Forgotten Edens* we were able to express that quite well. I worked with art directors, and we had a picture editor. They gave us a lot of freedom. Christine (Eckstrom, the writer of *Forgotten Edens*) has worked with the *Geographic* a long time, and saw to it there was a very strong story line.

SM: I enjoyed the writing very much too. I 'll do my best while looking at your book, looking at the first picture, the black lemur (in Madagascar), the cute furry creature leading you into the book. How long did you wait for the lemur?

FL: Oh, thirty-seven years, and 1/30 of a second!

SM: Okay, great, I love it. You can't plan for animals to do anything! And then the next picture (of elephants and a bird in Botswana), I think the way you used fill flash (it lights the bird) is very innovative for nature photography. I would say that was original, no?

FL: Yes, it's become more commonplace now, but when I started applying it, back in the early eighties, it was not often done.

SM: Yes. The next picture is flash, of a flying lizard with a black background. Very sharp. I assume it's done at night. And then a lovely panoramic landscape of a forest in Borneo. The gatefold [fold-out pages]. Do you do everything 35 (mm) or do you use a panoramic camera sometimes?

FL: Almost everything is 35. I do apply large format, or panoramic sometimes but only a fraction of the time.

SM: The fold-out pictures in this book, this Borneo tapestry, is that a panoramic shot?

FL: No, that's just a simple 35mm image, on Velvia.

SM: Velvia. Beautiful film. Beautiful color, that whole misty quality, very unusual.

FL: Yes. It was very unusual. It lasted five minutes, never happened again in the two months we were there.

SM: You have to be there, yes?

FL: And know what to look for.

SM: Did you study art?

FL: No, I never have. I would try to educate myself. But photography books. I could never get beyond page twelve of technical photography books. In the same way I have always found that books on theory of how to do composition are not useful.

SM: I'm still going through the book. This picture of orangutans, in the reserve in Sepilok (Borneo). Are you involved in the conservation movement, apart from your work, in any way, shape, or form?

FL: A lot of my photographic work is driven by awareness that by choosing my subjects carefully, and by timing them, I think I play a role in contributing to awareness of places that many people might not know about. The work I'm doing currently is in a remote part of the Amazon Basin, at present only a few dozen people have ever been there. There's a tremendous opportunity of preserving this huge area. I think a kind of outreach, with photos and words, will help.

SM: Just the way the American national parks were partly preserved because of photographs...

FL: It's not photography, or photographs alone of course. There's a whole network, a whole matrix. It's made up of scientists, conservationists, politicians, editors, publishers, the local people. Everyone has their own interest, their agenda. I think I can make a difference in that respect even though the effect is never measurable...

SM: Well, there's a tremendously increased public awareness of conservation issues in general...

FL: I think in the case of Madagascar for instance, that my work there did somewhat aid conservation...

SM: I spoke to a famous rain forest expert the other day, Dr. Tom Lovejoy. Perhaps you know him. I asked him what he thought about ecotourism. He said it was better for a tourist to climb on a tree, than for someone else to cut it down! Do you feel about the same way?

FL: In many areas, throughout the tropics in particular, in Third World countries, there are economic and ecological problems of an urgency we can hardly comprehend here. There have to be some benefits to the local people for setting aside land from development. This doesn't mean we should just give up on establishing refuges just for animals. Ecotourism is a new paradigm, it's becoming a buzzword that's overused. Inevitably, in a couple of years, people will see some of the pitfalls of it, and go on to the next concept.

I can't talk too much about the Amazon yet, my work for the *Geographic* there is still to come out. But there's a river that splits into two. As you go upstream, on the right-hand fork there's very active goldmining going on, on both sides. The result is many signs of occupation, and some tourism. The forest is no longer very interesting. On the other side, there's no gold; it's pristine forest. It's through such freaks of geology that we have places that are still untouched. It's a question of will goldminers get there first, or conservationists? I hope my work will help a little to preserve it.

SM: But with some provisions for visitors, obviously.

FL: I agree with Tom [Lovejoy] in that respect.

SM: He's not elitist about zoos either. There will always be zoos, because there are so many people, like kids here in New York for instance, who can't travel to see animals in the wild. And the good ones are involved in conservation.

FL: There are many reasons for zoos, one is there is something in human nature that wants to have access to animals. I was in the Bronx Zoo just a week ago. They have made tremendous changes, their exhibit of the jungle, a re-creation of the rain forest, is great.

SM: I'm now looking at the section of the book on South Georgia (island). I want to go there! The picture of the courting albatross with his beak in the air and outspread wings is extraordinary. Could I go to South Georgia if I had the money?

FL: Well, yes and no. Certainly my reputation does help me to get access to certain people and places. I don't have to explain myself now. I had to in the past. But, we have a saying in Holland, "Where there's a will, there's a way." I went places before anyone knew of me. I went to Falkland Islands and the Galapagos on a shoestring for instance.

SM: How long did you stay in South Georgia?

FL: I had a unique opportunity to circumnavigate it in a sailboat for three months, a rare opportunity. Most people stop there for two or three days on an Antartic cruise.

SM: I'm looking at the bird pictures at dusk, where you used flash. Did you camp out?

FL: Yes.

SM: If I may ask about logistics. Do you send film back when you are away for a long time?

FL: They don't have Federal Express to South Georgia.

SM: Anyway, it's cold there. What about hot places? The Amazon?

FL: Sometimes I send it back if someone is going. Or I store in a the refrigerator, if there's a hotel with refrigeration.

SM: How to you carry and store your gear in humid climates?

FL: I use the hard plastic cases. They don't look conspicuous, and handle a lot of abuse. They are waterproof and strong and help a lot.

SM: Now I want to ask you about the "Big Bang" — Madagascar. Did that become a book also?

FL: Yes, it was published two years ago. In 1985 the door of Madagascar cracked open. It had been politically isolated up until that point, like North Korea. It was an extraordinary opportunity for a journalist and naturalist like myself. It's truly a separate world. The original people came from Borneo, but there's so much intermarriage; a mixture of Arabic, Swahili, and Indian cultures. The wildlife is unique. And it lent itself to shooting as a story.

SM: I have heard that the Okavango (delta) is your favorite place. Or is Madagascar, or is the place you're working on now always your favorite place?

FL: They are all my children. Typically, I spend a year to two years being totally immersed in a project, focussed on one place. I don't rank the places. It's more like a relationship.

SM: You have had some very deep love affairs, or marriages! This extraordinary Okavango view of the huge water lilies taken from underneath, I first saw at the *BBC Wildlife* magazine annual nature photography exhibition in London. Purplish and green. An Art Deco image...

Do you have any words for young photographers starting out? Omit the word young. I just learned that Elliot Porter didn't publish his first book until he was sixty...

FL: I didn't start that young either. I think more important than say, any acquisition of equipment or class in technique, is an ability to sort of fall in love, to be passionate about the subject matter that you want to photograph. When that drive and passion is there, it will lure you on, make you determined to go to places, and be in places that might not otherwise be so comfortable. It will afford an entrance into the level of photographs that make a difference, aesthetically and otherwise.

SM: Thank you very much indeed.

An Interview with

Roger Tory Peterson

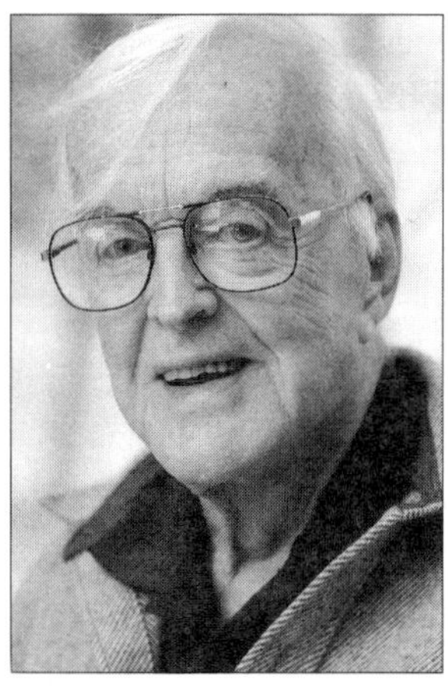

Roger Tory Peterson, one of the world's great artist/naturalists and nature writers, was born in Jamestown, New York, in 1908, and studied painting at the Art Students League in New York City. In 1934, he published his *Field Guide to the Birds,* which has been called the most successful and influential bird book of all time. He has illustrated, authored, and edited so many other field guides in the last forty-nine years that it is not possible to list them all here. Roger Tory Peterson has received twenty-two honorary doctorates, won the Gold Medal from the World Wildlife Fund in 1972, received the Presidential Medal of Freedom, the highest U.S. civilian award, from President Carter in 1979, was nominated for the Nobel Peace Prize in 1983, and received numerous other honors.

In addition to all this, he is a highly accomplished bird photographer.

I interviewed him at his studio in Connecticut.

RTP: Photography is my therapy. Painting is hard work. Not that I copy my photographs in my paintings, but I do study them.

SM: What is the most important quality for a good bird photographer?

RTP: He or she should be able to *see* a picture. Very often you've got to anticipate. If birds are getting restless, I know they are about to fly. Same thing if they defecate, birds kind of lighten the load first. So I'm all set for a quick flight shot, whereas someone who wasn't so aware might miss it. With water birds, watch for a feeding frenzy. If you see a lot of fish near the surface, and birds are being attracted, you can park in a good spot, and wait till the birds come into your range.

You don't frighten birds photographing from inside a car because to most birds a car is just a big animal with round legs; if you step out, they fly away. If you've got another person who can drive, sit in the back seat. Then you can slide across and work both sides of the car. You may have to make some adjustments, take turns driving.

The most important thing in working from a car is to have a good beanbag or steadybag that is nearly as solid as a tripod. Rest this on a lowered window. A problem with many rental cars is that you can't roll the windows down far enough, they are made to keep kids from falling out, not photography. Often it's a real effort to find the right car.

If I'm with a birding group, with other birders in a car or van, I may be a pain to them, and they certainly are a pain to me. Because if someone moves in the vehicle, you lose lens stability. It's rather good to have one like-minded person sharing driving with you, but not more.

SM: Do you have a lens that you like to work with? A focal length?

RTP: The lens that I am using most now is the Canon 300mm f/2.8, with a doubler (2X tele-extender) that makes it a very sharp 600mm f/5.6 lens. I find that when shooting from a car, a 600mm lens is ideal. I keep a 300mm lens handy also. At times I'd even like a 1000 (mm lens). The trouble is a doubler on a 500mm lens is not automatic. I rely on autofocus. I can no longer depend on my eyes, because I've had cataracts removed from both of them. Many people, especially old-timers who are conditioned to using manual focus, won't think of using automatic. Once they try it, they change. Because you can often get grab shots, instead of fiddling with the lens while the bird gets away. If you shoot through a window, use the lens flat against the glass, with a rubber lens cap.

SM: Do you use flash much?

RTP: At night, certainly. Or with birds on nests. And under the harsh light conditions of midday fill-in flash is advisable, if you can use it so it's almost not detected. Sometimes, you don't get light in the eyes without flash. But at night you have to watch for "red-eye." You must take the flash off the camera, to avoid that.

SM: You don't think that flash hurts birds?

RTP: No. Flash seems to bother them less than the sound of the shutter. The click of the camera will disturb them, but when a flash goes off they seem to ignore it.

SM: Here in Connecticut, they make the gyro-stabilizer [that permits hand-holding a camera at slow shutter speeds]. Do you ever use it?

RTP: I did, yes. On a rocking boat, it stabilizes things. Kenyon, the inventor, used to live near here. I owned a gyro-stabilizer years ago, when they cost around $400; I used it on my movie cameras. But I sold it back to the company when I was no longer doing movies. Now one of them costs about $4,000! But, be careful. I recently ordered a shoulder pod from a catalog; it was advertised as a "stabilizer" but it wasn't. It was just another gun stock, so you've got to watch what you're buying.

In zoo photography of birds, which I enjoy, you've got to get close enough to those wires, otherwise they show in the picture. Very few zoos are designed quite right for photographing birds. Often there's a gap between the railing and the wires. You can't lean over far enough to press the lens against the wires. Some zoos in Australia are the best I've seen, at least for the birds of prey. There are openings where you can stick a lens through, but which are too small to let birds fly out.

SM: Ann Guilfoyle said, "What I like about nature photographers is that many of them live to an enormous age, and have wonderful, open faces, because they are outside looking at beauty all the time." Like you!

RTP: I'm now in my eighty-fifth year, so it's easy to fall asleep, but I refuse to go to sleep forever. Eventually I'll have to go; some morning I'll probably not wake up. The fantasy for most people is that the hereafter is populated with people like themselves. I don't believe that.

To me God is the life force. I find it just as much in a blade of grass or a grasshopper, as in a bird or in myself. That word God is misleading, because to most people it is humanistic. It's also male. Where does that leave women?

SM: I read an article about you, by William Zinsser, in a recent *Audubon* magazine. He said you went to high school with Lucille Ball.

RTP: I was two years ahead of her in Jamestown High School. She was a sophomore when I was a senior. She was in my sister's class. Dropped out in her sophomore year to join George Jessell's "Follies." She was a bit of a wild girl. She became Mrs. Middle America, later!

When I was a kid in junior high school, a teacher started a Junior Audubon Club. This teacher, Blanche Hornbeck, was a terrific red-headed gal, about thirty-one. I was eleven. She said, "I'm going to start this club. I don't know anything about birds, but we're going to find out about them together." This for me was the right approach. Miss Hornbeck gave us these outline drawings to color. She said finally, "That's not quite the way to learn to draw, just filling in the colors." So she gave us each a box of watercolors, and a color plate by Fuertes to work from, and told us to start from scratch. I got a blue jay. Fuertes was the great bird painter early in the century, a great influence right up to this time.

SM: I think of Audubon as being the great influence, he's controversial.

RTP: Everybody's controversial if you look into them enough. I got bad reviews on my 1980 *Field Guide*, some hotshots who were trying to make a name wanted to shoot the big boy down.

SM: I read that your first field guide has gone into forty-four printings.

RTP: It's the most profitable book for my publisher, Houghton Mifflin, it even passed *Fanny Farmer's Cookbook*! It's been listed in the top thirty of all the books that have been published in this country.

SM: I like your *First Guide to Birds* for its simplicity.

RTP: The whole idea of my field guides was to make things simple for the beginner. Being trained as an artist, I am a visual person. Most bird books of my youth made things so difficult by describing a bird systematically from beak to tail. A robin was listed something like this: "Black tip on a yellow beak, three white spots around the dark eye, six black stripes on the white throat, head gray, darker on the back." Halfway down the page you would find it had a rusty breast!

I thought, go right to the point, describe the important thing first, and point to the main "field marks" with an arrow! But we never do anything by ourselves. My inspiration was a Scottish writer, Ernest Thompson Seton. He wrote a sort of novel called *Three Little Savages,* about a kid, Yan, who never could identify the ducks in the field. One day Yan found some mounted ducks in a display case. He thought that if he could sketch their uniforms on paper, simply, he could tell them apart when he saw them swimming at a distance. I thought that's a great idea, it could be applied to all birds. So I devised my schematic system, and added arrows [to the paintings in the field guides]. It is still called the Peterson System. It works for most field guides. Not for rocks, or the stars. We now have nearly fifty books in the series.

The idea was later picked up in England and Europe. My field guide *Birds of Britain and Europe* is now in twelve languages. When my first field guide was published in England it was sold under the name Roger Peterson, the publishers left out the Tory. They wanted to sell to bird watchers of both political persuasions! Actually I'm Swedish. My uncle's name was Turé. I was named for him. That's very difficult to pronounce, a teacher started calling me Tory, my mother liked it. Roger is an airman's acronym. It means Okay, in flight terms! Tory (tori) in Japanese, that means bird!

SM: I'm looking at a tufted titmouse through the window.

RTP: I bring birds in by feeding them and I enjoy this artificial pond, because usually a pair of mallards comes in, and sometimes wood ducks. If we keep watching, maybe a wild turkey will come to get grain. It's actually a many-faceted thing, to feed birds. It does raise the threshold of survival for some species that don't travel, like the Carolina Wren. During a cold winter it helps them to make it. But you can argue, "Let nature take its course"—just let the genetically strong survive. There's also the humanistic side, you feel compassion for the birds. In my own case feeding them is pure pleasure. As many birds are probably killed as saved by people who feed birds, because they fly into windows.

The number of birds that are killed by picture windows runs into the millions. With these big studio windows, a woodland bird thinks it can fly right through. Normally, I keep the curtains on one side closed so they can't see all the way through. It's mostly the birds of the shadows that get killed, like vireos, ovenbirds, wood thrushes, sometimes a morning dove. A sharp-shinned hawk is around now, looking for a bite to eat. Birds that try to escape might fly in the wrong direction, and crash into a window. Even the hawk itself might have an accident.

SM: You have a wonderful environment around here in Connecticut, with Long Island Sound, wetlands, woods. How many bird species can you spot?

RTP: On our seventy acres I've either seen or heard about 150 species. If I really tried, I could find others during migration, down by the marshy inlet out of sight of the house.

SM: Where should somebody who is starting out to photograph birds go? I know it's easiest to start with wading birds on rivers and lakes, and seabirds, rather than small perching birds.

RTP: Yes. With perching birds, it often becomes tripod work, with remote control needed near the nest. Often flash is needed. But certain waterbird hot spots are so good, you can shoot birds easily from a car. I was very much responsible, in East Africa, for the designation of Lake Nakuru as a national park. It is the best place in the world to see vast numbers of flamingoes, and is extremely good for Eurasian white pelicans. There are big mammals around there too. I was there as recently as last January. To the south of Nakuru are Lake Elmentaita and Lake Naivasha. Lake Natron in Tanzania, is also great for flamingoes. I've been going to Africa for more than thirty-five years. Seen a lot of changes. We don't live long enough to see what's going to happen eventually.

SM: Where's your favorite place in America that won't be ruined because of many people going there because you say so?

RTP: One place that is fairly well known, many people do go there, is the Ding Darling Wildlife Refuge on Sanibel Island in Florida. It's often crowded in winter, the best season. Go on weekdays. Go early in the morning; midday is the least productive time. Spoonbills may be especially good as evening approaches. You can go around the seven mile loop and find things dull, two hours later, everything can be there.

In the Northeastern U.S., there are certain good places, like Saybrook Point, here in Connecticut, but there are problems. Motor-bikes are a problem, because nesting birds birds like least terns and piping plovers are vulnerable to people riding over the land; they've had to fence things off to keep people out of nesting areas. In Rhode Island, piping plovers nested on a nudist beach. Part of it was closed to protect the birds. The nudists were not pleased. The world is getting complicated.

SM: The question of the northern spotted owl for instance.

RTP: That's not as simple as some people think. It's not just that owl, it's the whole ecosystem of old-growth forests. The southern race of the spotted owl lives close to Los Angeles, close to lots of homes. One wonders why the northern spotted owl can't as get as used to people as the southern population. The closest relative of the spotted owl, the eastern barred owl, is extending its range west and may eventually displace it, the two might even hybridize. Things are not as simple as we tend to make them, the whole ecosystem is what's important.

If you look at things historically, some birds today are better off than they were a hundred years ago when they were killed for the feather trade. Now that's out of the way. Environmental changes are much more dangerous in the long run. Many birds are losing their feeding and breeding grounds. The federal refuges have been extremely important in bringing back certain birds. Avocets and black-necked stilts have benefited greatly from protection. On the other hand, marshes along the Eastern seaboard are very much diminished. Here in New England, birds that were once common like bitterns are seldom seen. Even some open-country birds like meadowlarks are fewer because farmlands have been built on, or gone back to woods. There are so many factors. Today, all wildlife is under pressure, not just the birds. For some reason frogs and salamanders are disappearing, butterflies are scarcer. This might be because of acid rain, it could be some other factor. On the other hand, I have seen some things come back in the last half century.

SM: I'm so glad to hear some good news. What have you seen come back?

RTP: Mostly the big wading birds, because they were shot for womens' hats. The first Audubon warden in Florida was killed by poachers. In England there's a longer tradition of caring for nature.

SM: Heather Angel told me that in Britain there are laws prohibiting photographing endangered birds on their nests. There are no such laws here. What would you say to people about that?

RTP: Here, we have ethics. Use a long lens if you can, or work from a blind to avoid scaring birds off the nest. If you have a blind or any setup near a nest, don't trim branches away to get a better view of it. You might have to tie one branch back, but don't fuss with the place too much. Don't ever do as some photographers did years ago, cut off a branch with a noose on it, and drop it down.

SM: In his book of bird photographs, Elliot Porter said he did just that.

RTP: Elliot Porter did do it. I remember writing an article for *Audubon* magazine years ago, giving the ethics, mentioning not cutting off nests on branches. People thought I was aiming just at Porter, but I wasn't. You can photograph a nest from a blind. Now they have quick-to-set-up blinds. Or use a long lens, and trigger your camera by remote control.

There are ethics for even looking at birds. The American Birding Association has guidelines. Don't trespass, or tramp over somebody's lawn. Recently when a painted bunting showed up at a feeder here in Old Lyme, more than 300 people turned out to see it. It was right next to the church one Sunday, the minister thought he was going to have an overflow congregation, but most had come to see the painted bunting!

SM: What about photographing birds in cities?

RTP: Many parks are good. Central Park in New York can be a great place, because migrating birds travel at night, when all those buildings are lit up. The park to them is a dark oasis, birds concentrate there. Years ago, Robert Moses was parks commissioner of New York, he asked me what to plant in three areas of Central Park, for birds. I gave him a list of berry-bearing shrubs and trees. One area that was planted was the peninsula north of the 59th Street lake, today, that's wonderful. A second area was the Ramble near the Natural History Museum. A third was the lower end of the 110th Street lake. When I go through Central Park and see birds in these hot spots, I think "I had a lot to do with that."

SM: What can people do for wildlife? Pick a cause that they care about?

RTP: I think that helps a lot, but use common sense. There are so many organizations. Find the effective ones. Some are paying as much as 80 percent of their membership donations just for office staff.

I am called "special consultant" to the Audubon Society; I've seen it go through three major crises of identity in the last sixty years, but it seems to be on the right track again.

I'm still learning about photography even after seventy-five years behind the camera. You'd think I'd be better by now!

SM: Automatic cameras are different. You have to learn new skills. I feel as though I've been talking to God, as far as birds are concerned!

RTP: I'm not a god. What is God? Isn't it the life force?

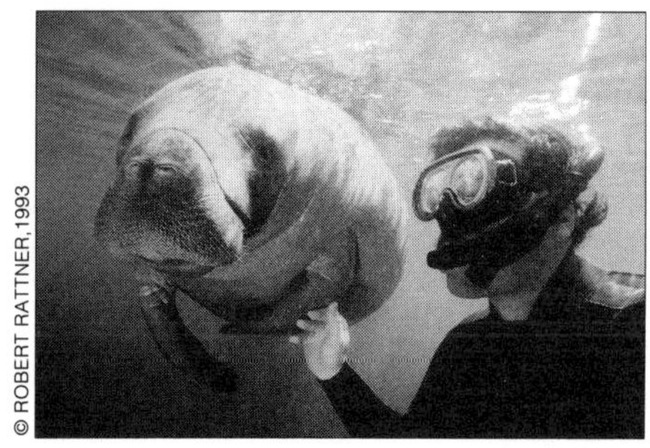

An Interview with

Robert Rattner

Robert Rattner grew up in Queens, New York, and has an M.A. in English from New York University. He made his first overseas trip to photograph wildlife, two months in East Africa, when he was twenty-three in company with his future wife and business partner Dian. Bob combines travel with nature photography, and his work has appeared in magazines worldwide. He specializes in underwater photography and endangered species. A commited conservationist, he is currently serving as president of the U.S. branch of the Wildlife Preservation Trust International, founded by the British naturalist and writer Gerald Durrell. The Rattners are personal friends. I interviewed Bob at his office in Connecticut.

SM: How would you describe what you do?

RR: This always has been a difficult question for me. I am a photojournalist—I explore and document. I strive to make photographs that capture an essence, a truth. I often work with nature and underwater subjects, but also photograph people and places. Too long away from nature and I need to get back to a desert or a rain forest or the marsh in my backyard, and especially miss the the underwater world. But I also enjoy the stimulation of peoples and cultures. Each one can make me miss the other!

SM: Some people have said to me that if you are not after deep-sea life, you get the best underwater pictures when snorkeling. Do you agree?

RR: Yes and no! If you are talking about snorkelers who stay right at the surface, those who aren't comfortable holding their breath and diving down, which is called skin-diving or free-diving, I'll say no. For a good free-diver, snorkeling and photographing can be great. Free diving, you are unencumbered by scuba gear, and really feel free. Also, you are working fairly close to the surface, which can reduce some of the problems that occur when photographing deeper. For me, the important issue is what do you need to make a good underwater photograph? Underwater photography can be very equipment intensive—scuba gear, underwater cameras, flashes, housings, etc. A person must decide what they're after—capturing an image of a passing fish or deliberately creating a photograph—and then choose the method and equipment.

SM: So learning to use scuba is a must for serious underwater work?

RR: The obvious disadvantage of snorkeling is that you can stay down only for as long as you can hold your breath, and you won't be able to reach all the underwater photographic opportunities. However, I have pictures that I made on a reef, free diving to about twenty feet, that are some of my all-time favorites. I had been doing a lot of free diving and was able to stay at twenty to forty feet long enough to compose and set my flash. I was glad not to be carrying all my heavy scuba gear, but this is not something a casual snorkeler could do. My manatee project, which has been going on for over ten years, has been done without scuba. Most of the photographs were done in five to fifteen feet of water.

SM: Do you wear a belt with lead weights when you dive?

RR: Always on scuba and usually when I'm free-diving. The weight you wear depends on body weight and individual buoyancy. On scuba with a full wet suit I wear thirty to thirty-five pounds of lead. To make myself more stable I make myself a little too heavy. I compensate with some air in my buoyancy vest. This is pushing safety a hair but I find it helpful.

SM: Do you recommend underwater-photography courses?

RR: Foremost is a good scuba course. You have to be certified to get air tanks filled. Unfortunately, a lot of places, especially in resorts, will give you quick certification. Many resort courses get you in the water but don't teach you enough to be a safe diver. A few hours during a week's vacation in St. Thomas cannot replace a complete month-long course. Take a good course near home and practice before you go.

This is especially important for underwater photography, because you can't concentrate on making photographs if you are not an adept diver. It's like driving. At first you can't even listen to the radio because you concentrate so hard. Eventually you drive almost instinctively and can pay attention to the traffic and the radio. It might even be unsafe to try to photograph if you are not a good diver. A commonly asked question is: Does a good diver or a good photographer make a better underwater photographer? The answer is you need to be both. For quality pictures obviously you want a photographer's eye and skills. But you also need to be proficient enough to position yourself underwater, as opposed to just grabbing pictures of fish as they go by. An underwater photographer has to do the things needed very very quickly. Later on you say, "Oh yes, I did that." Practice and experience are essential.

SM: So the underwater-photography course would be helpful?

RR: Yes. Underwater photography is normal photography — plus additional things that can go wrong. The more problems you are aware of, the more you can compensate for them. Some things require experience or fancy equipment. Others you can compensate for simply be knowing about them.

SM: Such as the very blue light underwater. Have you tried the new Underwater Ektachrome, the UW film?

RR: What Kodak has done, which is very clever, is to make the red layer of the film faster. The red layer is the equivalent of a 200 ISO film while the rest is a 64. Water absorbs the red end of the light spectrum turning everything more blue. To compensate, UW film is more sensitive to reds. The problem is, that there's not always the same amount of blue. At ten feet or thirty feet, in northern or southern waters, the color is different. It would be a mistake to see this film as a cure-all. Used judiciously it can be helpful but sometimes it will be too red. It will be very good to, say, photograph a shipwreck between twenty and thirty feet.

For underwater macro photography, though, 100 percent of your light comes from your flash. Most underwater flashes are biassed towards the warm side and even a housed land flash is working at such close range that color absorption is minimal. If you use the UW film in this situation you will get very red photographs. There is a filter you can use to correct this problem but it will cut light transmission considerably and you will have to compensate by using a wider f/stop.

SM: What are the options in underwater cameras?

RR: Single-use underwater cameras are fun, but are meant for casual snaps taken at or very close to the surface. I've found some underwater point-and-shoots unreliable, and they cannot go very deep. I suggest testing a new underwater camera for leaks in a bathtub before using it.

The Nikonos V is a wonderful underwater camera. It has evolved from four previous models based on the original Calypso camera designed by Jacques-Yves Cousteau. Of the older totally manual Nikonos models that are still around—you set the shutter speed and aperture and focus, they have to be taken apart to load, something like a Leica—I like the Nikonos III. You probably can find used ones quite cheaply. I didn't like the Nikonos IV, which was the first model with a built-in meter. It had big problems with flooding and other malfunctions.

Then Nikon came out with the great Nikonos V, which delivered the promise of the IV, but with the bugs removed. It has full electronics, is very automatic and is easy to load.

The Nikonos RS single-lens reflex camera has recently changed the state of the underwater art. Previous Nikonos cameras were not SLRs, and required that you estimate the distance to your subject to focus, and were approximate on framing. The RS is the first self-contained underwater SLR; it makes focusing and composition much more accurate.

SM: I have heard that the first of this model has some bugs. Should someone buying a new Nikonos RS reflex test it before using it?

RR: Any new technology will have a few bugs. It never hurts to wait a while for them to be worked out. All underwater equipment, especially new gear, should be tested before leaving for a vacation or a job.

SM: What lenses are currently available for the Nikonos RS?

RR: Nikon has come out with a good group of lenses: a 55mm macro, a 28mm and, the most interesting, a 20-35mm zoom. Most underwater photography falls into two categories: wide angle and close-up. The 20-35mm, for the first time, brings the convenience of a zoom underwater. The great thing about the new reflex is that you are viewing through the lens. What you see is what you get.

SM: What is your definition of wide angle underwater, given refraction which makes everything appear closer and larger down there?

RR: Underwater, things appear about 25 percent closer, or one-third larger, than they actually are. There are dome ports for camera housings that correct this, but Nikonos lenses, and lenses housed behind flat ports, are affected by refraction the same as the human eye. Therefore, in order to work as close as possible to your subject, wider usually is better underwater, as long as you don't get distortion. Nikon makes a terrific 15mm underwater lens that, in effect, is a 21mm. The effective focal length of the 20-35mm zoom would be about 28mm to 45mm.

SM: With older Nikonoses you have parallax and depth of field problems.

RR: Yes. You are looking through a fixed finder not your lens, so you will have parallax error. This gets worse with longer focal lengths. Also, since you guesstimate the focus, using a large aperture means shallow depth of field and a great chance for error. Say I'm going to photograph you underwater. We both are moving somewhat, so I will have a better chance of getting you in focus with a 15mm than a 35mm lens.

SM: Yes, but then I will be smaller in the frame.

RR: You have just defined the underwater wide angle situation. For the most part, you want to work as close as possible and as wide as possible. Two factors of photographing through water that in air usually are not problems are: Water absorbs color and water contains suspended particles that can blur your image. Water with a lot of particles appears cloudy and is obvious. But, *all* water contains sand, plankton, and silt, no matter how clear it appears. More water between lens and subject means that more color will be absorbed and more particles distort your image. Working close with a wide angle reduces problems.

SM: Underwater, the biggest problem I have is guessing focus.

RR: Wire frames are used for close-up focussing when the subject is a few inches from your lens. Further away than that, the best trick is to use a wide-angle lens and a small aperture for maximum depth of field.

SM: Underwater, there are few familiar things to help judge distance. RR: You can use your dive buddy as a point of reference. Or your hand. Stretch out your arm and see how far away your hand appears to be. I know that my finger tips are 2-1/2 feet away and I use this to "calibrate" my eye. With experience your mind will begin to adjust automatically. Remember that unless you are using a housing with a corrective dome, your camera sees what you see.

SM: You have to be careful stretching out your hand underwater. It can hurt if you touch some things.

RR: Hurt you and hurt many life-forms, especially coral. Underwater, the cardinal rule is don't touch anything. Coral is easily damaged or killed. "Hands off" includes avoiding brushing against coral and standing on it. Never hold on to coral to steady yourself to photograph. But, when diving wear gloves in case a surge pushes you into something.

SM: To put out your hand to stop being smacked into coral?

RR: Yes, but you should first try to swim out of the way rather than use your hands. Gloves are helpful around boat bottoms, docks, barnacles, and other rough surfaces also. Rubberized gloves are sold in dive shops, They are bright orange so you can find them if you drop them. In warm water I sometimes use thin cotton gardening gloves. Make sure you can comfortably operate your equipment with your gloves.

SM: About using flash. You talked earlier about going down and setting up lights. Do you use underwater flash on a stand off-camera?

RR: It can be done, but I mount my flash on a flash arm bracket. The flash is on a pole that can be angled and easily detached from its bracket. I decide on the lighting I want for a subject and position my light — above, to the side, high three-quarter, even backlight—almost as I would for a topside subject. I have even bounced light off a sandy bottom. Remember, all water contains some particles. If you leave the flash on-camera the particles will reflect light back into your lens and appear as out-of-focus blobs in your picture. By angling the flash, light is reflected to the side.

SM: How do you determine exposure underwater?

RR: Experience and an underwater light meter. There is some wonderful new totally automatic equipment. TTL works well underwater and solves many problems. Otherwise, for ambient light I use the Sekonic Marine Meter. My flash exposures are based on testing and experience. With a specific flash—my Ikelite Substrobe 150 is my workhorse—I know the correct exposure for specific flash to subject distances. Because so much is going on underwater I recommend a TTL system for all but the most serious photographers. And even professionals make some use of their high-tech features. But, TTL helps with exposure, not composition and lighting. You can use TTL to make a wonderfully exposed awful photograph. TTL is a tool, not a replacement for a photographer's eye.

I seem to be listing all the problems of shooting underwater.   Here's an advantage, a trick underwater photographers love. Underwater there are almost no straight lines, except for anchor lines. As you know, ultra-wide-angle lenses cause some distortion, which is most apparent in straight lines, therefore underwater you can make use of very wide-angle lenses more effectively. Look at this print of one of my manatee photographs from Florida. I wanted to show the manatee in its environment, among the huge stands of weeds growing from the bottom of the Crystal River. I shot through a gap in the weeds with a 16mm full-frame fish eye lens. There are no straight lines, no apparent distortion.

SM: The manatee looks as though it's in a clearing in a forest. At what depth was that picture shot?

RR: The bottom was about ten feet.

SM: The water is green with orangeish sun coming down and hitting the vegetation. No flash by the look of it. What exposure did you use?

RR: This was shot on 400 Ektachrome film, no flash, at about f/8.

SM: Many people say you can only use very slow film for saleable nature pictures. This is a big enlargement, beautiful quality. But you used 400 Ektachrome, not slow Kodachrome or Velvia.

RR: Ninety percent of my work is done with slow films. For macro work I use a lot of Kodachrome 25, the finest grain film of all. I shot most of my manatee work on Kodachrome 64; Kodachrome 200 was not available when I started the project. Working is shallow water at the right times of day, there was enough light. In the Galapagos I used Kodachrome 200 for available light work with sea lions. The weather and water both were gray. I was shooting at f/8, sometimes at f/5.6, with fast shutter speeds. Sharpness and grain were fine, the film's warm tone was what I needed.

For available light underwater, the best shooting times are between 10:00 A.M. and 2:00 P.M. The water surface acts as a mirror and reflects light as the sun gets lower. When the sun is overhead more light penetrates.

SM: Isn't sidelight more interesting?

RR: Early and late in the day only a limited amount of light penetrates and sidelight does not have the same effect as it would on the surface. Wind and waves also effect light penetration. More light gets through on calm days because the motion of waves reflects some light back. On choppy days you not only get less natural light but near the surface you have to deal with sea swells.

SM: What shutter speeds would you need to get sharp pictures in swell?

RR: 1/250. I advise using 1/125 whenever possible, 1/60 is necessary most times. I'm experienced, when it's calm I can use 1/30, even 1/15 with a wide lens. Whether or not your subject moves is a factor. A wreck is different from a dolphin. Action calls for faster shutter speeds.

SM: Which underwater lens would you recommend as a first lens?

RR: For the Nikonos the standard 35mm is effectively a 50mm underwater. It is inexpensive but hard to focus. The 28mm is better, its effective focal length is about 35mm. Nikon makes a very nice 20mm that costs much less than my favorite 15mm focal length, and is easy to use.

For Nikonos close-ups you use the 35mm with either the Nikon supplementary close-up lens or extension tubes, and compose with the appropriate wire frames. The 20-35mm zoom would be a good choice for the new Nikonos RS. First lenses with a camera in a housing could be a 20mm or 24mm used behind a dome port for scenics, and a 55mm or 105mm macro for close-ups.

SM: Do you prefer to use a Nikonos or a reflex camera in a housing?

RR: I use both. A housing is heavier and bulkier but is more versatile.

SM: What does a 35mm camera in a housing weigh on land?

RR: It depends. There is a lightweight system of plastic housings made by Ikelite and heavier high-end aluminum ones. The aluminum housings I use are made by Aquatica. They are precision products that can take a full range of lenses.

I like Ikelite housings because they are small and light. They are not as rugged as aluminum housings and are not as versatile, but they do a good job. Some of my professional colleagues look on these as amateur equipment, but I've shot magazine covers with them. Ikelites cannot do all that some aluminum housings can, but what they do they do well. I also use Ikelite strobes. They are top-of-the-line. I really like Ikelite, and have never found a more reputable company. Even before I was a published professional they were incredibly helpful and stood behind their products.

SM: Which strobes do you prefer?

RR: I use the Ikelite 150 and 225 substrobes. I set them manually because I am so comfortable working that way but they also work with TTL. Nikon strobes for the Nikonos V and the RS make full use of TTL. TTL really works and is a definite advantage, especially for the novice. Important features to look for in an underwater strobe are power and angle of coverage. To work at small apertures you need a pretty powerful flash; to use wide angle lenses you need to be aware of the angle of coverage. Underwater you may need to cover a 24mm, 20mm or even a 15mm lens. Get a unit that fits your needs. My Ikelite 150 gives me f/8 at three feet with 64 ISO film. This may not sound like much for an expensive unit but it is covering a 15mm lens.

Not many stores carry a full range of underwater equipment. Check out the *Helix Underwater* catalog for a good idea of equipment options.

SM: Tell me more about top-of-the-line aluminum housings.

RR: I use Aquaticas, made in Canada. They are sturdy, versatile and comfortable to use. I use them with Nikon F3s and action finders. The action finder makes it easy to compose and focus while wearing a mask. There are several different ports to accommodate a variety of lenses. There are Aquaticas for the Nikon F4 and top-of-the-line Canons.

SM: Do you suggest if you want to use a housing, trying the Ikelite first and seeing what it does for you?

RR: Unless you are committed to a top-of-the-line camera and lenses and are ready to spend almost $5000, more with a strobe. Ikelites are made for many cameras. Since most cameras don't take action finders they include a magnifying eyepiece. They make flat macro ports and dome ports for wide-angle lenses. Ikelites cost about $250, which is one-eighth the cost of an Aquatica. With one of their housings you might well be able to use a camera and lenses you already own. You can compose through the lens and, with a dome port, use wide angle lenses to their full advantage.

SM: But if someone is very serious you say go with an aluminum housing?

RR: Yes, or try a Nikonos RS. It is a fraction of the size and weight of a housing. Some people are wondering if the RS will put housing manufacturers out of business. A more important consideration for the professional is - have you ever done a job with a single camera body?

SM: Never, of course. The camera might fail.

RR: Exactly. And you can't change film underwater so two cameras are a must, actually a minimum. Professionals often hang several cameras from lines tied to a boat. To move around with two housed cameras requires an assistant. With the RS you can carry two or three cameras yourself. Remember, you can't change lenses underwater either. Back-ups are needed in case of failure too. I went fifteen years without flooding a major piece of equipment. But a few months age an o-ring gave out and put an end to my run of luck. On a job take spare cameras, lenses, flashes, and meters.

Aluminum housings are heavy and bulky. If you are a serious amateur going on vacation to the Great Barrier Reef you likely will take one. Most people don't want to be bothered carrying two housings. Take a Nikonos along. If one breaks or is lost or stolen, you have the other.

SM: Talk about maintenance. You have wash and clean the seals, the o-rings, use grease, clear out grains of sand, and so on, meticulously.

RR: There are passive and dynamic O-rings. Dynamic ones protect moving parts of cameras and housings and require special care. Keep them clean and replace them often. O-ring grease keeps rubber from drying out and becoming brittle. Wash salt water and chlorine off all gear. Soak gear in fresh water, then hose it, the sooner after use the better.

SM: You can rent basic underwater cameras in many locations. But, if they are anything like rented masks, they cannot be entirely trusted.

RR: No! Speaking of masks choose a well-fitting one and carry a spare. If you wear glasses, have one made with your prescription.

SM: Do you wear a wet suit?

RR: Often, especially if I staying down for some time. Even in warm water I wear a vest if I plan to stay in for a few hours.

SM: What underwater pictures sell best?

RR: The picture that "says" coral reef that could be used in an ad for Bermuda, the Bahamas, the Caymans, or wherever. A lot of Caribbean subjects are universal— a yellowtail snapper is a yellowtail snapper—no matter where you shot it. For saleable stock, look for the explosion of color you get when you light up a reef. Also an elegant shot of a colorful fish such as a French angelfish. For editorial work, look for behavior and subjects that help tell a story.

SM: Who's underwater pictures do you admire most?

RR: I think Douglas Faulkner is a first-rate artist. He was an important influence. Doug once said that swimming up to a sea anemone disturbs the currents, and its tentacles wave in all directions. He would wait until the creature returned to its natural flow in one direction before photographing.

SM: Patience is important underwater too. Thank you for your generosity.

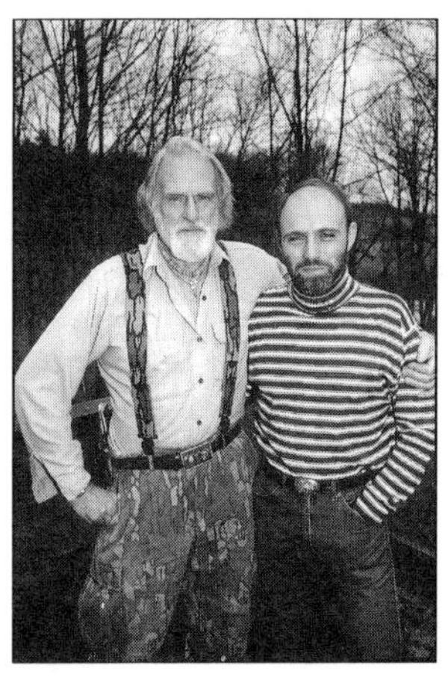

An Interview with

Leonard Lee Rue III
&
Len Rue, Jr.

Leonard Lee Rue III has been a world-class nature photographer for most of his forty-seven-year career. He was born in New Jersey, raised on a farm, and worked as a wilderness guide before becoming a full time professional nature photographer, writer, and lecturer. He is the author/photographer of twenty-two books including the bestseller _How I Photograph Wildlife and Nature,_ and writes a popular monthly column in _Outdoor Photography_ magazine. He is a noted authority on deer, and was recently awarded an Honorary Doctorate of Science by Colorado State University.

His son **Len Rue, Jr.,** also a New Jersey native, has a degree in professional photography from the Rochester Institute of Technology, and is recognized as an outstanding nature photographer in his own right. He also manages the family stock-picture business as well as Rue Enterprises, which supplies equipment to nature photographers.

Both photographers' favorite subject is big game species. I interviewed father and son at their office in northwestern New Jersey.

SM: Thanks for having me. This is such a beautiful place, I'm looking at a peacock on the deck outside the window! I thought it would be fun to talk to such a famous father/son team. Who wants to start?

LLR: I always say, I don't know anyone who has taken more pictures, but knows less about cameras than I do! The important thing about wildlife photography is that your camera should become a part of you, so that you can concentrate on the subject. An animal isn't going to stand there while you learn the equipment. Len is a much better technical person than I will ever be—when we do seminars and workshops together he fields all the questions about cameras! Of course, he's a very good wildlife photographer too!

SM: Were you self-taught as a photographer?

LLR: Yes. All the mistakes are mine! But I am a very good field naturalist. This is the keynote for wildlife photography, knowing the wildlife. I was a good enough trapper to be professional when I was seventeen. To give you an example, a fox has the whole wide world to run around in, and I could make him put his left front foot on a small piece of metal he couldn't see. If you can do that, you understand foxes. Or, take white-tailed deer. I've written four books and hundreds of columns about them and taken many thousands of whitetail pictures. I have over 200 hours of video. I don't know how many thousands of hours I've spent watching, working, studying deer.

SM: On the road coming up here, I passed a herd of about twelve white-tailed deer. But many people think there isn't any wildlife to photograph in New Jersey, or New York, or most Eastern states.

LRJr: There is a lot of wildlife around in northwest New Jersey. Wild turkeys come right down to the house here through the woods.

LLR: I lecture on deer all over the country. I just lectured in Michigan. Someone there said, "If you're so interested in deer, why do you live in New Jersey?" I said "How many deer does your state allow hunters to take?" They are allowed four in Michigan. In New Jersey, if you had all the possible permits, you could take twenty-two. We have so many deer, there isn't enough to feed them. We have to reduce the herd.

SM: A focus of my book is selling nature pictures. It's one thing to take photographs as a hobby, quite another to sell them. I'm sure that pictures of bucks with beautiful racks of antlers sell the best.

LLR: That's right.

SM: Are there many of those in New Jersey, or are they mostly in wildlife preserves?

LLR: We stress in our workshops that you cannot compete with the gun. Almost all pictures of big animals are taken in national parks, national wildlife refuges, private refuges, state parks, on private property, power plant property - any place where they are not hunted. That's where serious wildlife photographers, and all professionals, take their pictures.

SM: So you might be able to get pretty pictures of does and fawns and herds around here at the right season, but on the whole those aren't the bread-and-butter pictures.

LRJr: You're not going to get the big or huge racks, because around here, let's face it, bucks just don't grow old enough to grow racks...

LLR: Eighty-six percent of bucks in New Jersey are killed by the time they are one-and-a-half years old. They cannot grow big racks in that time. The big guys are in preserves. Of course they can come out to breed...

SM: In national parks in the the West you see big ones. How old do they have to be to have good-sized antlers?

LLR: Four years old.

SM: Your deer photographs are superb. I also love your pictures of Dall sheep.

LLR: Sheep are my favorite. Of all the things I can photograph, I prefer sheep. They don't sell! Because the average person will never be able to hunt sheep, it's too expensive. Everybody hunts deer, so that is where the market is.

SM: In your books, you show some of your many magazine covers. A great many of them are hunting magazines...

LLR: Oh, yes. I'm up around 1,800 covers now.

SM: Are ducks another big seller, because there is a lot of duck hunting?

LLR: Yes, ducks are big. I thought the wild turkey would be the next really big thing. But it isn't. It's the bald eagle.

LRJr: Because it's the symbol of our country. Bald eagles started to be big in 1976, with the bicentennial. In the 1980s there was the anniversary of the Constitution...

LLR: Symbolic of the Declaration of Independence, the Revolutionary War, you know, when we whopped the daylights out of you British!

SM: Ouch! Owls are very popular. They are symbolic of wisdom, they are cute...

LLR: Right! But not as popular as turkeys... Wild turkeys are very, very popular, but they have not replaced the bald eagle.

SM: Wild turkeys are not as handsome for one thing. They are kind of goofy looking.

LLR: But wild turkeys are hunted a great deal, this is the big thing. It is now spreading throughout the entire country... all the continental forty-eight states have the turkey, and I think forty-five states allow turkey hunting...

LRJr: Benjamin Franklin wanted them to be the national symbol of the country. He wanted the turkey over the eagle...

LLR: He said the eagle was a scavenger, and it's true. He's a fish catcher, but he scavenges a great deal upon dead fish...

SM: You have a big stock picture operation here, I've just seen it. You also deal with agents, one is Norman Owen Tomalin, of Bruce Coleman Inc. I just talked to him. Do you deal with agents in other countries?

LLR: Yes. And here too! Most people today are lucky if they can get one stock agent. Now, when you sign with an agent, they want you exclusively. There was a meeting with three big stock agents, up in Massachusetts, for a lot of aspiring wildlife photographers from a huge camera club. There was a lot of give-and-take. One guy asked why, if the agents gave only exclusive contracts, Leonard Lee Rue was with all three. One agent gave the classic answer. "Leonard Lee Rue was in business before we were!"

LRJr: When they were starting, they were only too happy to take the work!

SM: I'm quite sure that you guys have pictures that most camera club members couldn't get.

LRJr: There are certain camera clubs, like some out there in the Rockies, in the Denver area, where I tell you, they've got some excellent photographers. From Denver, from around Boulder, everything is at their doorstep. All they have to do is drive an hour and a half and they can be on top of Mount Evans and work on goats. A two-hour drive puts them in Rocky Mountain National Park, they can work on elk and all the Alpine high stuff. If they go in the other direction, they can get to the national grasslands, all the prairie stuff in Wyoming, the Dakotas, and Nebraska.

LLR: Prairie chickens, sharp-tailed grouse.

LRJr: Colorado people take trips down to Bosque Del Apache (Wildlife Refuge, in New Mexico) for the sandhill cranes. Even Yellowstone is only a day away.

LLR: For us it's a major expedition, Yellowstone is 2,090-some miles away from here. There's a very good camera club in Venice, Florida, too. Florida is a great state for wildlife. My opinion is that some of the finest nature work in the country today is being done in camera clubs. There are some that specialize in nature and wildlife. We know a lot of these people. I have a great deal of respect for what they can do.

SM: Your associate showed me your Airstream trailer. He said you were going to Alaska this summer.

LLR: That's what I work for!

SM: Do you have a favorite place? Would your care to mention it, or is it a deep secret?

LLR: Yellowstone National Park! It's the number-one spot in the entire world for me for photography. Denali (formerly McKinley) National Park in Alaska is number two, and the Ngorongoro Crater in Tanzania, Africa, number three.

SM: If you go to Denali, with your great names, are you given special permission to go off the beaten track?

LRJr: Denali is the most restrictive of all the national parks. They've got this one narrow, twisty dirt road, that goes for 112 miles out to one of the lakes. With the influx of visitors that they get these days, they bus everybody out. As professionals, you can get a professional photographic pass, and they give you an allotment of fourteen days for you to drive your own vehicle. Ten days in the prime time of August through September, four at another time. But it's very difficult to get the pass. You have to prove that you have had X numbers of pictures in magazines with a million circulation or more...

LLR: You can't just sell to a local paper like the Blairstown Press here... You have to qualify. We have very good friends who went in on a pass, that I thought shouldn't have had one. There are too many people that need them. There are just so many passes available. No more than ten professionals in their cars can be there at one time. August and September are the prime time, you get the best colors and so on... You can take your other four days earlier, or you can take all fourteen at one time earlier. We are going up there this summer. Len, Jr., will take his fourteen days in July, then we are going to work on brown bear, at Brooks Camp on the Katmai (peninsula) and then we'll come back, and I'll take my ten days in Denali from part way into August. We will not be there during the peak season, this year...

SM: How do you get the pass?

LLR: You have to send in twenty-five clips of pictures that you have sold as a magazine photographer, or, X number of books, or, X number of video tapes. You must send for the application for the pass to the chief ranger, no later than November or December for the following summer. He will send a list of all the requirements. Of the magazine clips, five of the twenty-five must have over 1,000,000 circulation. It's very difficult now.

SM: That's the best way to go. You can't do much from a bus...

LRJr: Yes, it's difficult, but there are only so many passes. But there are certain things in Denali, like the Dall sheep, that you do as a day hike. You can do that off the bus just as easily as you can from a car. Just take the bus to a trailhead, and hike up for sheep. But the primary thing people go to Denali for are the bears. Then you do need that vehicle, right next to you, so you can be there close, but have it as a sanctuary, to get into quickly!

SM: Yes! Your father says Yellowstone is his favorite place. What's yours?

LRJr: We're in agreement about that. Yellowstone is a fabulous place. One of the best in the whole world.

SM: Any time of the year?

LRJr: Spring is good for babies, but anywhere in the Rockies, they don't really get a spring the way we do here. Out in the Rockies, you'll get snow right into May sometimes, I've seen some really bad storms then. All of a sudden, the snow will go, and you'll get a week or so of green, then it gets so hot and dry it burns everything into the ground. September is best month of all.

LLR: Here, we have spring flowers, summer flowers, fall colors. In Alaska, you have about two good months... then, wham, winter!

SM: About Africa. You mentioned the Ngorongoro Crater, it's a fantastic place.

LLR: I would love to spend six months there. I was given a book by a German man who spent two years living in the crater, in a little stone cabin... He had access to everything. The pictures were unbelievable.

It's difficult to find that much time. People say to me, you're always in the out-of-doors. But I have written for four magazines this month. I've written twenty-two books. How do people think these things get done? Not when you are out in the field.

SM: Of course not.

LRJr: And selling pictures. I spent the whole day, down in my office, pulling pictures and making submissions. It's a labor-intensive business!

SM: I teach a class. Many people want to become professional. But most know little or nothing about the business side of photography. Writing lists and forms, and filing, and invoices, and copyright and caption imprinting, making sales calls.

LLR: When I started and someone wanted a picture, you quoted a price. Often $75 for one-time magazine use in those days. Now Lenny has a thick folder. He has to ask what it's going to be used for, and how many copies will be printed. Plus U.S. rights? Additional rights? Spanish rights, or world English-language rights? and so on. I never quote a price now. I let Len, Jr., negotiate. It's very complex, and takes time!

SM: Are you getting into marketing by CD-ROM, pictures on computer disc?

LRJr: Now you're hitting a touchy spot with me!

SM: I'm listening. I've met Jim Pickerell quite a few times...

LRJr: I get his stock report. I agree with him 100 percent. I'm not as versed of course as Jim is. He's made a career out of staying right on top of stock trends. Producers of CD-ROM "clip-art" discs as far as I'm concerned, are really trying to rip photographers off... There is no other way of putting it. As a free-lancer, as you are doubtless well aware, you live or die based on one-time use rights. Those clip-art people, first of all they come in on the bottom of the scale in terms of price, then they want to use the pictures in perpetuity, for everything under the sun! One company in California is offering two dollars a picture! For all rights!

SM: It's suicide to sell to those people.

LRJr: Yes, it is.

SM: The only protection is, of course, the good people, like us of course are not going to sell stuff to them. Can you talk about film?

LRJr: Films are so good now. I think it will be a long way down the road before digital or videotape or any new medium comes anywhere close to the quality of even 35mm film. For years, nature photographers shot almost all Kodachrome 64. Now it's being pushed aside somewhat by Fujichrome Velvia, which supposedly has the resolution of Kodachrome 25, and more vibrant colors.

SM: Have you changed films?

LRJr: I'm shooting more and more Velvia, not that I'm turning my back on Kodachrome, it's been a staple of the business for many, many years, but you can't ignore a new major addition to the film family like Velvia.

Other things are better too. There has also been a big increase in the quality of the printing industry. Back in the 1970s lenses were slower. We were still shooting with slower lenses, 500mm f/8 lenses and so on. Now there are 600mm f/4's.

SM: To change the subject. Do you ever go out and shoot for the market? If all of a sudden, clients want polar bears, do you run out and shoot polar bears?

LRJr: Sometimes. Or we go just to go, go somewhere we want to go. We've been up to Churchill [Manitoba] for the polar bears.

LLR: We've been up there a couple of times. Not so much for the market, but because it was the only large North American animal I had never photographed.

LRJr: You want everything than you possibly can have, for your files.

LLR: My trip to Antarctica. I came back with twenty-seven new species for the file. That's hard to do.

SM: A lot of penguins. What else?

LLR: Penguins, seals, sea birds, twenty-seven species, so I was very, very pleased. I had far more photographic opportunities there than I ever thought possible... Not that we've sold that much from down there, you get a surge of interest once in a while, then it goes by.

LRJr: For example, we went for years without much demand for all our African stuff. All of a sudden, in the 1980s, when poachers were starting to kill all the rhino and elephant in sight, everyone got on the bandwagon, and those subjects had a very high demand. They are still very popular now.

SM: One of the things that got me interested in doing this book was analyzing my stock sales. Lions and elephants outsold the other animals by a wide margin. I don't think I've ever sold a zebra picture, or a wildebeest, or a deer, even though I have lovely shots. I've sold a few giraffes and hippos. People seem most interested in the big, powerful animals, especially big cats.

LLR: And you'll go back. Africa is one of those experiences, if there's any way you can afford it, you'll go back. We hope to make it pay, but even if it doesn't you'll take it from somewhere else, just to go and see those animals again.

SM: I've done a lot of traveling on the beaten track, but now I'm concentrating on the places where you can photograph wildlife, Alaska, Manitoba, and so on. Normally, you make the money back if you take good pictures anywhere.

LLR: Yes. But whether it pays or not, if you can afford it, you'll go.

SM: You're a man after my own heart. If you don't love it, you shouldn't be doing it. If you love being out in wild places, you'll be rewarded no matter what you get, or don't get.

LLR: That's right! And I take notes when I'm not photographing. I sat in a blind for 21-1/2 hours once, in Denali, at a fox den, photographing when there was action, but taking hour by hour notes. I wrote a book on foxes, and I have my diary for the six weeks that we spent there. I have tremendous research on foxes' behavior. Knowing a lot about them to start with, I could study the nuances of fox behavior. Other people might see the fox, but not be aware of what certain behavior designates.

SM: Behavioral pictures are the key pictures. The little moments that reveal. As you said at the start, if you're using an unfamiliar camera you can easily miss them.

LRJr: But making it all pay, that comes down to marketing!

SM: I asked another famous wildlife photographer, Art Wolfe, if he ever used animal-model agencies. He said, "Certainly. For North American big cats for instance. It's much kinder to photograph them there than to drive them up a tree with dogs."

LRJr: Absolutely.

SM: Do you go to those game farms in Montana to photograph them?

LLR: I say, that anytime you see a picture of a cougar, you've gone down to your local Hertz Rent-A-Cougar shop!

SM: Having looked closely at a lot of nature pictures, there are some individual cats I now recognize. I see the same pretty gray bobcat over and over, she's in so many nature books, catalogs, and calendars!

LLR: I don't care what the caption says, or who took the picture. If it's a cougar, they either ran it with dogs, or it's a rented cat!

SM: So it's a pretty fair statement to say that most large and smaller wild-animal pictures are not taken just by people casually driving around in a car. Professional nature photographers go to find them, very carefully, at certain specified times, in well-known places. Sometimes you rent them, or keep them, or breed them...

LRJr: Yes. And you run into the same photographers, year after year. It's a circuit. Someone you met in Denali in August, you'll see them in the Everglades, in February...

LLR: If I'm not in Yellowstone, September 15th, I'm homesick. That's the peak of the elk rut!

SM: Is it crowded then? Do you need a permit? I've been in spring... I saw an elk being born.

LLR: No permit. But it can get crowded. I've stood there and had seventy-five photographers on either side of me!

SM: That's because it's you!

LLR: No. It's because the animals are there. Other photographers are no problem most of the time. You don't block each other's shots of course. Sometimes you get a few clowns...

Look at the red-winged blackbird on the feeder outside!

SM: And that peacock! Not your normal New Jersey bird.

LLR: He appeared one day from out of the woods. I suppose he escaped from a zoo or estate somewhere. Lots of birds come here, they like our woods and pond...

SM: Thank you both, very very much. It was a treat.

LRJr: We enjoyed it too!

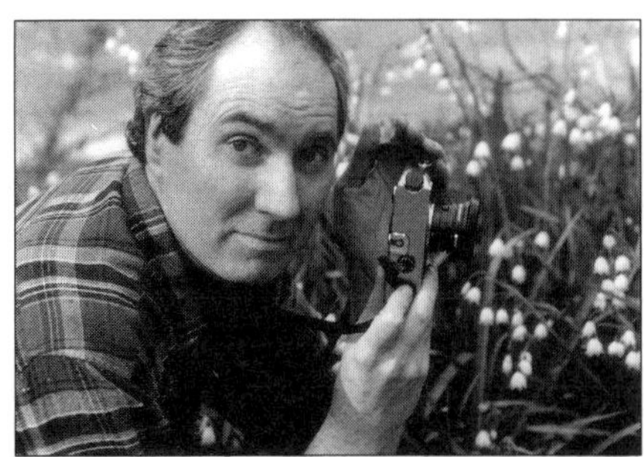

An Interview with

Curtice Taylor

Curtice Taylor grew up in New York, California, and Connecticut, studied film at UCLA, and has a degree in anthropology from the State University of New York at Purchase. One of his specialities is gardens, and his color pictures have appeared in most of the leading garden and shelter magazines in the U.S., Britain and Europe. His hand-colored fine-art photographs are exhibited in galleries, and represented in many corporate and private collections. He has just completed a book on the gardens of Holland and Belgium, which will be published late in 1994. Curtice is a colleague who teaches some classes at the School of Visual Arts in New York. I interviewed him at his studio.

SM: How did you get started?

CT: Recently I found some old pictures I had totally forgotten. They were chromes taken in the summer of 1962 with my brother's little Yashica, of gardens. I was twelve years old. Today, thirty years later, I'm still photographing gardens. There was something there that I guess I didn't tune into until much later. I'm not exclusively a landscape or garden photographer. That is my commercial and editorial work. My art work is hand-painted black-and-white and manipulated photographs. I keep the two very separate, the subject matter is totally different.

I have never taken a formal photography course, I learned mostly from a woman I lived with who was a photographer. I was in New York, and became a struggling photographer, having abandoned film and anthropology because I found that with both of those professions you needed to be fund raising all your life. That wasn't for me. I photographed people, just scraped by, and for a year taught anthropology, film making and photography. It was a rather schizophrenic existence!

How the commercial garden thing started, my father had a very close friend, Russell Paige, an Englishman who only died a few years ago, who was considered the great garden designer of the midtwentieth-century. Russell was in New York with Lanning Roper, also a great English garden designer and a writer. Roper was doing a story on a garden that Russell Paige had designed for William and Babe Paley (the owner of CBS at the time) on Long Island. The photographer never showed up! Lucky for me. My father and I had been invited later that day to meet Roper and see the garden, so I got the job. I was very nervous, but borrowed cameras and went out five or six times, and thoroughly overshot, but it came out well and was published in the British magazine *Country Life.* For almost no money, but to have that garden in my portfolio opened a lot of doors!

I was also lucky that Americans became very keen on gardening at just about that point. There was a market for garden photography, and good garden photography took off. As late as 1979, the garden books were bad. Still black-and-white predominantly, and the color separations were terrible. Magazines like the late lamented *House and Garden* at that time used the same photographer who shot the house to shoot the garden, even if they had no feeling for gardens. A breakthrough was a beautiful color book called *Visions of Paradise,* pictures of gardens all over the world, by Marina Schinz. That became a best-seller, and soon, in the 1980s, many many expensive garden books were being published, $65, $75 books! There were too many of them. I think now the bubble has burst.

SM: The important question is, how do you capture the soul of a garden?

CT: I don't know that you can do it in one picture. Most good gardens have "rooms" or parts to them. You could get up very high and shoot down on them, you can get the plan, but I don't know that that gets to the spirit or the soul at all. Formal gardens are the ultimate manifestation of man's trying to dominate nature, trying to put chaos into order; I think you first have to figure out what the designer or owner is trying to do. Sometimes that's obscure, sometimes it's straightforward.

A lot of people think garden photography is only about flowers, which is a problem. Even some magazines think this. The editors like something floriferous! But a formal garden is a design, not just a random collection of pretty flowers or massed bright colors. I have often had this dialog with picture editors: "This is a story about a garden designer, and you have chosen nothing but close-ups of plants. He or she is going to be upset when they see this! Those pictures don't illustrate at all what this person is about. You must show the overall design."

To me, to show flowers alone would be like photographing the Seagram Building [a much admired skyscraper in New York] and only doing the lobby. You have to do a long shot, you have to see what the garden is about. The lobby certainly reveals a lot about the Seagram building, so you need the close-ups as well. In editorial photography as you know, they call that the "in-and-out." In garden photography you need the long shot, and the intimacy of the plants too. By the way, I'm no horticulturalist. I sometimes give lectures and have to tell the garden club members I don't know the Latin names of all the plants! A good garden is not solely about color. A good garden is about texture as much as it is about flowers. Contrasting textures, all that stuff.

SM: Isn't it also about paths and grottoes, and pools, and niches?

CT: Yes. That's why there is never enough space in a magazine to do a big garden real justice. You must select what you think most important. But in this book I have just finished on gardens in Holland and Belgium, we made a decision to show fewer gardens in more detail. I would rather have many pictures of one great garden, than show four or five that merely tantalize you, don't really show you their breadth. We dropped a few gardens we had originally planned on including, to do this in the book. It's going to irk some people. By the way, Low Country gardens may sound like a very esoteric subject, but they have a very long history. There's some argument that English garden style as we know it actually came from Holland, was brought over the North Sea by William and Mary!

SM: Do you try to read about the designer or history of the garden?

CT: I like to. I also like to work with an author. I think that's something you often have to do. If there's a text-driven article and you don't know what the author is saying, you are often working at cross-purposes. He or she is going on and on about the grotto, and you didn't even know it was there! I read, but also go with an open mind. You have a view of what it's going to be like, and how you are going to react, but it's never what you think. I tell always myself not to take any pictures when I first arrive, to first walk through the garden, experience it, let it wash over me. But then when I do arrive, I invariably get very excited, and start taking pictures right away! I think, "This isn't going to last another five minutes."

SM: Do you have a kind of set picture, that you know will be safe, will cover you if it's in the camera?

CT: The long shot from above. Marina Schinz is funny about that. She is rather short, and always insists on having plenty of tall stepladders around when she works. Being tall, I'm not as wedded to that as she is, but I suppose that is the one safe shot. Marina likes to shoot from seven or ten feet up, even from a wall or window twelve or twenty feet But, I write this in the introduction to my book, the real secret of garden photography is long lunches on sunny days! From about eleven in the morning till around four in the afternoon; even having a glass of wine, and a nap after that nice lunch is a good idea. Not just because of greed or sloth! You have to be up at about 5:30 or 6:00 A.M., to be there when the light turns pretty. This early arrival can be a problem when the anxious garden owners want to welcome you, they hate to get up then. It's a problem also with public gardens, which don't normally open until around 9:00 A.M. But at 9:00 A.M. the best light has gone in summer. If you have an assignment, try to arrange for early admission, to be there alone. In places like Italy that's almost impossible. Dealing with Italian bureaucracy can be frustrating. The secret of photographing gardens as a tourist, I've done it many times, is to remember tourists' schedules. They are on vacation, they don't like to get up early. So get there the moment the gate opens. In the late afternoon, the gardens get packed. So go as early as possible. Sometimes closing time is great. I got great, very long soft shadows in spring evening light at Keukenhof (tulip gardens) in Holland around 4:30 P.M. one April, the tour busses had all gone. It is a waste of film and time to shoot gardens in the middle of the day. You want sun. But hard noon shadows and crowds are both awful.

SM: What camera format do you use?

CT: I use a Leica, and medium format. Lately I have been using the new Mamiya 6 MF (a 6x6cm rangefinder). I like rangefinder cameras. I have a tall Linhof tripod. Here's a good tip for your readers. Dragging equipment around all day in a big garden gets exhausting. I use a golf cart. Mine cost about $120 from a discount sporting goods-store. You can fold up the wheels and ship it on a plane, with your tripod and light stand securely covered. The ball pocket is for carrying film. I hang my carry-on camera bag from it when shooting. It may look strange, but it's practical. You can hook a small stepladder to it if needed.

SM: What if you must shoot at noon? Last August in Butchart Gardens (in Victoria BC) the shadows were hard, and Japanese tourists were endlessly taking pictures, even standing in flower beds. They don't do it at home.

CT: Japanese tourists always do that in flower gardens. I think it's because the point of Japanese gardens is design. They have few flowers. Finding a big shady tree is a good idea if you must shoot at noon on a sunny day. Just hope there are some flowers under it.

SM: What about wind? That is a problem when photographing flowers.

CT: Wind is a problem because you must use small f/stops and slow shutter speeds for maximum depth of field. Early there tends to be less wind. In a breeze, I wait between the puffs. You can't shoot in a gale.

SM: Where are your very favorite gardens?

CT: I would have to say in Italy. Those are my personal favorites. In this country, the deep South and the Pacific Northwest have the climate needed for the best gardens. Some desert gardens are beautiful too. The gardeners who have the toughest time here live in the cold upper Midwest, they must be very dedicated. They mostly have to plant annuals.

SM: Thank you so much.

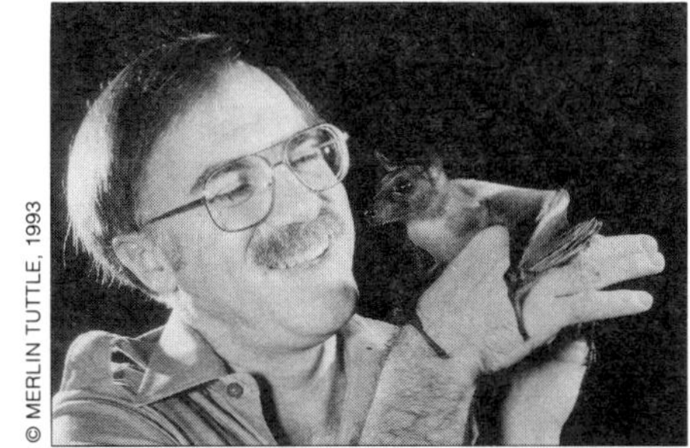

An Interview with

Merlin Tuttle

Dr. Merlin D. Tuttle is one of the world's leading authorities on bats, and on bat photography. His pictures have appeared in top magazines, and books and calendars around the world. He is the founder of Bat Conservation International, based in Austin, Texas.

These remarks are excerpts from a telephone interview.

MT: The key to doing the best possible nature photography is to love and befriend animals. Noone should ever needlessly hurt or scare any creature just to make a few bucks with a picture. I don't photograph any bat until it is contented and relaxed. I became a photographer in self-defense, when I wrote the chapter on bats for the National Geographic Society book, *Wild Animals of North America,* in 1978. The bat pictures then available were awful, mostly of tormented bats who were snarling in self-defense. I could see fright and pain in the animals' expressions in those pictures. To the casual observer, the bats appeared to be mean and aggressive. But happy bats are just as inquisitive and cute as chipmunks, or any other animal, and many are just as pretty. I protested that pictures of defensively snarling bats would only foster peoples' misconceptions and harm my efforts to educate people to understand and appreciate bats, which consume countless insects each night. They are extremely important to the balance of nature, and contrary to ancient fears, do not attack people or pets. The *Geographic* saw my point, and sent me out to take more appropriate pictures with photographer Bates Littlehales for six weeks. He taught me my original field techniques. I have since learned a great deal more.

My first bat stories for *National Geographic* were lit with Vivitar flash units with the power turned down. I now use high-speed flash units custom-made by Ken Olson, an engineer in St. Paul. It took years to perfect my lighting. I don't use beam triggers. I travel with hundreds of pounds of equipment, and a portable studio. It often takes hundreds of frames to get one that shows a bat in just the way I want.

An Interview with

Art Wolfe

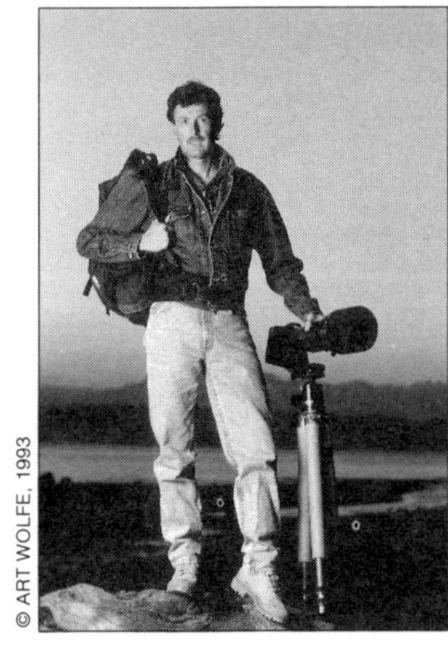

Art Wolfe is one of the most celebrated and successful nature and wildlife photographers in the world. He has eleven photography books to his credit to date including favorites of mine, *The Kingdom* and *Bears.* He is currently concentrating on big cats, primates, and endangered peoples for other books. His pictures have appeared in top nature magazines worldwide, and in many books and calendars. His video *On Location With Art Wolfe* is a bestseller, and his new how-to book, *The Art of Nature Photography,* a collaboration with writer/picture editor Martha Hill, is headed that way also. Art is a painter as well as a photographer, and has had one-man shows of photographs and watercolors at the Frye Art Museum in Seattle. I interviewed him when he was visiting New York.

SM: Thanks so much for coming.

AW: As long as you understand the publisher of my new book *The Art of Nature Photography,* won't be too happy if I answer a lot of technical questions!

SM: I am more interested in how you think and see! First, the usual question, how did you get started?

AW: I grew up in Seattle, where I still live. As a kid I used to run around among the pine trees, looking at butterflies and birds, going hiking and camping, all that stuff—I've always loved nature and the outdoors. I studied English and painting in college. For several years I taught high school English, and photographed in the summers.

SM: What was the big breakthrough?

AW: Like a lot of other photographers, I went to see *National Geographic.* I had been photographing owls very seriously — my ambition was to document all the owls in America—I suggested the story to an editor, and showed her the work to date. She suggested that I concentrate on eared owls. I did, and finished the story in about three months. I wrote it too. It was published in January 1980. After that, my serious career got going.

SM: I'd like to ask how you do your research.

AW: That's a good question. I do it by telephone.

SM: I saw a superb picture of yours, of scarlet ibis, taken at the Caroni Bird Reserve in Trinidad (in *Audubon* magazine, November 1992). I've been to the Caroni mangrove swamp, it's surrounded by water, you are a long way from the birds. How did you approach that whole thing?

AW: I knew of a hotel that caters to naturalists in Trinidad, part of the Asa

Wright Nature Center. I called them from Seattle. They recommended a guide. I called this man, and we talked for about an hour on the phone, then I flew to Trinidad with my assistant and met the guide. He had a big flat-bottomed boat for taking people through the swamp. He had done what I asked, and cut quite a lot of nine- or ten-foot poles and they were lying in the boat. We started out in the afternoon and took the boat to within about 100 yards of the trees where the ibises roost. We drove poles deep into the mud all round the boat, and lashed it to them until the boat was a very stable platform. It took quite a time. Then my assistant and I set up my Nikon and 800mm f/8 lens using two tripods, one for the tripod socket of the lens, one for the camera, and waited. When the ibises showed up, I had about ten minutes to shoot; the birds only come in just before sunset. I used Fuji 100 film and shot as fast as possible. Sometimes I used a 1.4X extender [making a 1100mm f/11 tele-extender/lens combination]. All three of us had to keep as still as possible, because the exposure times were between two and three seconds in the very low sunlight! Then in the tropics, the sun goes right down. The birds spend the day in Venezuela somewhere. I suppose I could have gone there to shoot them, but didn't. I needed ibises for my stock. You have to have as many species as possible; if people don't find what they want when they call you, they soon stop calling.

SM: How much do you rely on stock?

AW: At this point, almost totally. It has been like that for seven or eight years. I am with Allstock agency in my hometown of Seattle. I have an exclusive agreement with them. They give me a guarantee. Marty Loken (Allstock's founder and president) says I am his most productive photographer. I met him when he was picture editor for *Alaska* magazine. I like the freedom stock gives me, to do whatever I am most interested in. It now finances my travels all over the world.

SM: What interests you the most?

AW: Well, I'm a generalist. Some people, like Tim Fitzharris say, who's a superb bird photographer; or John Shaw, who is marvellous at close-ups, mostly do one thing. I do birds, animals, landscapes, close-ups—I often use long lenses to shoot landscapes by the way—and next year I will be doing a book on indigenous peoples, their traditional way of life; mostly the small tribes of the world. They are endangered too. From Indians in the Brazilian rain forest to Pygmies in Africa, to the Aborigines in the outback of Australia.

SM: What advice would you give to nature photographers starting their careers?

AW: People do sometimes ask my advice. Especially people in midlife, like a doctor or a lawyer say, who has somewhat of a cushion of money, and wants a complete career change. Quite a lot of these people are very, very good. Usually, they think they can make money in nature and wildlife photography by selling fine-art prints. I tell them not to rely on that. I sell prints, originals and reproductions. I was here in New York autographing posters in March last year at the paper-goods show, but truthfully prints don't produce that much income for me. I tell people who are good, if they have $10,000 or $20,000 to invest, to shoot for stock. Good stock will give a much better return for the money.

SM: Do you use the places where they breed and keep animals for photography and filming? Wild Eyes Game Ranch, in Montana, is said to be very good. They currently charge about $350 for half a day with a bobcat, for instance, and the cat comes with a trained handler.

AW: Yes, I use them. I've used that one. As I said before, for stock, you have to have as many different species as possible. The only way to photograph bobcats in the wild is to tree them with dogs, which of course is extremely stressful to the animal.

SM: Where do you like to shoot best?

AW: In the wilderness, away from crowds. I like to hike into back country.

SM: You shoot with very long lenses; you need a big tripod. How do you carry all that stuff, plus camping gear?

AW: As I said, I always use a field assistant, who of course carries a lot. Also, I never found a backpack I really liked, so I've designed one. It will be on the market soon and it will take the longest lenses made.

SM: I went to Washington State for the first time last summer, to the Olympic National Park. The beach section to me was especially wonderful.

AW: And the best part is, most of those beaches are wilderness. You just hike in from the road.

SM: Where are some of your other favorite places?

AW: Alaska. In the backcountry.

SM: Denali National Park is very busy in summer.

AW: I don't work along the road. July and August there the road can get quite crowded. You don't see that many animals. No problem for landscape. If you hike away from the road it's fine.

SM: Do you use a ball head on your tripod?

AW: Yes. I use the old Arca-Swiss. I left mine behind by mistake when I went to photograph at the Jurong bird reserve in Singapore recently, so I bought one of their new model at one of the big camera stores there. The small screw adjusting the tension fell out and got lost, and the whole thing came apart on me.

SM: If you had one gadget you wouldn't leave behind on any trip, what would that be?

AW: Gadget or lens?

SM: Anything!

AW: It's a lens. My 200-400mm zoom [Nikkor 200-400mm f/4 ED zoom lens]. It's just the right length for everything from big birds to mammals to landscapes. Nikon doesn't make it anymore. The lens used to cost about $3,000 new. I was afraid to have just one. I recently found a second one, mint, used; it cost $6,000. I was glad to get it.

SM: This may drive the price up! Thank you so much for talking to me.

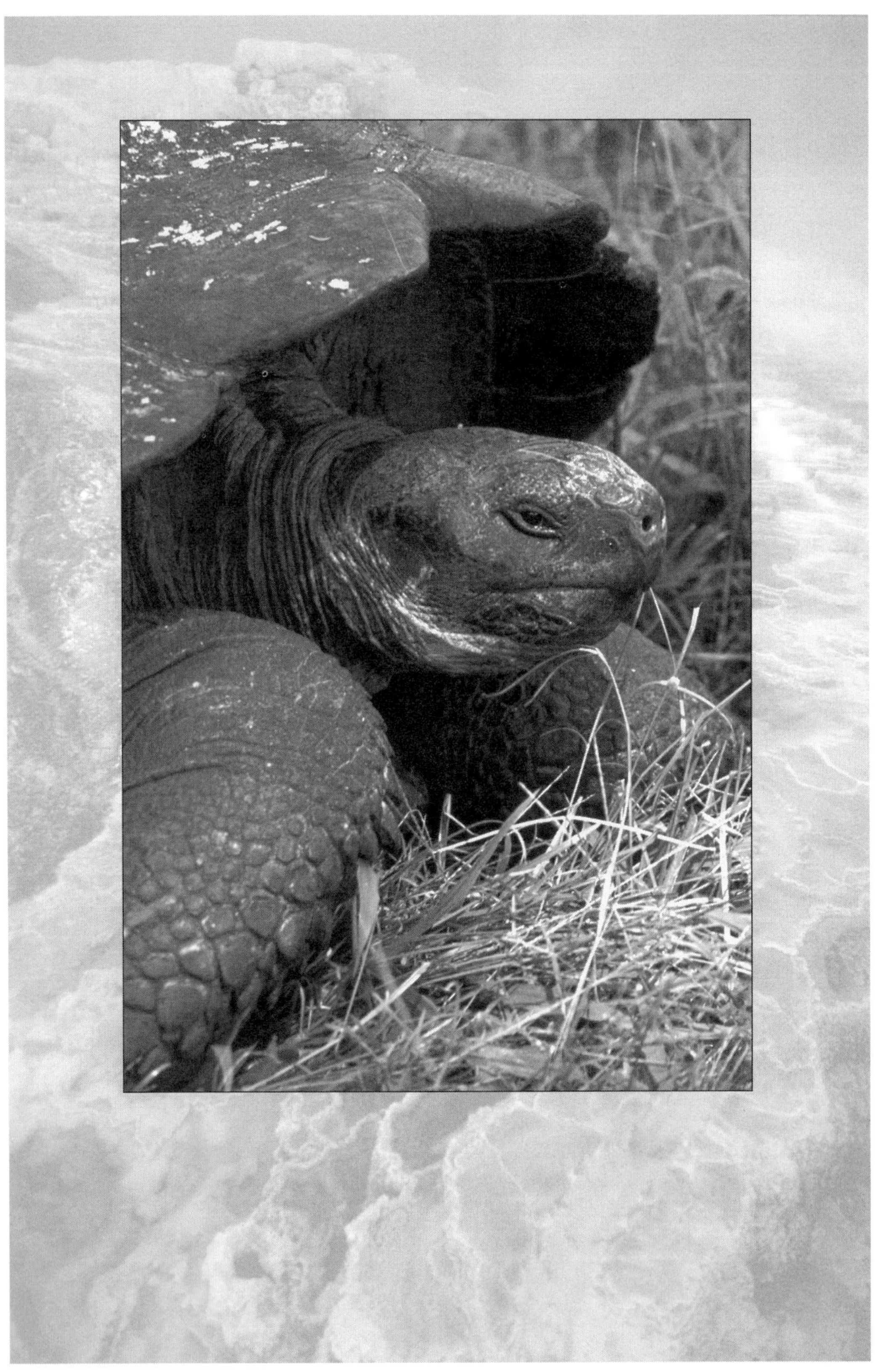

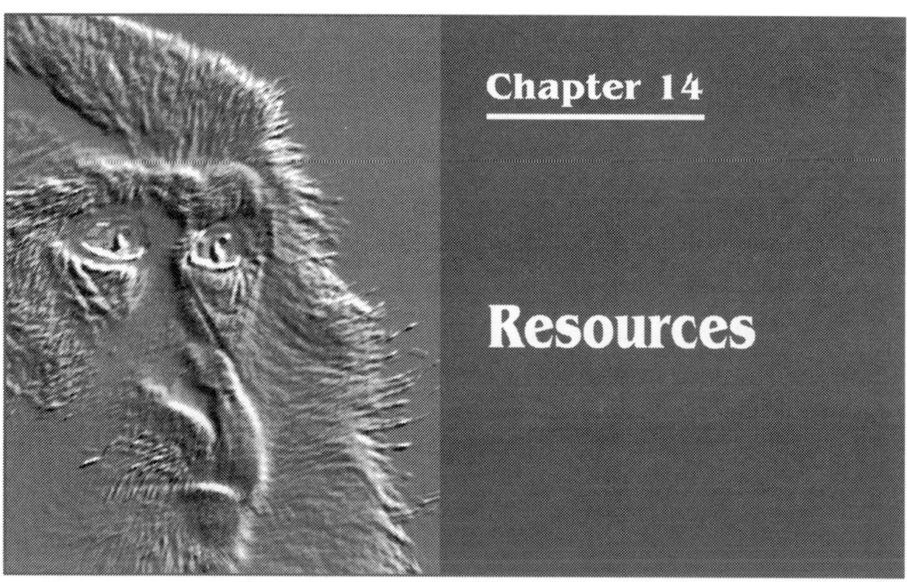

This chapter of the book is to help you look, learn, take action, plan, and more. The listings run the gamut from accessory manufacturers and dealers to conservation organizations, helpful government agencies, and a directory of zoos. I have tried to make it as complete as space permits, but I will be glad to hear from you, in care of the publisher, if you have additional helpful sources that could be included in future editions of this book.

Listings

Note: Phone numbers and addresses change quite frequently; check telephone directories, information operators, or toll free [800] information operators in case of difficulty.

Official Government Information

Canadian Department of External Affairs
Phone: 613-992-3705
(Official advice for traveling Canadians.)

Canadian Wildlife Service
Phone: 819-997-1095

Environment Canada
351 St. George's Blvd.
Hull, QC K1A 0H3
Phone: 819-997-2800
Toll free in Canada only: 800-668-6767
(They will send free illustrated information on Canada's thirty-nine national parks and park reserves)

U.S. Department of the Interior
1849 C St.
Washington, DC 20240
Phone: 202-208-1100
(Agency responsible for most Federal lands, conservation of wildlife)

U.S. Fish and Wildlife Service
Publications Unit
Rm 130, Webb Building
4401 North Fairfax Drive
Arlington, VA 22203
Phone: 703-358-1711
(Free list of all refuges, with phone numbers and names of managers; individual guides to most refuges noting species, best seasons to go)

U.S. National Park Service
Office of Public Enquiries
1849 C St.
Washington, DC 20240
Phone: 202-208-4747
(Free illustrated brochures on individual parks, general information)

U.S. State Department
Citizens Advisory Center
Phone: 202-647-5225
(Telephone service giving advice and official warnings on travel to problem areas; also health requirements, more. Have pencil and paper handy, and be patient when calling.)

U.S. Environmental Protection Agency (EPA)
401 M St.SW
Washington DC 20460
Phone: 202-382-5700
(Environmental and clean water information)

Note: Foreign government tourist offices, consulates and airlines are also good sources of travel information.

Some Conservation Organizations

Bat Conservation International
P.O. Box 162603
Austin, TX 78716-2603
Phone: 512-327-9721

Greenpeace USA
1436 U St. NW
PO Box 96128
Washington, DC 20090
Phone: 202-462-1177

MERI — Marine Environmental Research Institute
Main Street, P.O. Box 300
Brooklin, ME 04616
Phone: 207-339-2553 or 212-721-6243

National Audubon Society
700 Broadway
New York, NY 10003
Phone: 212-979-3000
(State and local chapters nationwide)

National Wildlife Federation
1400 Sixteenth St. NW
Washington, DC 20036-2266
Phone: 202-797-6800

Nature Conservancy (U.S.)
1815 North Lynn St.
Arlington, VA 22209
Phone: 703-841-5300
(Chapters nationwide)

Sierra Club
730 Polk St.
San Francisco, CA 94109
Phone: 415-776-2211

Wilderness Society
900 Seventeenth St. NW
Washington DC 20006
Phone: 202-833-2300

Wildfowl and Wetlands Trust
Slimbridge
Gloucestershire GL2 7BT,
UK

Wildlife Conservation International
New York Zoological Society
185th St.and South Blvd.
Bronx, NY 10460
Phone: 718-220-5155

Wildlife Preservation Trust International
3400 West Girard Ave.
Philadelphia, PA 19104
Phone: 215-222-3636

World Wildlife Fund (U.S.)
1250 Twenty-Fourth St. NW
Washington, DC 20037
Phone: 202-293-4800

Camera/Lens Manufacturers:

Bronica
GMI Photographic Inc.
1776 New Highway
P.O. Drawer U
Farmingdale, NY 11735
Phone: 752-0066

Calumet/Cambo *(see under catalogs)*

Canon USA
One Canon Plaza
Lake Success, NY 11042
Phone: 516-488-6700

Fuji *(see under film)*

Hasselblad
10 Madison Rd.
Fairfield, NJ 07004
Phone: 800-338-6477

Leica
156 Ludlow St.
Northvale, NJ 07647
Phone: 800-222-0118 or 908-767-7500
Fax: 908-767-8666

Mamiya America Corporation
8 Westchester Plaza
Elmsford, NY 10523
Phone: 914-347-3300
*(Also Toyo cameras, panoramic backs;
PermaPak rechargeable batteries)*

Minolta Corp.
10 Williams Drive
Ramsey, NJ 07446
Phone: 201-825-4000
(Also meters)

Nikon Inc.
1300 Walt Whitman Rd.
Melville, NY 11747-3064
Phone: 516-547-4200

Olympus Corp.
Crossways Park
Woodbury, NY 11797
Phone: 800-221-3000
Fax: 516-349-2471

Pentax Corp.
35 Inverness Drive East
Englewood, CO 80112
Phone: 800-877-0155 or 303-799-8000

Polaroid *(see under films)*

Tokina Lenses
THK Photo Products
1512 Kona Drive
Compton, CA 90220
Phone: 800-421-1141 or 213-537-9380
Fax: 516-496-8524
(Also Hoya filters)

Sigma Corp. of America
15 Fleetwood Court
Ronkonkoma, NY 11779
Phone: 516-585-1144

Custom and Specialized Equipment and Accessories

Arca-Swiss ball heads *(see Calumet, under catalogs)*

Armato Industries
6717 Myrtle Ave.
Glendale, NY 11385
Phone: 718-441-441
(Modified Vivitar 283s and Sunpaks, custom work)

Aqua Vision Systems Inc.
804 Deslauriers St.
Montreal, QC H4N 1X1
Phone: 514-336-7051
Fax: 514-745-1780
(Underwater camera and strobe housings)

Bogen Photo Corp.
565 East Crescent Ave.
Ramsey, NJ 07446
Phone: 201-818-9500
(Bogen/Manfrotto tripods, heads, clamps, stands. Metz flash)

Chimera Photographic Lighting
1812 Valtec La.
Boulder, CO 80301
Phone: 303-444-8000 or 800-424-4075
(Folding fabric light boxes, all sizes)

Cougar Design
220 East 23rd St.
New York, NY 10010
Phone: 212-685-2310
(T-bars and plates for joining Vivitar 283s; lightweight stands)

Dyna-Lite Corp.
311-319 Long Ave.
Hillside, NJ 07205
Phone: 908-688-3210
(Dyna-Lite studio strobes. Jackrabbit portable flash power packs)

Ivan Eberle
P.O. Box 51307
Pacific Grove, CA 93950-6307

Phone: 408-373-8476
(Light-beam trigger setups)

Four Designs Inc.
9400 Wystone Ave.
Northridge, CA 91324
Phone: 818-882—2878
(Old folding Polaroid cameras modified. Reconditioned models sold)

Gitzo Tripods
Karl Heitz Inc.
34-11 62nd. St. Box 427
Woodside, NY 11377
Phone: 718-565-0004

Holly Enterprises
7555 Woodley Ave.
Van Nuys, CA 91046
Phone: 818-988-7111
(Replacement metal feet for Vivitars)

Ikelite Underwater Systems
50 West 33rd St.
Indianapolis, IN 46208
Phone: 317-923-4523
(Underwater housings, strobes, and accessories)

Kenyon Gyro-Stabilizers
Ken Lab Inc
P.O. Box 128
Old Lyme, CT 06371
Phone: 203-434-1619

Kirk Enterprises
4370 East US Hwy 20
Angola, IN 46703
Phone: 219-665-3670 (Information) or 800-626-5074 (Orders only)
Fax: 219-665-3670
(Camera car window mounts, beanbags, custom work for Nikons and Canons)

Minolta meters *(see cameras)*

MC Photographics
2235 Harris circle
Cleveland, TN 37311
Phone: 615-339-1898
(Cara Gear equipment wraps, insulated film bags)

NPC (Photo Div.)

1238 Chestnut St.
Newton Upper Falls, MA 02164
Phone: 617-969-4522
(Polaroid backs for 35mm and medium-format cameras)

A. Kenneth Olson

3 Woodhill Ln.
St. Paul, MN 55127-2140
Phone: 612-484-0150
(Custom-made high-voltage, ultra-high-speed flash units)

Prestoflash

c/o Dr. John Cooke
P.O. Box 171
Dutch Flats, CA 95714
Phone: 916-389-2167
or, c/o Tony Tilford
3 Newmarket Rd.
Cringleford, Norwich NR4 6UE, UK
Phone: 0603-504710
(Ultra-high-speed, high-voltage flash equipment, and accessories)

Protech Inc.

5710-E General Washington Hwy.
Alexandria, VA 22312
Phone: 703-941-9100
Fax: 703-941-8267
(Dale Beam Triggers)

S.A.I. Photo Products

126 Somers Court South
Moorestown, NJ 08057
Phone or Fax: 609-778-0261
(NVS-1 Double Power Vivitar 283 conversions. Wild Bird lighting kit)

Saunders Group

21 Jet View Drive
Rochester, NY 14624
Phone: 716: 328-7800
(Benbo, Domke, Lepp, Patterson, Stroboframe, Wein equipment, more)

Quantum Instruments

1075 Stewart Av.
Garden City, NY 11530
Phone: 516-222-0611
(Rechargeable battery packs, radio slaves and triggers)

Visual Departures

1641 Third Ave., Ste 202
New York, NY 10128
Phone: 800-628-2003 or 212-534-1718
(Handy gadgets, portable blinds, beanbags)

Wein triggers/slaves *(see Saunders)*

Zing Designs

865 Florida St.
San Francisco, CA 94110
Phone: 415-282-9119
(Protective/thermal Zing stretch SLR camera covers)

Free Nature Related Catalogs

Cabela's

Sidney, NE 69160
Phone: 800-237-4444
(Over two-hundred pages of hunting, fishing, camping gear; waders, clothing, blinds, camouflage, towers. Much that outdoor photographers can use, budget prices. (Don't send for this if pix of guns, etc., upset you)

Calumet Professional Imaging

890 Supreme Drive
Bensenville, IL 60106
Phone Orders: 800-225-8638
Fax: 708-860-7105
(Very complete photo catalog. Stores in New York, Chicago and Los Angeles)

Connecticut Valley Biological Supply

P.O. Box 326, 82 Valley Rd.
Southampton, MA 01073
Phone Orders: 800-628-7748
Phone: 413-527-8286
Fax: 413-527-8286
(Ant farms, aquariums, bird feeders, butterfly chrysalides, insect collecting gear, microscopes, science specimens, slides and instruments, books, videos)

Edmund Scientific Company
101 East Gloucester Pike
Barrington, NJ 08007
Phone:609-547-3488
(Microscopes and camera attachments, optical tubing, much more for the science photographer and do-it-yourself gadget maker)

Helix Underwater Catalog
310 South Racine
Chicago, IL 60607
Phone: 800-334-3549 or 312-226-3727
Fax: 312-421-1586
(Very complete. Also u/w book catalog with twenty-six pages of listings)

Images Products
Gould Trading
7 East 17th Street
New York, NY 10003
Order Phone: 800-367-4854
Phone: 212-243-2306
Fax: 212-243-2308
(Some hard-to-find books, plus videos, equipment, gadgets)

Light Impressions
439 Monroe Ave,
Rochester, NY 14603-0940
Phone: 800-828-6216 (orders)
        or 800-828-9859 (customer service)
(Archival storage supplies)

L.L. Rue Catalog
Leonard Rue Enterprises
138 Millbrook Rd.
Blairstown, NJ 07825
Phone: 908-362-6616
Fax: 908-362-5808
(Equipment and accessories for nature photographers, including beanbags, clamps, lures, pop-up blinds, vests, more; plus books, videos)

Photak
180 Main St.
Menasha, WI 54952
Phone: (Orders) 800-723-9876,
        or 414-722-8733
(Useful photo gear, some unique, plus books)

Recommended Professional Dealers:

Adorama
42 West 18th St.
New York, NY, 10011
Phone: 800-223-2500 (Orders)
        or 212-741-0052 (Customer relations)
(Discounts. Photo books, videos. A major underwater dealer)

B & H Photo
119 West 17th Street
New York, NY 10011
Phone: 212-807-7474
Orders: 800-221-5662
(Huge-volume pro-discount dealer. Books too)

Calumet *(see under catalogs)*

Helix *(see under catalogs)*

Ken Hanson
920 Broadway,
New York, NY 10010
Phone: 212-777-5900
Fax: 212-473-0690
(For my money, the best professional dealer in New York. The specialist staff know digital imaging and a lot about esoteric camera gear)

Lens and Repro Equipment Corp
33 West 17th Street
New York, NY 10011
Phone: (212) 675-1900
(Professional dealer with excellent large-format department. Panoramic specialists; good used stuff too)

Recommended Repair Services:

Professional Camera Repair
37 West 47th St.
New York NY 10036
Phone: 212-673-0550
(Custom and rush work too. Ask for Rick Rankin or Herb Zimmerman)

Flash Clinic
9 West 19th Street
New York, NY 10011
Phone (212) 673-4030

Film, Chemicals, and Paper Manufacturers:

3M Corp.
3M Center
St. Paul, MN 55144-1000
Phone: 612-733-1110
Environmental: 612-733-1135
(Scotch films, more.)

Agfa
Division of Miles Inc.
100 Challenger Road
Ridgefield Park NJ 07660-2199
Phone: 201-440-2500

Eastman Kodak Corp.
343 State St.
Rochester, NY 14650
Phone: 800-242-2424 or 716-724-4000
Professional Imaging Ext. 19
Environmental Support Ext. 444
Scientific Ext. 12
CIESS phone: 716-477-3194
Fax: 716-724-0663

Fuji Photo Film USA
2490 Black Rock Turnpike, Ste. 212
Fairfield, CT 06430
Phone: 800-736-3600 or 914-789-8100
Environmental phone: 800-473-3854
Fax: 914-789-1000

Ilford Photo Corp.
West 70 Century Rd.
Paramus, NJ 07653
Phone: 201-265-6000
Fax: 201-265-0894

Polaroid Corp.
575 Technology Square
Cambridge, MA 02139
Phone: 800-343-5000 or 617-577-2000
(Also cameras, and free information on macro and micro photography)

Recycling/Recovery/Waste Disposal

Boston Recycling
960 Turnpike St.
Canton, MA 02021
Phone: 800-229-3456 or 617-828-5445

CPAK Division of Trebla Corp.
2364 Leicester Rd.
Leicester, NY 14481
Phone: 716-382-3223
(IMG silver recovery tanks)

Eastman Kodak
(See under film)

Publications:
(You should be able to find most of the magazines listed at a good magazine store. In case of difficulty, check Yellow Pages under Magazines — Distributors for local suppliers in your region.)

Animals
Airone (Italy, sold in U.S.)
Audubon
BBC Wildlife (U.K., sold in US)
Backpacker
Birding
Buzzworm
Dive
Geo (Germany, France, both sold in U.S.)
Harrowsmith (Canada, sold in U.S.)
International Wildlife
National Geographic
Natural History
Organic Gardening
Outdoor Photographer
Outdoor and Travel Photography
Ranger Rick (Children, uses many animal/nature pictures)
Scholastic Magazines (Student, use many animal/ nature pictures)
Terre Sauvage (France, sold in U.S.)
Wildlife Conservation
Wild Bird

Directories, Newsletters, Professional Publications

AAZPA Directory
(American Association of Zoos, Parks and Aquariums)
Publications Div.
Oglebay Park
Wheeling, WV 26003
Phone: 304-242-2160
(Membership directory lists facilities and spe-

cies for more than 150 U.S. and Canadian zoos,
nature parks and aquariums)

The Green Book Directory of Natural History and General Stock
and The Guilfoyle Report
AG Publications
41 Union Sq.
New York, NY, 10003
Phone: 212-929-0959
(The Green Book is the indispensable nature
stock directory, the Guilfoyle Report an impor-
tant newsletter)

Photo District News
Subscriptions
P.O. Box 1983
Marion, OH 43305
Phone: 800-669-1002
(Indispensable professional trade monthly)

Photo Traveler Newsletter
P.O. Box 39912
Los Angeles, CA 90039
Phone: 213-660-0473
(Nature—destination oriented.)

Professional Associations

ASMP (American Society of Media Photographers)
14 Washington Road, Ste. 502
Princeton Junction, NJ 08550-1033
Phone: 609-799-8300
Fax: 609-799-2233
(Chapters nationwide. Useful publications)

NPPA (National Press Photographers Association)
P.O. Box 92397
3200 Croasdaile Dr.
Durham, NC 27705
Phone: 919-383-7246

PACA (Picture Agency Council of America)
currently, c/o Third Coast Stock Source Inc.
P.O. Box 92397
Milwaukee, WI 53202
Phone: 800-457-7222
(Publishes a directory of members and special-
ties, $10)

PP of A (Professional Photographers of America)
1090 Executive Way
Des Plaines, IL 60018
Phone: 708-299-8161

Stock Interest

Green Book directory and Guilfoyle Report
(see under Directories etc.)

PhotoSource International
Pine Lake Farm
Osceola, WI 54020-9530
Phone: 715-248-3800
Fax: 715-248-7394
(Fax/mail service of specific stock needs; daily,
weekly or monthly)

Stock Direct
10 East 21st St., 14th Fl.
New York, NY 10010
Phone: 212-979-6560
(Directory, individuals can advertise stock pic-
tures)

The Stock Photo Report
7432 Lamon Ave.
Skokie, IL 60077
Phone: 708-677-7887

Taking Stock
Pickerell Marketing
110 Frederick Ave., Ste. A
Rockville, MD 20850
Phone: 301-251-0720
(Also publisher of Negotiating Stock Picture
Prices.)

Nature Tours and Travel

Ecotourism Society
P.O. Box 755
North Bennington, VT 05257
Phone: 802-447-2121
Fax: 802-447-2122
(Association dedicated to ecologically respon-
sible travel. Information on member companies
available)

International Expeditions
One Environs Park
Helena, AL 35080
Phone: 800-633-4734 or 205-428-1700
(Rain forest specialists. Member of Ecotourism Society)

Joseph Van Os Photo Safaris
P.O. Box 655A,
Vashon Island, WA 90870
Phone: 206-463-5383
(Operator of wildlife/outdoor photo tours, many led by top-name nature photographers. F.I.T. [foreign independent travel] safaris also)

Adventure Associates
13150 Coit Rd., Ste. 110
Dallas TX 75240
Phone 800-527-2500
(U.S. representative of Metropolitan Touring, Quito, an Ecuadorian company, who in my opinion give excellent service on the mainland, and have the best guides and boats in the Galapagos)

Sierra Club Outings *(see under conservation)*

United Touring International (USA) Ltd.
400 Market St, Ste. 260
Philadelphia, PA 19106-6486
Phone: 800-223-6486 or 215-923-8700
(U.S. office of old established Kenyan company that I have used. Well-priced group and F.I.T. [foreign independent travel] in East Africa. They can also make arrangements for travel in other areas of the African continent)

Private Property/Animal Model Release

I, _______________________________________ the owner of the private
(print name)

property/animal located at/described as

____

____

hereby give ____
(photographer's name)

The right to use, copyright and publish the pictures taken of my
property/animal for purposes of advertising and trade in all lawful media.

Signed_______________________________________ Date ______________

Address____________________________________ Phone #___________

Standard Short Form Model Release for People

Date:____________

Place____

I ____(please print clearly)

hereby grant ____

Permission to use, copyright and publish the photographs taken of me today
for purposes of advertising and trade in all lawful media.

Signed_______________________________________ Date ____________

Bibliography

All U.S. publishers are in New York, all U.K. publishers in London, and all books illustrated with color photographs, unless otherwise noted.

Some of the Most Beautiful Nature Photography Books

Adams, Ansel. ***Images of the American Wilderness.*** Richard Wrigley, Ed. Smithmark. 1992. Black-and-white master's landscapes.

Angel, Heather. ***A World of Plants, Treasures from the Royal Botanic Gardens at Kew.*** Boston. Little, Brown. 1993. In U.K.: Kew, A World of Plants. Collins and Brown. 1993. Lovely flowers, exotic plants. See anything else by Angel.

Anthology. ***Colors in the Wild.*** Washington, D.C.. National Wildlife Federation. 1988. Best-seller; colorful, graphic photos by famous nature pros.

Beard, Peter, ***The End of the Game.*** San Francisco. Chronicle Books. 1988. (Revised, first published 1963.) A classic, b/w pictures. Life and death in Africa.

Brandenburg, Jim. ***White Wolf, Living With an Arctic Legend.*** Minneapolis, MN. 1990. Northword Press. A bestseller, the most spiritual, intimate book of photographs of wild creatures I know of. See his new book ***Brother Wolf*** also.

Brown, Richard. ***Moments in Eden.*** Boston. Little, Brown. 1989. Gorgeous color photographs of gardens in U.S., Europe, Japan. See Brown's other books too.

Cavagnaro, David, and Frans Lanting. ***Feathers.*** Portland, OR. Graphic Arts Publishing. 1982. A beautiful book about birds, with many close-ups, by an influential nature photographer; also includes some early work by Lanting, a famous disciple of Cavagnaro's. See both mens' other books also.

Cook, Ferris, Ed. ***Invitation to the Garden.*** Stewart, Tabori and Chang. 1992. Color anthology with pictures by nine photographers, including Curtice Taylor.

Dalton, Stephen. Text, Jill Bailey. ***At the Water's Edge, the Secret Life of A Lake and Stream.*** Random House. 1989. A year in one small ecosystem with many high-speed close-ups, by a British master. See anything else by Dalton.

Doubilet, David. ***Light in the Sea.*** Charlottesville, VA. Thomasson Grant. 1989. Inspiration by one of the world's top underwater photographers.

Haas, Ernst. ***The Creation.*** Penguin Books. 1989. First published in 1971, a nature classic photographed in Africa, the Galapagos, Hawaii, and other places.

Farb, Nathan. ***The Adirondacks.*** Rizzoli. 1988. Best-seller, large-format color landscapes of upstate New York mountain park; can serve as a model on how to extract the most from any scene. Also see Farb's ***The Galapagos,*** 1989.

Iwago, Mitsuaki. ***Serengeti.*** San Francisco. Chronicle Books. 1987. Stunning color pictures of the migration, taken over a two-year stay in Tanzania.

Kuhn, Dwight. ***My First Book of Nature.*** Scholastic Books. 1993. Colorful, many fine close-ups. Inspiration for those aiming at the youth/textbook market.

Lanting, Frans. Text, Christine K. Eckstrom. ***Forgotten Edens, Exploring the World's Wild Places.*** Washington, D.C. National Geographic Society. 1993. Wildlife in the environment, some landscapes; taken on extended stays in Borneo, Botswana, Madagascar, Maui, South Georgia Island. Interesting text.

Muench, David. Text, Stewart Udall, and James R. Udall. ***National Parks of America.*** Portland, OR. Graphic Arts Center Publishers. 1993. Large-format landscapes by the Californian master. Stewart Udall is a former Interior Secretary.

Norfleet, Barbara. ***Manscape with Beasts.*** Harry N. Abrams. 1990. Wildlife in weird places. Beautiful, funny, fine art by a Harvard photography professor.

Neubert, Christopher. ***Within a Rainbowed Sea.*** Honolulu, HI. Beyond World's Publishing Co. 1989. One of the finest underwater books ever printed.

Rowell, Galen. ***Mountain Light.*** San Francisco, Sierra Club Books. 1986. A modern classic with fabulous color pictures. Some "how-to" information also.

Wilkinson, Peter, FRPS, Picture Ed. ***Wildlife Photographer of the Year, Portfolio One.*** U.K.: Fountain Press, 1992. Images from the BBC Wildlife contest/U.K. Natural History Museum exhibit, by professionals and amateurs.

Wolfe, Art. Text, Douglas Chadwick. ***The Kingdom.*** San Francisco. Sierra Club Books, 1992. Gorgeous photographs of major species of North American wildlife from the Aleutians to the Florida Keys. Also see the range of Wolfe's work in ***The Art of Nature Photography*** (listed under "how-to" books).

My Choice of the Best "How To" Books

Angel, Heather. ***Animal Photography.*** U.K.: Oxford Illustrated Press. 1991
Fine pictures, planning, how to find animals, checklists for travel, more.

Caulfield, Patricia. ***Photographing Wildlife, Techniques for Portraying Animals in Natural Habitats.*** Amphoto. 1988. A specific and honest "how-to" book; beautiful pictures of the Everglades. Strong on reptiles, amphibians. See her ***Capturing the Landscape With Your Camera*** also.

Eastman Kodak, Eds. ***Kodak Pocket Guide to Nature Photography.*** Simon and Schuster. 1985. Text by Michael Freeman, author of many good photography manuals. This tiny book contains a lot of hard information.

Fitzharris, Tim. ***The Audubon Society Guide To Nature Photography.*** Boston. Little Brown. 1990. Lovely pictures, useful diagrams, photographs of blinds in use. Techniques and field craft strong on water birds, amphibians, insects.

Freeman, Michael. ***Light.*** Amphoto. 1988. The best general book I know on "seeing" and using daylight;

plus small-flash and studio techniques, more.

Gravé, Eric. ***Using the Microscope, A Guide for Naturalists.*** Dover Publications. 1988. Very clearly written beginners' guide. Techniques for photo microscopy, preparing slides, etc. (Camera/film information dated.)

Hill, Martha, and Art Wolfe. ***The Art of Nature Photography.*** Crown. 1993.
More than 250 superbly reproduced color photographs showing the master's range from landscape to close-up, which illustrate text by a former *Audubon* magazine picture editor; it covers everything from seeing to shooting, selling to ethics. The standard by which such books will be judged for years to come.

Hill, Dr. Mike, and Gordon Langsbury. ***Field Guide to Photographing Birds in Britain and Western Europe.*** U.K.: Collins, 1987. Good photographs, extremely detailed on techniques, also lists top birding destinations.

Kodak, Eds. ***Closeup Photography,*** 1989, ***Electronic Flash,*** 1988, ***Landscape Photography,*** 1987, ***Photography Through the Microscope,*** 1988 and ***Using Filters,*** 1989. Rochester, NY. Four relevant titles from the Kodak Workbook series. Clearly written, these all start with basics, continue with surprising detail, and give professional-level technical information and formulas at the end.

McDonald, Joe. ***The Complete Guide To Wildlife Photography.*** Amphoto. 1992. Fine photographs, good text. Helpful pictures of flash set-ups in use.

Meehan, Joseph. ***Panaroramic Photography.*** Amphoto. 1990. Thorough introduction to cameras, techniques; some color landscape illustrations.

Seaborn, Charles. ***Underwater Photography.*** Amphoto. 1988. Fine pictures of marine life, and underwater photography gear in use. Clearly written text.

Shaw, John. ***The Nature Photographer's Complete Guide To Professional Field Techniques.*** Amphoto. 1984. Best-seller, concise and well organized; splendid pictures.

Zuckerman, Jim. ***The Professional Photographer's Guide to Shooting and Selling Nature and Wildlife Photos.*** Cinncinati, OH. Writers' Digest Books. 1991. Quality nature pictures; good story/stock shooting and marketing tips.

Recommended, Out of Print; Find These in Libraries and Used Book Dealers:

Life, Eds. ***Photographing Nature.*** Time-Life Books. 1973. Still a fine book.

Porter, Eliot. ***In Wildness is the Preservation of the World.*** San Francisco. Sierra Club. 1962. With Thoreau's text. The now rare book that revolutionized nature photography. See ***Birds*** and anything else by Porter also.

Rowlands, Peter. ***Underwater Photographers' Handbook.*** Van Nostrand Reinhold, 1983. Specific on techniques, safety. Diagrams, maps of dive sites. Good pictures.

Rue, Dr. Leonard Lee III. ***How I Photograph Wildlife and Nature.*** W.W. Norton. 1985. The stalking and tracking sections are unsurpassed. Tips for using blinds, attracting insects, climbing trees, handling snakes, more.

Angel, Heather. ***Nature Photography, Its Art and Techniques.*** U.K.: Fountain Press. 1979. Mostly b/w pictures. Excellent on birds, insects, plants, the shoreline. Studio flash setups for tiny subjects covered in detail. Diagrams.

Biography, History, and Regional/Specialist Nature Photography Books

(Some are out of print, but worth hunting for in specialist libraries.)

Imperato, Pascal James, and Eleanor. ***They Married Adventure. The Wandering Lives of Martin and Osa Johnson.*** New Brunswick, NJ. Rutgers University Press, 1992. Illustrated biography of wildlife photographer/filmakers of the 1920s and 1930s.

May, John. ***Greenpeace Book of Antartica.*** U.S.: Doubleday. 1988. U.K.: Dorling, Kindersley Ltd. 1988. Good photos, text, history. Field guide, maps, etc.

Rosenblum, Naomi. ***A World History of Photography.*** Abbeville Press. 1984. Scholarly, copiously illustrated, an enjoyable standard reference work.

Guggiswell, C.A.R. ***Early Wildlife Photography.*** Taplinger Pub. 1977. An entertaining, well-illustrated history. Some of the pictures are still great.

Shiras III, George. ***Hunting Wildlife With Camera and Flashlight,*** Washington, D.C. National Geographic Society. 1936. Classic early wildlife pictures, text.

Nature Guides

Angel, Heather. Text: Duffy, Miles, Ogilvie, Simms, Teagle. ***Natural History of Britain and Ireland, The.*** U.K.: Mermaid Books. 1985. Fine land/seascapes, flora and fauna, macro and micro pix. Scientific ecosystem guide. Maps.

Imes, Rick. ***The Practical Botanist.*** Simon and Schuster. 1990. Lay person's guide to plants, with nice photographs, information on classification, etc.

Jenner, Janann V. ***The Birdwatcher's Companion.*** Smithmark. 1991. Popular ornithology. How to get close to birds in habitats. Anthology of photographs.

Reess, Sr., Robin, Exec. Ed. ***The Way Nature Works.*** Macmillan. 1992. Detailed, popular encyclopedia, illustrated with paintings, based on TV series. Indexed.

Houk, Rose. ***Eastern Wildflowers.*** San Francisco. Chronicle Books. 1990. Interesting facts and legends about wildflowers; stunning picture anthology.

Schnek, Marcus. ***Your Backyard Wildlife Garden.*** Emmaus, PA. Rodale Press. 1992. How to attract wildlife with plantings. Photos, diagrams, field guide.

Tuttle, Merlin D. ***America's Neighborhood Bats.*** Austin, TX. University of Texas Press. 1988. Thorough introduction, high-speed flash photos.

Travel Guides

Buzzworm Magazine, Ed. ***Buzzworm Magazine Guide to Ecotravel, The.*** Boulder, CO. Buzzworm Books. 1993. Listings of 100 worldwide adventure trips. Maps.

Insight Guides to Wildlife. Eu, Geoffrey, Series Ed. ***Amazon Wildlife,*** 1992. ***East African Wildlife,*** 1989. ***Indian Wildlife,*** 1988. ***Southeast Asia Wildlife,*** 1990. APA/Prentice Hall Travel. Splendid. Color pictures, national park lists, etc.

National Geographic Society, Ed. ***A Guide To Out Federal Lands.*** Washington, D.C.. 1984. Detailed listings by state. Index, maps, facilities. A few fine pictures.

Rachowiecki, Rob. ***Ecuador and The Galapgos Islands.*** Lonely Planet. Berkeley, CA, and London. 1986. Color photos, maps. Field guide to Galapagos.

Riley, Laura and William. ***Guide to the National Wildlife Refuges.*** Collier, Macmillan. 1993. Text and maps. Listings by state/region of over 500 places in the U.S. to view/photograph wildlife. What is where, and when to go. Recommended by the National Audubon Society, the National Wildlife Federation, and me.

Showker, Kay and Gerry Ellis. ***The Outdoor Traveler's Guide to the Caribbean.*** Stewart, Tabori and Chang, 1989. Solid information, color pix, hotels, etc.

Stephenson, Marylee. ***Canada's National Parks, A Visitor's Guide.*** Scarboro, ON. Prentice Hall Canada. 1991. Solid info on flora and fauna, maps, B/W pix.

Field Guides

These all have descriptions plus photographs, drawings, or paintings, plus range maps; aid in identification of species. Most list local and Latin names.

Golden Press Guides: ***Butterflies and Moths; Flowers; Mammals; Venomous Animals,*** etc. many others in series. Golden Press, var. dates. Pocket size.

Danks, Dr. Hugh, ***Bug Book.*** Workman Publishing, 1987. A cute little basic field guide to insects, meant for kids, comes with a bug collecting jar.

Peterson, Roger Tory. ***Eastern Birds.*** Boston, MA. Houghton Mifflin. 1980. (If you live west of the Missisppi, of course get ***Western Birds.***) The ***Peterson First Guide To Birds,*** 1986, is tiny; easy to stick in a crowded camera bag. (The rest of the Peterson Guides and First Guides series are valuable also.)

Business, Environmental, and Miscellaneous Books

ASMP, Ed. ***ASMP Stock Picture Handbook.*** American Society of Magazine (now Media) Photographers. 1988. Bible of business practices for stock. Text only.

Campbell, Joseph, with Bill Moyers. ***The Power of Myth.*** Doubleday, 1988. Coversations between the scholar and the TV journalist, based on PBS series.

Davis, Harold. ***Successful Fine Art Photography.*** Images Press. 1992. This photographer uses a lot of nature images to illustrate his business text.

Eastman Kodak, Eds. ***Disposal and Treatment of Photographic Effluent, In Support of Clean Water***. Rochester, NY, 1989. 28 page pamphlet.

Heron, Michal. ***How to Shoot Stock Pictures That Sell.*** 1991. Detailed business and copyright information, more, b/w pictures. ***Photographer's Organizer,*** 1992. Text.

Heron and David MacTavish. ***Pricing Photography,*** 1993. Extremely specific guide to assignment and stock pricing. Allworth Press.

Hollenbeck, Cliff. ***Big Bucks Selling Your Photography.*** Seattle, WA. Hot Shots. 1990. Photographic business/marketing tool. Text, sample forms, specifics.

McCartney, Susan. ***Travel Photography, A Complete Guide to How to Shoot and Sell.*** Allworth Press, 1992. My first book has specifics on travel, lighting, more, b/w pictures.

Naar, Jon and Naar, Alex J. ***This Land is Your Land, A Guide to America's Endangered Ecosystems.*** HarperCollins. 1993. How to take environmental action. Resources, maps, some b/w pictures. An important book. See Naar's other books also.

Pickerell, Jim. ***Negotiating Stock Picture Prices.*** Rockwell, MD. Pickerell Marketing. 1993. Extremely specific, a must for those who market their stock.

Shaw, Susan, and Monoma Rossol. ***Overexposure, Health Hazards In Photography,*** Allworth Press. 1991. Data on handling chemicals etc. Important.

Index

ALLWORTH BOOKS

Travel Photography: A Complete Guide to How to Shoot and Sell *by Susan McCartney.*
This unique and complete guide tells how to shoot the best possible photos — and earn money
doing it. Includes ten self-assignments, world travel highlights, and releases in twenty-nine languages. Brian Seed's *Stock Photo Report* comments,"Technical information is presented in a read-
able style that's useful to both neophytes and pros, without insulting the intelligence of either....More
than an excellent travel photography guide, this is one of the best and most practical guides to professional photography in general. Highly recommended." According to Bob Krist, *Travel and Lei-
sure* magazine, it is "one of the best books ever on the subject — a lively, personal and comprehen-
sive treatment." Bill Black, Photography Director for *Travel Holiday* magazine, says it "should be
mandatory reading for all travel photographers, from amateurs to professionals...packed with practical and invaluable advice." (384 pages, 6 3/4" X 10", $22.95)

Pricing Photography: The Complete Guide to Assignment and Stock Prices
by Michal Heron and David MacTavish
Written by successful free-lance photographers (Heron is also the author of *How to Shoot Stock Photos
That Sell*), this essential resource for photographers, art directors, and graphic designers explains how
to price and negotiate both assignment photography and stock photography. Included are extensive and
detailed pricing charts compiled by the authors. The book concludes with pricing guidance for photography buyerswho will also find this information indispensable. "The definitive guide..." — *Light and
Shade.* (128 pages, 11" X 8 1/2", $19.95)

How to Shoot Stock Photos that Sell *by Michal Heron.*
Everything you need to know for success as a stock shooter, from how to shoot to how to sell. Contains
25 unique self-assignments to let you create images that buyers want today. "One of the top publications
in today's hottest photographic area." — *Studio Photography* (192 pages, 8" X 10", $16.95)

The Photographer's Organizer *by Michal Heron.*
The Photographer's Organizer is for every photographer who wants to organize photographs, shoots,
travel resources, clients, markets, and the business of photography. (32 pages, 8 1/2 x 11", $8.95)

Stock Photo Forms *by Michal Heron.*
Here are 19 forms that will organize your stock shoot and help you achieve success. Included are
a stock job form, estimate for shoot expenses, a shooting day organizer, pocket-releases, and more.
A Main Selection of the Photography Book Club. (32 pages, 8 1/2" X 11", $8.95)

Business and Legal Forms for Photographers *by Tad Crawford.*
Twenty-four essential forms covering all aspects of photography, plus careful explanations and
negotiation checklists. "A simple one sentence review: Every photographer needs this book." —
Shutterbug. (208 pages, 8 1/2" X 11" book, $18.95; Computer disk with forms only, in WordPerfect
format, $14.95, specify MAC or IBM)

The Photographer's Assistant:
Learn the Inside Secrets of Professional Photography — and Get Paid for It *by John Kieffer.*
The only book to explain how to break in as an assistant, needed skills, business practices, equip-
ment and film, finding work, and more. Seven top photographers tell what they want in an assistant.
A must for assistants and photographers who use them. (208 pages, 6 3/4" X 10", $16.95)

Overexposure: Health Hazards in Photography *by Susan D. Shaw and Monona Rossol.*
This highly acclaimed work is completely revised from its 1983 edition. It offers a complete guide
to all risks that photographers, lab personnel, and others using photographic chemicals face — and
tells how to protect health and safety. (320 pages, 6 3/4" X 10", $18.95)

If you wish to order a book, send your check or money order to:

Allworth Press, 10 East 23rd Street, Suite 400, New York, NY 10010. To pay for shipping and
handling, include $3 for the first book ordered and $1 for each additional book ($7 plus $1 if the order is
from Canada). New York State residents must add sales tax.